No Greater Love

"Greater love hath no man than this,
that a man lay down his life for his friends."

Harper & Row, Publishers
New York

No Greater Love

THE JAMES REEB STORY

By DUNCAN HOWLETT

To
Marie
John, Karen, Anne, and Steven
and to
Mae and Harry Reeb
whose loss no man can repair

Contents

Introduction

JAMES REEB went to Selma, Alabama, on the night of Monday, March 8, 1965, in answer to a call from Martin Luther King following the beating of civil rights marchers there the day before. Tuesday night, when the march was over, he fell on the sidewalks of Selma, a victim of the same brutality that had hospitalized nearly eighty marchers on Sunday evening; the same brutality that had kept the Negro in bondage since the white man first enslaved him more than three hundred years before. Through the efforts of modern medicine, James Reeb was kept alive for nearly forty-eight hours, but it was no use. The single blow that struck him down had been so vicious that he was beyond human help from the start.

As he lay dying in Alabama, the entire civil rights struggle suddenly came to a focus in him. It all fitted together as if by design. He was a white minister who had come to Selma to support the Negro cause. He was a peaceable man who became the victim of a wholly unprovoked attack. Defenseless himself, he was felled by a man with a club. He was struck from behind by an adversary he hardly saw.

When the world looked beyond the attack to the man who was its victim, the feeling began to grow that it had all happened in accordance with some grand design. For James Reeb in his personal life had been the epitome of the ideals of the civil rights movement. His concern first became articulate while he was a chaplain at the Philadelphia General Hospital. It became more explicit during his work as Youth Director of the West Branch YMCA in Philadelphia. At All Souls Unitarian Church in Washington, D.C., he increasingly gave his time to programs designed to assist the poor in the area of the church, most of whom were Negroes. He went to Boston under the auspices of the American Friends Service Committee in order to give full time to this type of work. There he moved his family into the neighborhood where he worked. The father of four, he had gone to Selma because he thought he could help there at a crucial moment in the struggle that was closest to his heart. He went, having first faced with his equally courageous wife the risk he ran in going.

James Reeb also symbolized in his personal life the ecumenicity that has increasingly marked the progress of the civil rights movement and was conspicuous in the Selma marches. His father's religious background was Reformed, his mother's Roman Catholic. He was christened in a Methodist church, joined a Congregational church when he was twelve, became active in a Presbyterian church as a youth, attended a Lutheran college, a Presbyterian seminary, and was ordained a Presbyterian minister. While serving as Protestant chaplain of a nonsectarian hospital, he became a Unitarian, primarily as a result of the impact of psychiatry on his orthodox theology. During this period of deep religious transition, he served as a YMCA youth director. He then entered the Unitarian ministry, where he developed an inner-city project sponsored by a group of churches, including his own, and a neighboring university. When he died he was the director of an inner-city project for the Friends.

This was the man the world discovered when it looked to see who had been felled on the streets of Selma. The bare outline of facts reported in the newspapers was just enough to make people want to know more about him. Who was this extraordinary man whose death had lifted him from obscurity to martyrdom and worldwide fame? What was he like? What was his background? What was his life story?

Many profess to see the hand of God in the martyrdom of James Reeb. The story lends itself to myth-making. If you were to search the entire civil rights movement for the most suitable person for the role of martyr, you could hardly find a better candidate. Yet he would be the first to denounce any such effort. He himself had explicitly rejected belief in a God who interferes in human life. But he deeply believed in the spiritual forces that guide the lives of men and strengthen them in time of need. He deeply believed in the power of the spiritual forces that rise within us to guide us in the right path even though all the world stand against us.

It was this conviction that took him into the ministry, this that took him into Unitarianism, this that took him to Dorchester, to Selma and to his death. The story of James Reeb is the story of a man who above all else loved and believed in his fellow man. He was a human being with his faults like the rest of us. But unlike most men, his faults were not many and his virtues were constructed on a grand scale.

There is no need to mythologize such a man, no need to suppress the blemishes, no need to exalt the virtues. The need is rather to see him as the human being he was, as he himself tried to see whomever he dealt with. The need is to see the boy with his parents and how they molded him consciously and unconsciously in accordance with their ideals; to see his sufferings and struggles and how they, too, strengthened his character; to see how he grew in accordance with his own unfolding ideals, and how men and events played their part in the story. The need is to see the man who became a martyr, not a martyr made into a myth. The need is to see the man who lived and loved, whose death made those who knew him poorer, but whose life, illumined by his death, has made the world a better place.

Except for sermons, letters, and an occasional report, the source material for the biography had all to be created. This was done through personal interviews and visits to the various parts of the country where James Reeb had lived. I have striven for the utmost accuracy in telling the story, and in most instances have been able to verify the material through more than one person: usually through several. Sometimes there is a difference in the way people remember things, which makes the verification process essential. Thus, the final responsibility for the story in the following pages must be mine alone.

The following persons granted me formal interviews; to them I shall always be grateful: Mark Almli, Ruth Batson, Prof. Wilbur Beeners, Frank Bowran, Mr. and Mrs. Chester Cable, Rev. Gilbert Caldwell, Rev. Fred A. Cappuccino, Alberta Cole, Rev. Howard Cole, Mr. and Mrs. John Coleman, Dr. Edward Cooper, Nathala Cox, Prof. Harold H. Ditmanson, Mr. and Mrs. J. Ronald Engel, Frances Ferris, Elizabeth Forslung, Rev. Robert G. Foulkes, Mr. and Mrs. Kenneth Fox, Inez Frayseth, Sara Dulaney Gilbert, Carol Glaser, Charles Groesbeck, Robert Gustafson, Margery Hall, Jean Hellmuth, Gwendolyn Hill, Waco Hill, Herbert Hillman, Robert Hohler, Dean Elmer G. Homrighausen, Albert Howlett, Prof. Lloyd Hustvedt, Lowell Johnson, Harold Jordan, Bernice Just, Jack Lamb, Jack Laugen, Suzanne LeBovit, W. Byron Lukens, Rev. John G. MacKinnon, Prof. Donald Macleod, Rev. Kenneth Marshall, Charlotte Meacham, Rev. Orloff Miller, Verna Schwalm Miller, Anne Montgomery, Mr. and Mrs. Harry Mozenter, Dr. Joseph Murphy, Rev. Truman D. Nabors, Jr., Dr. William Stuart Nelson, Rev. Alex Nemeth, Prof. John H. Ness, Prof. Arthur L. Olsen, Rev. Clark B. Olsen, Harold Olsen, Dr. Richard Oman, Rev. David P. Osborn, Mr. and Mrs. Thomas O'Sullivan, Rev. William B. Payne, Robert Post, Darold Powers, Adam Rape, Mary Rape, Rev. Robert Reed, Mildred Reynolds, Daniel Richardson, James Robinson, Dr. Harry B. Scholefield, Prof. Joseph Shaw, Rev. Benjamin Sheldon, Margaret Shidler, Iva Smith, Susan Snell, Nora O. Solum, Jack Soronen, Helen Stouffer, Rev. Frank Stroup, John Sullivan, C. R. Swanson, Edna Stowe Thomas, Clifford Trent, John Traut, Sterling Tucker, Rev. Herbert F. Vetter, Howard Wahrenbrock, Rev. John Wells, Rev. James P. Wilkes, Rev. Griffith Williams, Rev. Virgil Wood, J. Allen Young, F. Jackson Zylman III.

There were many others who related various incidents, many who wrote, some who telephoned. These also helped greatly, and I only regret that all their names cannot be included here. I owe particular thanks, however, to Jean Dulaney, who edited, informally, all of James Reeb's sermons; to Maurine Mulliner, who analyzed the underlinings in some two hundred volumes selected from his library; and to Helen Herrick, who gave many hours of time typing manuscripts, sermons, and interview recordings. To my secretary Ruth Blitman I am grateful for untold hours of typing and administrative work over and beyond the call of duty as the manuscript went through successive stages; to the people of All Souls Church for giving me the time to write the story and their understanding of my need to concentrate on the task; to Marie, and Jim's father and mother, for their help and unfailing cooperation in what was for them a very difficut undertaking; and lastly to my wife, Carolyn, who endured the isolation the writing made necessary and who helped, as always, in uncounted other ways.

DUNCAN HOWLETT

Washington, D.C.
December 8, 1965

No Greater Love

1 ଙ

Clear and Ever-Present Purpose

MAE REEB lay on a stretcher waiting to be wheeled into the delivery room. It was quiet in the hospital, for it was New Year's Eve and only a skeleton crew was on duty. Somewhere down the corridor her husband Harry waited. Outside, Wichita, Kansas, like cities all over the United States, was preparing to greet the New Year, 1927.

The pains were increasing now. Mae closed her eyes, and, her mind released momentarily from her immediate surroundings, slipped back seven years. She had been going to have a baby then, too, but her child was premature and had been stillborn. In her weakness she had caught the flu. Soon she was running a fever. It became alarmingly high, and for several days her life hung in the balance. Her hair fell out and later grew in gray, though she was but twenty-one years of age. As she came out of her delirium, Mae had said a prayer she still remembered.

"O Lord," she prayed, "if thou wilt heal me and give me another child, I will give him to thee. Whatever you may wish to use him for, that he shall do. Wherever you need him, there he shall go."

That had been seven years ago.

Now her lips moved in prayer once more as she renewed her pledge.

"O Lord, make me a good mother to this child," she said silently. "I give him to thee. Take him, make him thine. Use him as thou wilt."

Prayer came easily and naturally to Mae Reeb, for she had been reared in a family in which devout Protestantism and devout Catholicism merged. She had grown up in the little town of Wurtemberg in northwestern Pennsylvania. Her father was a Methodist, her mother an Irish Catholic. Since there was no Roman Catholic church in the area, her mother soon joined her father in attending the Methodist

1

church, although she herself never joined it. There the children were brought up under the strictest religious regimen.

Mae's mother was not merely pious, but practical in her religious devotion. She began assisting the doctors in Wurtemberg long before there was a hospital in the area and long before the profession of nursing was established there. When later the family moved to Ellwood City, a few miles away, she helped at the hospital there. As the hospital expanded its facilities, the knowledge and skill of Mae's fun-loving but peppery mother increased, together with her reputation, and she was legendary before she died. Mae's father, on the other hand, was Alsatian, of stern, censorious mien. Only Mae among the children dared stand up to him. Both parents were strong in character and neither was able to dominate the other. The Fox home was never a happy one and the marriage eventually broke up.

Harry Reeb came of a family no less devout. They were German Lutherans and were marked by the strong strain of piety that characterized most German immigrants to America, in particular those who settled in Pennsylvania. Like Mae's, Harry's ancestors had also settled in northwestern Pennsylvania, but much earlier, in the area around Zelienople, the next town to Wurtemberg. Harry Reeb grew up as Harry Rape, "Rape" being the anglicized form of the original German name "Reeb," sometimes also spelled "Reep." The name did not sound strange in Zelienople, for it had been in common use there for more than a century.

The baby born to Mae and Harry Reeb that night was a boy, and he was all they could have hoped for: healthy, strong, and perfectly formed, a truly beautiful child. It was past midnight when he came. That made his birthday January 1, 1927. It seemed an auspicious beginning for the New Year.

They named him James Joseph. James was the name of Mae's brother, who had recently died, of whom she had been very fond. It was also the name of her mother's father. Joseph they thought went well with James and it was the name of a man who had befriended them during the first years of their married life. Those had been terrible years. They first lived in Augusta, Kansas, a little town of three thousand people where Harry had a job in an oil machine shop with his brother Harvey. There they had rented a small two-room house. Pay was low and it was the best they could afford. But in winter when the winds swept across the plains, they had to chink up the walls and windows and put newspapers under the mattress to keep out the cold. Sometimes salt water from the natural gas wells that heated the house got into the pipes and put the fire out.

In the spring they rented rooms in the home of Joseph Marlow. Their first child was to be born in the early fall, and they could not face another such winter in the little drafty two-room house. Then came the tragedy of the stillbirth and Mae's bout with the flu. Her illness was so severe she remained an invalid for almost seven years afterward. Meanwhile, Harry came down with sciatica and was out of work for a year. They could no longer keep up the payments on their furniture and the store took it all back. During this time they knew real privation, but Mae never complained. Hard as life was, she met every reverse with a stern determination and a quiet fortitude and slowly but steadily regained her health.

In 1923, the Bridgeport Machine Company for which Harry worked moved its shop from Augusta to Wichita. Harry and Mae moved too. Harry was still making only forty-five cents an hour, but it was steady, dependable pay. Mae could make a dollar go further than anyone, and their horizon began to brighten. They began to hope for another child, and prayed fervently that such a thing might come to pass. They wanted another son to take the place of the one who had been denied them. When James Joseph was born healthy and whole, all the years of privation and suffering were forgotten. It was one of the happiest moments of their lives.

But joy and ease, comfort and freedom from anxiety, were not to be their lot. In the hospital the baby caught cold and came home a sickly child, and so he remained for many years. His mother devoted her full time and attention to him, and under her care he got along, if not too well, at least satisfactorily. But as the months passed they were slowly forced to the conclusion that Jimmie Joe's eyes, which were big and beautiful, were crossed. He was too young for an operation, the doctor told them, but glasses would help. Jimmie Joe, only eighteen months old, began wearing glasses.

This handicap only increased his mother's efforts on his behalf. Determined to give him every advantage and to endow him with the strongest Christian character, she now resolved somehow to compensate for the glasses which set Jimmie Joe apart from other children and handicapped him in his attempts to play with them. As a result, though by nature a strict disciplinarian, she indulged the boy. He in his turn, full of energy, became very mischievous and required the constant attention of an alert parent to keep him in hand.

He also became very demanding. Accustomed to the virtually un-divided attention of his mother, he could not understand why when people came to call she seemed to pay no attention to him. True, he was frequently the center of an admiring circle of adults. He liked that very much, but it made him feel all the more lonely when they moved on to grownup talk and acted as if he wasn't there at all. If this happened when his father was home, he liked to crawl up in his lap and lie there quietly. His father didn't say much when people were around, but he smiled at the boy and nudged him from time to time, and this made him feel that he was still a part of things. He saw little of his father, but he always waited eagerly for him to come home for supper. He loved to be swung up to the ceiling in his big, strong arms. Somehow it made him feel bigger and stronger himself. The child of a happy home, little Jimmie Joe was happy too. Usually the center of attention, he learned early both to demand it and to respond successfully to it. He was at once mischievous and quiet, demanding and obedient, and very endearing.

Mae and Harry quickly made friends wherever they went. Always they joined a nearby church, and Mae, particularly, was soon active in its affairs. Harry, who usually worked seven days a week, was not able to be. But their lives were constantly disrupted by the desire of Harry's brother Harve to open a new shop. Harry, as shop foreman, was the one chosen for the new enterprise. Mae and Harry had come to Kansas in 1919 immediately following their marriage. In the space of a few years they had moved from Augusta to Wichita to McPher-son. When, in 1933, they were asked to move to Canton, Kansas, just as Jimmie Joe was entering kindergarten, they refused. It was only ten miles from McPherson. Harry said he would prefer to com-mute.

They found some relief from this constant uprooting because each year Mae returned home to Ellwood City with her son for the sum-mer. The heat was almost unbearable in Kansas in July and August. The wind blew constantly and the sun beat down on the flat, shade-less plain. Back in northwestern Pennsylvania, it was cool and green.

And there, too were their own people—the friends and relatives they had known over the years. Harry always joined her for his two-week vacation at the end of August, and those summer visits became for them a kind of oasis in a rather dreary life.

Jimmie Joe entered kindergarten at McPherson in September, 1932. A year later, fed up with commuting, Harry moved the family to Canton, and there Jimmie Joe entered the first grade. But hardly had they settled down in Canton when Harry's brother Harve talked of opening still another shop, this time in Russell, Kansas, seventy-five miles away. They held off for a while, but in the end, only a little more than a year later, they moved again and glumly set themselves to starting a new life in still another small Kansas town.

It proved to be too much for them. They moved in the dead of a hard Kansas winter, and both Jimmie Joe and his mother came down with influenza as a result of it. In the wake of the flu, Jimmie Joe was stricken with rheumatic fever. He must lie flat on his back in bed to prevent strain on his heart, the doctors said. He could not lift his head or feed himself or even hold a book to read, and he was not to be excited. Sparing no expense, they got him a nurse, and she and his mother gave him their undivided attention.

"We spoiled him, I suppose," his mother said later, "but it was the only way."

The patience of Mae and Harry with their son was inexhaustible. But not that of the nurse, who was of a different temper and who did not have so much at stake. One day, her patience tried beyond endurance, she slapped him smartly on the face. His mother was terrified. Jimmie Joe apparently survived the blow unharmed, but that was the end of the nurse. Mae summarily dismissed her and took on the whole burden of caring for her son herself. She became his nurse, his companion, and his tutor. She talked to his teacher, and got the loan of the books and the assignments the second grade was to use that year. Each day she saw to it that Jimmie Joe did his lessons in step with his classmates. She joined the Junior Literary Guild to provide extra reading for her son, and from the Russell Public Library she got still more books for supplementary reading.

Mae Reeb was a person of iron will, resolute in her intent that her son should neither risk his health nor fall behind in his schooling. Deprived of the chance for an education for which she herself had yearned, and knowing its importance, she was determined that nothing should interfere with his progress eventually into college and perhaps graduate school.

She was succeeding remarkably well when yet another disaster struck them as it did thousands upon thousands of others in that area: the dust storms. In 1934 the people of Kansas witnessed a series of devastating storms. Then on the morning of February 25, 1935, the dust struck again, perhaps the worst storm of them all, but not the last. That spring, storm after storm after storm swept through Kansas. Mae was faced with the task of not merely caring for her bedridden son, but of keeping the dust from him as well, for coughing could be dangerous. Shutting the windows and doors helped only a little. The wind was so strong and the dust was so fine that it sifted into the house, filled the air and covered every object, clinging to the walls, now and then cascading down them like flour in a bin. She kept wet clean cloths over Jimmie Joe's body to keep the dust from his lungs. Somehow she succeeded, for his recovery from rheumatic fever was total.

But when in the winter of 1936 the doctor at last said Jimmie Joe might be up and about again, he had now missed most of the second grade and the first half of the third. The school authorities in Russell naturally thought he should repeat the second. But not his mother. She had not tutored him for a year for nothing. Could he not be put in the third grade on trial, she begged. Under her importunity, the school officials yielded and Jimmie Joe went into the third grade where he soon demonstrated to everyone's satisfaction that he could do the work.

His long illness had made him very weak, but what he lacked in strength his mother made up in devotion. Each morning she drove him to school. At recess time she was there with milk, cookies, and fruit. At twelve o'clock she returned to drive him home to rest through the noon hour. She then drove him back to school, returning to pick him up at the close of the day to take him home and put him to bed. He was not permitted to run and play with the other children. Going up and down stairs he had to take one step at a time. But his strength was slowly returning. Entering the fourth grade, Jimmie Joe was able to walk to school alone, play as he wished in the school yard, romp with the children after school, and generally live the life of a normal child once more.

But trouble came again the next year. The doctor felt Jimmie Joe was not yet strong enough to risk inoculating him against whooping cough. Better to take a chance on the disease itself. However, because he was still weak, Jimmie Joe duly contracted whooping cough when it went around the fifth grade. He developed a pain in his heart. Even after the disease itself had passed, the cough still hung on, a hard, hacking, nerve-racking cough. They worried now about tuberculosis.

Take him to Arizona or New Mexico, the doctor urged. The cough must be brought to a stop. It was not an easy decision, for their resources were still very meager. But if a few weeks' stay in the Southwest would cure him, they would manage somehow.

Mae took her son and went to Albuquerque. But the move, even though temporary, brought up the old problem of education again. She no longer felt equal to the task of tutoring her son. One of her new friends in Russell, however, Mrs. Edith Jones, a graduate of the University of Kansas, came to her aid. She moved in with Mae and Jimmie Joe, and began to tutor him so that he might go on with his class into the sixth grade in the fall. During the next four months Mrs. Jones kept up the program of study. She made no charge for her work. It was enough, she thought, to help where she was needed, particularly among people who so much appreciated what she did and profited so much from her efforts. As a result of her work Jimmie Joe again was able to keep up with his class despite his poor health. On returning to Russell, he took an examination which permitted him to enter the sixth grade. He had no trouble keeping up with the work. Meanwhile he grew rapidly in physical strength also.

The return from Albuquerque marked a turning point in the lives of Harry and Mae. It proved to be the last in the long series of hardships that had been their lot ever since their marriage fifteen years before. The unthinking would say their luck had changed. The more perceptive who saw how they met privation and tragedy, disaster and disease, would say that slowly, by virtue of the utmost determination, severe self-discipline, self-denial, and unswerving application to the task in hand, they had surmounted every obstacle in their path.

They had succeeded because they had a sense of purpose that was completely clear and ever-present. Determined that their son should have every advantage: health, a clear mind, a good education, a strong Christian character, and a deep religious faith, they themselves, in no small part had endowed him with these assets.

Jimmie Joe was now a thoroughly normal boy. As his thin body grew stronger, his alert mind and studious nature made him a front-rank scholar by the time he reached the freshman class at the Russell High School. There his ease of manner and readiness of speech put him on the debating team, and while still in his freshman year he was elected to the Junior National Honor Society. Mae and Harry were very happy and very proud. It had been a long road since the stillbirth of their first child and the coming of Jimmie Joe seven years later. The sacrifices they had made for him now seemed like nothing. In joy and gratitude they had given their all for him. Looking ahead, they knew they were ready to make whatever further sacrifice on his behalf might be asked of them.

2

A High School Boy Learns Compassion

HARRY and Mae Reeb found themselves uprooted for the last time in the summer of 1942. Owing to the disruption of the oil industry because of the war, Harry was unemployed for the first time in his life. There were many openings with other firms, however, and after giving the matter some thought, he took a job with the Western Oil Tool and Manufacturing Company of Casper, Wyoming. It was not because he liked the job particularly or knew much about the firm, but because Casper seemed to him and to Mae to be a good place to bring up a boy. It was a clean, neat city of some size with a large new high school built not many years before. That determined their choice. Serving the whole surrounding area, it was called the Natrona County High School. Its size, facilities, and unornate collegiate Gothic style symbolized the belief of the citizens in the highest standard of education for their chilrden. The teachers were held in the highest esteem by the citizens. Indeed, in character, intelligence, and dedication they were outstanding. Every honor won by the students, whether on the athletic field or in the scholastic area, was acclaimed by the people as an honor to Casper itself.

Jimmie Joe entered as a sophomore in September, 1942, determined to succeed here as he had as a freshman at the high school in Russell, Kansas. His teachers were impressed with his seriousness of purpose and his industry. They were struck with his clarity of mind. He had a neatness of appearance that was noticeable, a courteousness of manner that was exceptional, and a moral commitment that was outstanding. Never obsequious, he was considerate of everyone with whom he came in contact. He seemed to have a deep sensitivity to,

9

and understanding for, the feelings of his fellow students.

He was also argumentative—some said contentious. He would follow a discussion all the way to the end if anyone would continue on with him, and sometimes was so persistent that those who disagreed with him thought him obstinate. Yet he never failed to grant a point to the other side if he could be made to see his error or that there were weightier considerations he had not thought of. There were many who felt, however, that persuading him to see an error in his argument was something of an accomplishment.

The move to Casper marked the beginning of a basic change in his relationship to his parents. They had begun to sense vaguely that it was taking place, but it all came into focus one day when he came home from school and announced to his mother that she was to call him Jimmie Joe no longer. Not even Jimmie. From now on she was to call him Jim. The little boy whom they sometimes thought headstrong, but who could always be made to conform to their wishes, was developing a personality of his own and a will of his own as well. Where previously their family had consisted of two adults and a child, now it consisted of three people, one of whom sometimes seemed like a strange new adult standing apart, watching them. This was what they wanted. They had always tried to teach their boy to be independent, to make up his own mind and be himself. But it was hard when he stood over against them: harder still when his sudden assertion of his own desires meant their giving up a name that would be forever precious in memory. But they went along, because he had asked it and because they knew he was right.

Jim got off to a good start at the high school in Casper. His record at the Russell High School won him a place in a special English class taught by Miss Frances Ferris. Not everyone who wished to could enter her class. It was a select group of students who had already shown outstanding ability in literature, composition, and speech. But as the pupils themselves were the first to say, it was the teacher, Frances Ferris, that made the difference. She designed the program they followed. In the hands of anyone else it might have been one more course in literature, composition, and speech. In her hands it was an adventure. Short, alert, attractive, always smartly dressed, she injected her own spirit into her teaching in a manner that left her spent at the end of the day. Quick of mind, she was never trapped in argument. On the other hand, she knew the adolescent mind and could often see what a student was trying to say when he was not quite sure himself and help him get it into effective words.

Membership in Miss Ferris' English class also provided an important social milieu for Jim. Her room was a sort of center for her students, who tended to regard one another with a certain sense of superiority. They had much in common. All were serious students and found in one another the stimulus they sought and the opportunity to discuss questions of importance. Often they would gather in Room 209 after school for extra work or for preparation for interscholastic debating. At Christmas time, when the graduates were home from college, they would drop by to see Miss Ferris, talk over old times, and meet one another.

Another teacher who had great influence on Jim was Miss Margaret Shidler whose subject was Latin. He found Latin difficult and dropped the subject at the end of his sophomore year, but in that one year he made a lasting impression on his teacher and she on him. Miss Shidler first noticed Jim because he was so different from the other students. He enjoys a good joke, she thought, and he enjoys his fellow students, but there is nothing of the roughneck about him. She noticed something else. While he seemed to take little interest in Latin vocabulary and constructions, he had the deepest interest in what the Latin text described.

In the second semester they began reading about Caesar's treatment of conquered peoples. They read about the slave rebellion and the fight of the common people for rights. Discussing these events, the normally mild and courteous Jim sometimes became quite pugnacious. On one occasion the discussion moved from Gaul to Casper and from the plight of the conquered peoples there to the plight of those on the welfare rolls in Casper. The argument became very tense, with the majority of the class on one side along with the teacher, and the minority on the other side with Jim. He argued that people on welfare rolls didn't deserve to be there; that they needed help, social as well as monetary, and ought to be given it. The others felt that people on welfare had not tried hard enough to help themselves. Miss Shidler emphatically disagreed with his point of view, but she was impressed with the earnestness of the young man's defense of the poor and with the skill with which he marshaled his arguments.

Another day when the discussion again became intense, Miss Shidler made a statement, the exact nature of which she does not now remember. But she remembers Jim's response.

"But that's not right," he said. Miss Shidler, a person of strong character, strong convictions, and a strong sense of right of her own, was surprised to find that she was not ruffled by this retort. Ordinarily she did not permit answering back of any kind in her classes. But somehow this was different. This earnest lad had not been discourteous. He had not been denunciatory or dogmatic, although the words taken by themselves might easily have sounded that way. There was nothing sharp in his tone. It had been one of surprise more than anything else. Above all, he had obviously spoken out of deep moral conviction.

The practice of making swift moral judgments was characteristic of Jim in formal debating also. Although an excellent speaker and a careful, intelligent reasoner, Jim never made the debating team, for he was never able to argue with any persuasiveness for a point of view in which he himself did not believe. The students noticed this quality in him, as did his teachers. Both respected him for it, not only because of the obvious sincerity that lay behind his convictions, but even more because he himself lived by them. His standards of conduct were impeccable. His was a missionary spirit. He never ceased to try to draw others to his point of view, and would argue with whoever differed with him as long as they cared to continue. And yet with all the ardor of his convictions he had a sweetness of temper that was disarming. He could be censorious. He could become fierce in argument, but he never personalized the issue. He could become angry in argument, but when it was over, his anger was over, too. It was directed at the issue, never at the person with whom he was arguing.

In class and on the football field, on the playground, at church, and at home, the war was never very far away. Casper boys by the hundred were enlisting or being drafted. Casualty reports were already coming in. Many students were dropping out of high school to enter the service. Jim, though tempted, did not. A boy should finish high school before enlisting, he held. He should get his basic education first and then be ready to go. A little older and better educated, he would be a far more valuable soldier.

Jim solved the problem for himself by entering the Junior ROTC unit of the high school. True to character, he gave it his best. Soon he was known as a regular spit-and-polish cadet, immaculate, dependable, conscientious. His uniform was always pressed and spotless; his brass and his leather shone. He was always prompt, completely faithful, and drilled as if he meant it. He rose to be commander of the corps in his senior year, a signal honor to win at the high school, particularly in wartime.

Yet Jim was not one of the group that ran the school, and he would like to have been. The boy who had been nursed by his mother to the health he now enjoyed and who had had little chance for normal play contacts until he was in the sixth grade did not quite know how to adapt himself to the ways of his teenage peer group. In character and personality he was markedly different even from the other serious students. He was not only highly moral and eager to make the world a better place, he was deeply religious as well. It was generally understood that he planned eventually to enter the ministry. The average boy at the high school talked about who was dating whom, what club to join, the type of thing teen-agers think about most of the time. But not Jim. He always wanted to discuss world events: the war, its moral justification, the kind of world organization that would follow, human society, religion, and the church. Joseph Murphy, now one of the leading physicians in Casper, who was vice president of Jim's senior class and who hardly knew him more than to say hello, remembers the one personal contact he had with Jim. It was a conversation on the steps of the First Presbyterian Church. Jim was on his way into the church and Joe Murphy was about to join the class in-group at the local ice cream parlor across the park. The two boys earnestly discussed the meaning of war. For the class vice president, it was an event that still stands out in his memory.

There were other class leaders like Joe Murphy who admired Jim even if they did not chum around with him. Most of the students respected him but the opinions of some were strikingly negative. "Yes, I remember him," said one when the story of his death first broke in the papers. "He was a creep." This harsh judgment, to be understood, must be set over against the reaction of most of his classmates when they heard the Selma story.

"Yes, I remember him," they said. "Thinking over all the boys in

the class, Jim is the one I would have expected to risk his life in a
freedom march in the South."

But over and beyond his strikingly high moral character and religious intensity, Jim had two severe handicaps which would have set
him apart under any circumstances. One was his crossed eyes. It was
a very noticeable defect. No one ever mentioned them, but he knew
how greatly they handicapped him. The high school students were
considerate in this respect, but he still remembered the fun they made
of him when he was in the grammar school back in Russell. He could
never be sure, of course, but often he felt a boy or a girl might have
been friendly to him, but they seemed to draw back because he was
funny-looking. Always a realist, Jim faced the fact that this was so.

In the summer of 1944 he went back to Wichita with his mother
for the long-awaited eye operation. The doctor thought the best time
to do it had now come. It was a complete success. Thereafter Jim's
eyes were normal. Although their alignment was not always perfect,
few ever noticed it. He always wore tinted glasses which also helped.
But the operation itself was a traumatic experience because its outcome meant so much for his future. He was unable to speak for
several days afterward, but his joy was complete when he finally
realized that now he would be like other boys and girls. The following
school year nearly everybody, it seemed, was a little more friendly,
though Jim never became one of the in-group—his habits and their
attitudes were already too well fixed for that. But there was a difference; of that he was sure. He always felt that his election to the post
of Cadet Colonel, the commander of the ROTC Cadet Corps, a high
honor to win, was made possible by the removal of this defect.

During his high school years, Jim lived under an equally serious
handicap, however, the importance of which he himself never quite
saw: his name. His father still used the anglicized form of the family
name, Rape. Because Jim had always been used to it and the family
made nothing of it, he himself didn't think much about it. Men sometimes would tease Harry a little about it, but among their friends no
one ever suggested to them that their name was odd. At school it was
the same. No one made fun of Jim's name to his face, but behind his
back he was the butt of many an obscene joke. He never knew,
because he was not there to hear, the damage others did to him by
coarse wordplays on his name, jokes which in their thoughtless

cruelty sealed off from him friendship with all but the brave or forlorn.

One day a group of boys were discussing the matter. They agreed they were thankful not to have been born with a name like that.

"He's going to be a minister, isn't he?" one said.

"Imagine a name like that for a *minister!*"

"Imagine the newspaper! Jim comes to town. 'Rape in the pulpit' go the headlines. Imagine *that!*" They shouted with laughter. Others standing nearby came over to see what the big joke was. In twenty-four hours virtually the whole school had heard the story. Jim never knew why he felt so oddly uncomfortable the next day. He never knew why the teachers and a few students seemed solicitous, almost overfriendly, while others seemed ill at ease in his presence. He never knew because he never heard the story.

Nevertheless, during his senior year Jim rose rapidly toward the social acceptance for which he longed. Already respected as a first-rate student, as commander of the ROTC Cadet Corps, and as a person of the highest integrity, he now became less quiet and reserved in his manner. Because of his increasing self-confidence, the students began to see the joyous, friendly side of him previously known only to his friends. His easy, outgoing manner was infectious, and in the latter half of his senior year there was a noticeable increase in his popularity among the girls in his class. As always, Jim responded with natural grace and affability. The boy who took his diploma at the Natrona County High School in June, 1945, seemed hardly to be the same person as the sophomore from Russell, Kansas, who had entered the school three short years before.

Yet basically Jim was still the same, essentially the product of his home and of the single-minded devotion of his father and mother. He was still the center of their thought. His mother, in particular, followed his every move with solicitous care. She constantly strove to arouse his intellectual curiosity and his will to succeed by holding the highest goals of achievement always before him. No grades could be too high in his courses to satisfy her, no honors too frequent or eminent. Some of her friends thought she kept at him too much, but as a person Jim did not seem driven by an overbearing or over-ambitious parent. The gleam was in his own eye. He always seemed to be beckoned on by the future, not driven from behind.

The goal his parents held before their son was not one of simple

worldly success. It was always success with a purpose as they saw it.
Jim was preparing himself for a great work that he would do one day.
They were not sure just what it was to be: nor was he. But it was to be
centered in the church, and animated by the ideal of service. That
was clear. His mother did not consciously mold her son in the image
of her own mother, whom she adored, but no doubt she tried unconsciously to do so. Certainly the Christian ideal which was clearly
articulate in both parents and which both put into practice, early became articulate in Jim. From the time when he was a little boy, he
wanted to help where help was needed. He believed that he could.
The determination that marked his parents through all their trials became his, and this above all else sustained him at the high school. He
knew that it did not really matter in the end how the others treated
him. He believed in himself because his father and mother believed in
him, and because a certain few adults and fellow students whom he
respected did also.

When Jim graduated from the Natrona County High School in
June, 1945, he was in many ways less mature than the average student. But in certain ways he was far more so. Alone among his
classmates, perhaps, Jim had learned while still very young how it
feels to suffer social exclusion because of a physical characteristic
with which you had nothing to do and could not change. In his case
he had been able to change through the eye operation. Then people
changed toward him. But supposing the operation had failed? He
dared not think about it.

Because he was basically so attractive and increasingly stood on
the edge of great popularity, Jim learned in high school what it was
to belong and not to belong. Such an experience has made many men
bitter. It made Jim compassionate. His religion taught him that it is
the task of men to relieve the sufferings of one another. This he always
strove to do thereafter. For now he knew how men can be made to
suffer, not because they are unworthy but because they are different.

3

The Fuller Life in Christ

IT WAS the church above all else that had sustained Jim's parents through their years of privation in Kansas. In Augusta it was the Christian Church; in Wichita, the Baptist Church; in McPherson, the Christian Church again. At Canton they had gone to the Methodist Church where Jim was christened, and at Russell, to the Congregational Church which Jim joined at the age of twelve. They were not religious floaters. There were always good reasons for the choice they made. Sometimes it was the only church in the town.

In Casper, the family began attending the First Presbyterian Church, a large red brick American Gothic structure, with soaring roof, easily the leading church in town. As always, Jim's mother became an active member of the Women's Federation. Jim joined the Westminster Fellowship, the high school youth group. Soon he was its head. With characteristic verve he helped extend its religious, social, and service activities. They went tobogganing in the winter and on camping trips in the summer. He was ready to help in getting speakers, ready to conduct the worship service himself when asked. There was always work to be done around the church, still unfinished since the Depression. Noticing a large unused coal bin in the basement of the education building, Jim organized its refinishing and painting as a chapel.

He also developed a series of interfaith meetings to enable the members of the various youth groups in Casper to meet each other and exchange views. It was a time of real cooperation and mutual helpfulness among the churches, and his program enhanced what today would be called the spirit of ecumenicity which then prevailed. In all these activities his father and mother were never far away, assisting with transportation, providing refreshments or meals, acting as chaperons on overnight expeditions.

17

In the circle of the church Jim was not an outsider. He was highly regarded. His enthusiasm, friendliness, sense of responsibility, and willingness to work, together with his obvious religious devotion, made him very much sought after by both old and young. It was because of the way people received him there that Jim found the confidence in himself to sustain him at the high school. In the church he discovered that he had the capacity for leadership.

During the spring of 1944, when Jim was a junior in high school, he became involved in a church program which further developed his talents. Robert Reed, a mechanic at the Air Base, looking for something to do in his spare time that was worthwhile, had organized the North Casper Boys Club. He called them the Christian Rangers after the Ranger Commando Unit in the army the boys so much admired. Bob was also a regular attendant at the First Presbyterian Church and was often among the boys Jim's mother took home to Sunday dinner in an attempt to relieve their loneliness. Soon Jim was helping him with the Boys Club after school, and his mother, as always, was supporting the program with good food.

Bob Reed was but two years older than Jim and soon they became fast friends. When Bob shipped out in January, 1945, in the middle of Jim's senior year, Jim took over the Boys Club himself despite his heavy load of work at the church and the high school. Now alone, he proved to be a very successful leader. His method of handling the youngsters was to mix right in with them on their level, an approach he had learned from his father.

"To handle men you can't boss them," he had often heard his father say. "You have got to be one of them." It was a lesson he learned early and made use of all his life.

Jim was lonely after Bob Reed left. Somehow the club wasn't as much fun any more. There had been a deeper aspect to their relationship. Both boys expected to enter the Presbyterian ministry as soon as they could complete their education. They had talked much of religion during the year they spent together. In March, Bob mailed a devotional book to Jim. When Jim wrote back later, he said he hadn't been to a movie since he read it, which gives some indication of the character of the book.

For some time Jim had been trying to decide whether to enlist in the Army. Bob had consistently urged him not to. As a candidate for the ministry under the Casper Presbytery, he would not be drafted, Bob argued. The Army would be a terrible bore and an evil influence. But Jim was unpersuaded. "I am under no illusions about army life," he wrote shortly after V-E Day, "but I know I will be sorry if I don't go." June 14, 1945, his high school diploma safely in hand, he was duly inducted into the armed forces of the United States. To all who protested his failure to claim exemption, he made the same answer.

"If everyone else has to go, then I must go too. The fact that I intend to enter the ministry should not make me exempt." And he often added a supporting reason, not determinative in itself. "I think I will be a far better minister if I have been through the same experiences as my people. If I know what they know and they know that I know it, I will be able to serve them much better." He had another reason that he seldom expressed. He knew that army life would help him develop into the well-rounded man he wanted to become.

Once inducted, he found that all the time and attention he had given to the high school ROTC unit meant nothing. He and the other members of the corps were thrown in with the rank-and-file draftees who had had no training whatever. Because he had been corps commander they allowed him to carry the company flag, small compensation, it seemed to him, for his long hours of drilling on the high school athletic field. Sometimes it took all the patience he could muster to sit through lectures on military service given by men who obviously knew less about the subject than he did.

Jim did not regret joining the army, he wrote Bob Reed from the induction center. But less than a month later, when his basic training had begun at Fort Roberts in California, he wrote, "They are trying to make a killer out of me: that is something I must decide for myself." During the seventeen intensive weeks of basic training, he tried to keep up his practice of daily devotions and a daily letter home, but it proved more than he could manage. The purpose of the program was to toughen men and prepare them for battle, and it left little time for anything else. Learning how hard it was for him to find time to write, his mother suggested that he not try to write her every day, which he found a great relief.

In August, his father and mother drove out to visit him, and his mother stayed some time. She was greatly worried about him, particularly by the fact that there seemed to be no suitable recreation available on weekends when the boys were permitted to leave camp. Paso Robles, the nearest population center of any size, had a Presbyterian Church, she found, but no minister at the time. So she went to the Methodist Church and put her problem squarely in the minister's lap. Was there not, she asked, a member of his church to whose home Jim could go on weekends where he would find himself in congenial surroundings and could seek the kind of recreation and activity in the church to which he was accustomed? The arrangement was easily made and thereafter Jim's leisure time was absorbed with the kind of things he enjoyed most.

Nevertheless, he became increasingly discouraged with army life. They practiced with live ammunition and he was terrified lest he kill one of the men inadvertently. By now he was sorry he had entered the army and would have gotten out if he could. He turned down an opportunity to go to Officers Candidate School because he wanted to get out of the army as soon as possible.

Perhaps in reaction to his military training, perhaps as an outgrowth of his deeply religious nature: perhaps because of both, Jim became increasingly devout during his tour of duty. Encouraged by Bob Reed, he had taken with him to training camp his Bible, which he read daily, a Bible commentary, and a selection of devotional books of which he made constant use. *Strength for Service to God and Country* was one of his favorites. He went to Los Angeles several times to hear a well-known evangelist at the Church of the Open Bible and also attended the fundamentalist Christian Missionary Alliance Church there. He found several friends among the servicemen, all, like himself, of fundamentalist persuasion, but he knew his religious outlook created problems for him with the other men in his unit. "I am trying to strike a happy medium," he wrote Bob Reed, "between a holier-than-thou attitude and not giving in an inch on principle."

His basic training completed, Jim found himself at Fort Ord in California, an embarkation point. The two atomic bombs had now been exploded. V-J Day had passed, but the men expected to be shipped to Japan as a part of the army of occupation. Jim was happy at Ft. Ord. He found a group of committed Christian friends there, and thought Monterey beautiful. "I feel joy in my Christian experience," he wrote Bob Reed one day. "It tells me I am just touching on a fuller life in Christ."

That sense of a fuller Christian life was deepened by a profound religious experience he had in Alaska to which he was next assigned. One night soon after arrival, feeling a strong urge to pray, he entered an army chapel. Inside all was blackness, but suddenly there seemed to be light all around him. He did not doubt that it was of heavenly origin. Now he knew that the beliefs he had always held were true. Now he knew what the fuller life in Christ really was, for he had experienced it in his heart, seen it with his eyes and known Christ at firsthand in his soul. What doubts he may have had as to his call to be a minister were all dispelled. He had been chosen, and having been chosen, he would serve to the utmost of his ability.

Jim was stationed at Ft. Richardson in Anchorage and assigned to the Headquarters Company, Special Troops. He was soon made Technical Sergeant 5th Class, became a clerk typist, and was promoted to Technical Sergeant 3rd Class. In the city of Anchorage he early made friends with the Presbyterian minister and was soon deeply involved in the life of the church. Each Saturday night he attended Youth for Christ rallies, taught Sunday School the next morning, had a mission class in the afternoon, and helped with the Christian Endeavor Society in the evening. As if this were not enough religious exercise, on Monday and Friday evenings he met with a group of like-minded servicemen for study and prayer.

But the work at the Presbyterian Church soon became routine; the Youth for Christ movement was a failure—nobody came—and he found the church itself quite resistant to change. Always ecumenical in spirit, he tried getting the Protestant churches of the city together much as he had the youth groups in Casper, but he found little support and a lot of opposition. By mid-March he was homesick. He bought a camera and began taking color slides of the Alaskan scenery, and started going to the movies again. He did not give up teaching his Sunday School class, but his enthusiasm for work at the church steadily declined. The purchase of the camera was a small but real symbol of a shift in emphasis from the religion of the church in which he still deeply believed to the religion of nature to which he was beginning increasingly to respond.

Jim thought the Anchorage area in Alaska the most beautiful he had ever seen. He hated his Quonset hut which made him feel closed in, and he hated the enveloping fog which often rolled in. But when the weather was clear and he was able to get outside, it seemed to him that his very soul expanded. Alaska was wide and open like Wyoming. All around, it seemed, snowcapped mountains towered. Behind the city rose the Chugach Range, to the north lay the Talkeetnas, and across the Inlet, the peaks of the Alaskas. It was as if the Tetons had been bent around Anchorage like a great horseshoe with a bay on the open end. But the Northern Lights impressed him most of all. He had never seen anything so beautiful, he wrote Bob Reed. He related them to his vision in the chapel. The two experiences were not the same, he realized, and yet whenever he saw the Aurora, it stirred within him the same mystical feelings he had felt in the darkness that night.

Jim got out of the Army just before Christmas in 1946. He had been gone just eighteen months. It was a happy homecoming and a happy reunion for them all. But as with many returning servicemen, the excitement of the homecoming soon began to wear off. A mood of depression set in. To his amazement, Jim found himself restless, unhappy, and bored.

As they had always done with his problems, Jim, his father and mother faced this one together. They talked about his taking a job, but at best that would only be temporary: in the fall he would go to college. Then why not start now? It was of course too late to enter a college of any consequence, but he could begin right there in Casper in January and perhaps get a little head start on his college work. A few months before, the Casper Junior College had been founded by a group of enterprising citizens who foresaw the necessity of helping to provide for the great number of returning servicemen who would be seeking an education under the "G.I. Bill of Rights," as the act of Congress to provide for the free education of servicemen was popularly called. Classes were held on the third floor of the high school.

Jim found he could be enrolled in time to begin with the January quarter. It seemed good to be back in the familiar surroundings of the high school again. He stopped by to see Miss Ferris, Miss Shidler, and some of the other teachers he liked best. It was good to talk to them, good to be back in a normal environment once more. It was the same and yet not the same. Outwardly everything looked just as it always had, yet everything also seemed different. For one thing, he was sure they were admitting students to the high school at a much earlier age than they used to. But it was not long before he realized that any change was really in himself. Eighteen months in the army had made a difference in him of which he had not been aware.

Nevertheless as he had in high school and while he was in the Army, Jim immediately plunged once more into the work of the church. During the late winter of 1947 the minister of the First Baptist Church was taken sick. With no one to fill the pulpit for him, he turned in desperation to Jim. Could he fill in temporarily? Jim was glad to do what he could and handled himself very creditably. The people left the church that first Sunday assuring each other that here was a young man with a great future in the ministry. His clarity of mind, his earnestness of manner, greatly impressed them all.

Jim preached a number of times to the Baptist congregation. Much as they loved their own preacher and dearly as they wished to see him return to health and strength, few were sorry on the Sundays when they found the tall, thin young man with black curly hair in their pulpit. But this arrangement did not last long. In the great influx of people during and just after the war were a number of Southern Baptists who insisted on closed communion. Through their efforts the bright young ex-serviceman who was soon to enter a Presbyterian seminary was dismissed with thanks.

Jim was never idle. He was in constant demand among the church people of Casper. The Winter Memorial Presbyterian Church on the north side of the city had never been able to afford a minister of its own, for the congregation was too small to support one. Would Jim conduct evening services for them, they asked. He said he would be glad to try, and again he was an immediate success, so much so that preaching there on Sunday evenings became his regular assignment for the remainder of the winter.

But Jim was not satisfied with merely preaching the Word. From his mother he learned early that a true believer is also a doer of the Word. And there was much to do. Young Western cattle towns like Casper were hardly conspicuous for observing the respectable virtues. In the boom following World War I, Casper had become primarily an oil town. The early oil towns were no more notable for sober respect-

ability than the cattle towns had been. Casper at that time offered a
real challenge to churches wishing to do more than preach the gospel
with averted eyes.

But any effort in this direction became impossible with the establishment of the great Army Air Base during World War II. The
Casper Diamond Jubilee Souvenir Program tells the story of the
"Sandbar," the town's red light district. When it was declared off
limits to the Air Base, the managers of the district countered by
buying a few fine homes in the residential area where they continued
business as usual. The neighbors were outraged but their objections
availed nothing.

After the war this situation was rectified, but there was still much
to be done. Jim had not been home long when, not yet twenty-one
years of age, he was caught up in a reform movement in Casper
churches. In a cooperative project in which almost all of them joined,
they rid the city of slot machines. The townspeople still recall seeing
women with little enough for meat and groceries emptying their
pockets into the slot machines in the vain hope that by spending a
small sum they might win and for once be able to buy the things they
really wanted.

The churches also undertook to get the police to enforce the rule
against serving liquor to minors. To establish their case they needed
evidence. Jim volunteered to get some pictures, and did so. When
they were presented to the police with the demand that something be
done, the police acted. Nobody was brought to trial, but thereafter
tavern owners were more particular to whom they served their wares.
The reform movement instituted and carried out by the churches with
Jim's help indicated a new mood of maturity in Casper. It marked the
transfer of the city's affairs into the hands of a group of responsible
citizens.

During this period Jim's religious fervor was very intense and his
fundamentalist convictions were still very strong. Besides his work
among the churches and in the reform movements, he was always
ready in discussion or reading to pursue any religious question. He
was endlessly probing, endlessly inquiring, endlessly seeking the
truth. One evening when his father and mother had some friends in
for dinner, the discussion turned to the ancestry of Jesus and the two
genealogies given in the Bible for his paternal descent. The argument

became very hot. At this Jim disappeared down the back stairs to his room, got out all the books he could find that dealt with the question, and except for meals scarcely emerged for three days, while he pursued the question as far as his books and his own thought would allow.

How deeply his convictions ran, how far he expected to follow their implications, and what he thought those implications might be, Jim revealed to an old friend Jack Lamb one night. Lamb, newly out of the service like the others, was in Casper waiting for a teaching post. He was a college graduate whom Jim had come to know while still in high school. Back then they used to argue religion far into the night. Now they were at it again. On this particular night when Jack dropped by for a visit, they sat up late talking about what it means to be religious and how far you have to go in your religious commitment. Jack already knew that Jim's religious fervor had increased markedly since his high school days. Now he learned that his religion centered in a verse in Paul's Epistle to the Romans:

The Spirit itself beareth witness with our spirit, that we are the children of God:
And if children, then heirs; heirs of God, and joint-heirs with Christ; if so be that we suffer with him, that we may be also glorified together.

If all believers are heirs of God and in consequence joint heirs with Christ, Jim insisted, it must follow that all true believers are called upon to suffer with Christ. If we do, we shall achieve his glory, he said. Jack thought it a good Bible quotation, but didn't think it need be carried that far. He was glad to be one of the joint heirs with Christ if he could qualify, but he did not see that it necessarily involved suffering. But Jim did. In the chapel in Alaska he had found the fuller life in Christ, he said. And since then he had come to see that it would involve suffering. But why, Lamb found himself asking on the way home afterward. Is it true that man has to suffer for his religion? Apparently Jim thinks it is.

4

Total Christian Commitment

"I CANNOT remember a time when I wasn't in church on Sunday, nor can I remember a time when I haven't studied the Bible through some means. When I was still very young I joined a church and started to take part in young people's activities. About the time I entered high school, I began to study the Bible more intently. As I grew in knowledge of the claims of Christ upon all men and with the conviction that Christ died for me and that through him I had received life, I was continually confronted with his words, 'Follow me.'

"Just before leaving high school I made my decision to enter the ministry and was taken under care of Presbytery. Since that time I have never been without the conviction that I must carry the news of salvation to men.

"I believe that in the Bible God has revealed himself to men and in Christ he redeemed man unto himself and called them to fellowship in his church. It is essentially this message and the Lord who gave it which constitute my reasons for entering the ministry."

In these words Jim Reeb summarized his feelings about his boyhood and youth, the place of the church and the Christian faith in his life. The statement appears in his own handwriting on his application for theological school under the heading "My Reasons for Choosing the Ministry as a Life Work." It reveals what his life in this period also shows, an unusually devout young man of strict undeviating, unquestioning Christian orthodoxy.

Yet it was just at this time that the winds of change began to blow in his mind. As with so many young people, it was the impact of his college years that made the difference. Jim went to St. Olaf College, a Lutheran school at Northfield, Minnesota. It was evangelical in its emphasis, but stanchly academic also. The change in James Reeb's thinking that began there was not suspected either by his teachers or by himself, but it can be seen even in his handwriting as he wrote out his reasons for making a career of the ministry. The writing slants to the right, it stands erect, and it slants backward. It is both school-boyish and mature. This is just what we see in Jim as we follow him through his college years, basic changes taking place, the direction of which is not yet clear.

He entered St. Olaf in the fall of 1947 and was fortunate to be admitted. Flooded with applications from returning G.I.'s and beset by a policy of preference for Lutherans, the admissions board was confronted with a difficult decision in Jim's case. This young man was a transfer student and their experience with transfers in the past led them to be cautious. But Jim was only technically so. His semester at Casper Junior College stood in his favor, for he had gone there only while waiting to enter an older, well-established school. So did the straight A-B record he had made there. He was accepted, but on condition that he demonstrate his capacity to do St. Olaf-level work.

He was accepted also on the basis of a warm recommendation from an alumnus of the school, Rev. Griffith Williams, pastor of Our Savior's Lutheran Church in Casper. He and Jim had become good friends during Jim's later high school years. It was to Griff that Jim had turned when he entered the service and was faced with the prob-lem of what to do with the North Casper Boys Club. Griff had taken it over and through it had become a close friend of Jim's father and mother as they helped him with it. In fact he became a kind of second son to them.

Bob Reed, now out of the service, had meanwhile entered Wheaton College in Illinois and had been writing to urge Jim to join him there. Griff, on the other hand, argued for St. Olaf. Because of Jim's fervent evangelical turn of mind he felt very strongly that a more objective academic atmosphere was desirable for him. St. Olaf was church-centered, but it was not nearly so fundamentalist as Wheaton. A visit to the two schools in the spring of 1947 settled the matter. Wheaton was in a cramped urban setting, but St. Olaf was on a hilltop in the gently rolling hills of Minnesota. This greatly impressed the boy from Wyoming. He was impressed, too, by the people he met there and by the academic standards the school maintained.

At St. Olaf, Jim's special character and personality were soon
recognized by his fellow students. He was seen to be devout, filled
with evangelistic fervor, and a strict fundamentalist in his views of the
Bible, all of which were thought to be quite proper in a candidate for
the ministry. He went out for none of the athletic teams or for the
famous St. Olaf Choir. He gave his time to his studies, and, for
extracurricular activities, to the church and social service. He was
an honor student and graduated *cum laude*. Moreover, by taking
extra courses and going to summer school, he completed his academic work in two and a half years. He wanted to get on with his
education, he said. The army had delayed him a year and a half, and
he wanted to make up the lost time if he could.

The campus in those days was dominated by older men who had
had several years' service in the armed forces. Many of them had
been under fire. They were not accustomed to ask philosophical questions. Most of them wanted an education only in order to earn a
better living when they got out. They were sophisticated, they had
learned long since not to volunteer for anything. They picked and
chose whom they would associate with and they ignored the rest. Few
if any were marked by the bright-eyed enthusiasms that so easily
swept through Jim. The main part of the student body hardly knew
him. As before, he was not a part of the in-group.

But Jim easily achieved a sense of belonging in the smaller, religiously oriented groups on campus. He was, for example, very much
a part of the beginning Greek course, where rapport among the
students usually developed early and lasted throughout the year.
Almost all who took it were, like Jim, preseminary students. They
often twitted one another about their differing religious views, and
in the course of it more than one serious attempt was made to
bring Jim over to Lutheranism. One evening, pressed hard to give
reasons for holding to his Presbyterianism, he said:

"The Lutherans are not sufficiently involved in life for me. I like
your theology better than my own. Some of the Presbyterian ministers
compromise with modernism to the point where you wonder how
God's Word can any longer guide their lives. You wonder how they
can any longer preach from the Word. Among the Lutherans there is
no question on this score. But the Presbyterians are involved to a
greater degree in the lives of the people, and I think that is just as

important as sound doctrine. The one leads straight to the other."

They challenged him to give examples of what he meant, and he told them about his work with the Boys Club in North Casper. This was Jesus' teaching, he reminded them. To support his point he quoted the passage in which Luke relates how Jesus, going to the synagogue, was given the Scriptures to read. Jesus chose the opening verses of Isaiah 61, and read:

The Spirit of the Lord is upon me; because he hath anointed me to preach the gospel to the poor; he hath sent me to heal the broken-hearted, to preach deliverance to the captives, and recovering of sight to the blind, to set at liberty them that are bruised. To preach the acceptable year of the Lord.

The discussion moved on to the war, still so vivid in the minds of them all. Most of them had been on active duty; some had actually been in battle. Many of them had intimate friends who had died. The war was a struggle against fascism, they all agreed, and for this reason it had to be won. The Lutherans were haunted by the fact that Nazism had come to flower in the midst of the largest concentration of Lutherans in the world. The discussion moved to Dietrich Bonhoeffer, at the time virtually unknown among American theologians. They candidly faced the fact that Bonhoeffer was their hero because, unlike most of the German clergy, he had involved himself in the struggle against Nazism and had given up his life in doing so. In Bonhoeffer's sacrifice they recognized the truth of what Jim was saying.

The argument shifted to the United States. Here, most of them agreed, things were different. But on this point too Jim stood out against them. The difference was more apparent than real, he argued. With the same forces at play, under the same circumstances, the same thing would happen here. Man's tendency to evil and sin is universal. We who are the believers must always be ready anywhere and at any time to participate actively in the struggle for what we believe, he said. We must be willing to take our stand against the evil forces of our day and to run whatever risks such a stand might involve. As they listened, the students knew that Jim was not merely developing a theory. It was clear to all that what he believed he was prepared to live out in his own life.

In his first year Jim found himself, along with most of the other freshmen, in Ytterboe Hall, a large ugly, four-story structure of red brick that contrasted sharply with the newer white stone buildings the college had been erecting since the 1930's. The counselor in his wing was Lloyd Hustvedt, an older man who had seen combat duty during the war. His role was not merely to maintain discipline, but also to provide guidance and help to the students in his charge. Jim took to the slender yet rugged Norwegian at once, and Lloyd responded to him. He saw that beneath Jim's earnest exterior there was a lot of sparkle and fun. He used to like to needle him about his fundamentalist views. Jim took it in good part because he knew Lloyd's own faith was strong, but he didn't take it lying down. One day he challenged Lloyd on his views of the Bible.

"How are you able to take some parts of the Bible literally and others not?" he asked.

"I think some things are to be taken literally and some only figuratively," Hustvedt replied.

"But which ones?" Jim persisted. Hustvedt tried to explain, but it was useless.

"You take literally what you want to and you take figuratively what you want to. Isn't that it?" Jim asked.

"I suppose I do."

"Then you have no guide at all," said Jim. "Once you admit that any one part of the Bible is not to be taken literally, then you have to go all the way. Then your guide is not God's Word any longer. It is your judgment of God's Word. If you can't accept the whole Bible as literally true, then you cannot accept any of it as necessarily true."

Jim's strict fundamentalism brought on many an argument during his years at St. Olaf. Sometimes half a dozen students would gang up on him and try to move him off his literalistic base. He always had an answer. It was all or nothing, he insisted. Once you begin the sorting process, there is no place to stop. Some of them secretly agreed with him. Once you began, where *could* you stop, they wondered. But that thought was intolerable, and they quickly thrust it aside. If applied, it would mean the end of the Christian religion, for Christianity was founded on the Bible. Yet they had to make some concessions. After all, you couldn't take everything in the Bible literally—the story of Jonah and the whale, for instance. The men in the dormitory who cared about such things admired Jim for his consistency and the good humor as well as the determination with which he held to his position. They had no wish for compromise either. But they also realized even Biblical literalism can be carried to the point of absurdity.

By his second year at St. Olaf Jim was already in the junior class as a result of the accelerated program he was pursuing. His credits at Casper Junior College, his extra work during his freshman year, and summer school at the University of Colorado had advanced him a full year. Lloyd Hustvedt, now a senior, had meanwhile been promoted to the office of Head Counselor at Ytterboe Hall. Contrary to the usual practice, he had asked and had been given permission to pick his own staff of assistants. Among them he included Jim. He had observed at close range his young friend's sense of responsibility and his deep interest in the needs of people. Jim wondered if he was equal to the task, but wanted to try. He was glad to be back with Lloyd, even if it meant his spending another year in old Ytterboe rather than going over to the new and handsome men's dormitory across the campus.

Hustvedt soon discovered he had chosen a far better man than he realized. Most of the counselors were so eager to advance the cause of their own charges, they would do so to the disadvantage of the dorm as a whole. The result was an inevitable clash. Then the Head Counselor was called upon to do some counseling on his own. He tried to give his staff members a sense of proportion and persuade them that they had to manage the corridor assigned to them with the other groups always in mind. Jim was the lone exception. He always seemed to see the needs of his corridor in relation to those of the dormitory as a whole.

Hustvedt discovered two other unusual characteristics in Jim: the thoroughness with which he followed through on whatever he undertook, and his deep concern for individual human beings, whether fortunate or unfortunate. A series of thefts occurred on his corridor during the middle of the year. Jim took measures to uncover the thief, but the thief proved elusive. He then began marking money and luncheon tickets and put watchers where the boy using the tickets or money could be spotted. Soon the thief was identified. When Jim laid the evidence before him, he confessed.

The boy was then taken before the Men's Senate for "trial." But instead of acting in the role of prosecutor as he was expected to do,

Jim defended him. No disciplinary action was necessary or proper, he argued. The demoralization of his corridor resulting from the thefts had cleared up as soon as it was known that the thief had been found. The thief himself was now penitent; genuinely so. He had learned his lesson. Only harm could come from exposing and publicly punishing him. The Senate accepted Jim's recommendation, and his faith in the young man proved to be justified, for he never stole again.

Jim was tireless in his role as confidant and guide to his freshman charges. The time he would give them seemed endless and his patience was inexhaustible. He was at his best sitting alone with a boy face to face while the boy poured out his troubles. Always he listened closely, making suggestions, offering advice, helping where he could.

But Hustvedt also had his problems with this high-principled young man. Every now and then Jim would get after him because one of the other junior counselors was not attending to his duties. There were times when it seemed to Hustvedt that Jim in his earnestness was taking the whole dormitory as his responsibility. He had to face the fact that this rather brash young man occasionally got under his skin. He would have been glad if Jim had confined his thought and attention to his own corridor. Once Jim awakened Hustvedt in the middle of the night regarding a problem he was having to deal with.

"Can't that wait until morning?" Hustvedt demanded with some irritation.

"No," Jim replied, "it cannot wait. This is important." Hustvedt does not remember now what the problem was. He remembers only that he got reluctantly out of bed because Jim said it was important and reminded him that important things cannot wait.

Through Hustvedt Jim sought to understand the psychology of men under battle conditions.

"How did you find that men acted in moments of crisis?" he asked. "What did they do when they faced the possibility or even the probability of their own death?" Jim supposed that a man facing death confronts the meaning of life, but he wanted to know. Hustvedt confirmed his surmise. He told of giving communion before landing in the face of enemy fire to men who had never had communion before. Jim seemed to understand why this would be so. Hustvedt, like most returning servicemen, did not like to talk about his war experiences.

He wanted to forget it all as quickly as he could. But with this young man who so eagerly sought to understand life in all its phases, he would often reminisce. Jim's rapt attention always drew more from him than he originally intended to say.

Hustvedt could accept almost anything from Jim because in him the distance between conscience and act was exceedingly short. More often than not they were coexistent. Jim's conscience could be a stern taskmaster. Yet for all his idealism, he was not a crusader or even a reformer in the traditional sense of these terms. He preferred quiet reason and personal influence to mass persuasion, Hustvedt reflected. This man was trying to make himself fit for the world, not the world fit for him. His convictions were many and they were firm, but they were not barbed. They were not harsh. In a remarkable way Jim seemed to have reconciled high principle with understanding and love for his fellow man.

A literalist as far as belief in the Bible was concerned, Jim was never legalistic in his approach to Scripture. For him the Bible was an unfailing source of inspiration and light. One Sunday afternoon, after a long session with the Bible, he walked into the room of Howard Cole, one of his close friends, a pretheologue like himself. Jim's eyes were ablaze. He had again been reading Paul's letter to the Romans. The Bible open upon the palm of his hand, he began reading:

God; who will render to every man according to his deeds:
To them who by patient continuance in well doing seek for glory and honour and immortality, eternal life:
But unto them that are contentious, and do not obey the truth, but obey unrighteousness, indignation and wrath,
Tribulation and anguish, upon every soul of man that doeth evil, of the Jew first, and also of the Gentile.

The meaning of these words had struck something deeply responsive within him. "If there is tribulation and anguish upon the soul of every man that doeth evil," he said, "then there is tribulation and anguish upon my soul too: on everyone's. That means that our task as ministers will be to lift the burden of anguish from those who do wrong, and that means just about all men, for all men are sinners. Their anguish then becomes mine."

"Yes, probably," Cole replied, "but the passage doesn't hit me that hard. I'll do what I can, but the anguish, no. I guess I just don't feel it. Not yet, anyway."

Going back and forth from Northfield to Casper with his fellow Casperite Arthur Olsen, by train if necessary, by car if either happened to have one, provided an opportunity for protracted theological argument. On one memorable ride when Howard Cole was with them, they got into a discussion about the value of great cathedrals. Olsen and Cole took the position that they were necessary and proper monuments to the glory of God and his worship by man. Jim held that a modest building without any frills was far more appropriate for a church.

"The first responsibility of a church is the needs of its people," Jim retorted. "It would be testimony to their integrity as churches if they were to build cheaper buildings with smaller and less pretentious roofs. As it is, each tries to put up the most expensive and lofty structure it can afford." Like most such arguments, it was a draw. But the discussion reached heights of such emotional intensity that none of them ever forgot it.

His father and mother, had they overheard, would not have been surprised at the position their son took or at the points he marshaled to support it. While he was in high school there had been many an argument in his own living room over the same issue. And it had not been theoretical. At that time the people of the First Presbyterian Church were worshiping in the basement while above the low ceiling over their heads soared the great vaulted auditorium of their new sanctuary, still unfinished because of Depression debts. How much better off they would be had the builders of the church been more modest in their plans, his father and mother argued. But how much better to build a noble church in which to worship eventually, their friends replied, even if you can't afford it all at the outset.

Jim never stopped thinking about such problems. He took nothing for granted. Always he was trying to fit the pieces together into a pattern both consistent and meaningful. One day he said to Howard Cole:

"There is something that has been troubling me a lot lately. When I was home for vacation I began discussing the Bible with my Dad and he told me he had been having some difficulty with it. He had been reading Joshua and Judges and had got to thinking about all the killing you read about there. It's pretty bad, you know."

Howard Cole agreed.

"It has bothered me some, too, because God ordered it," Jim went on. "But it's funny. What bothered me most was to find out that it bothers my Dad. He is pretty devout as men go, and I've never known him to question anything in the Bible before. I've got to think about this some more," he concluded. "God's vengeance gets harder for me to understand. I can repeat all the arguments they use to justify it, but it still goes down hard. Yet it's got to be right. There it is in the Bible as plain as day."

Jim would engage any student who would talk to him on any point in Scripture. One day he asked a group of them to weigh the familiar words from the Sermon on the Mount. He read:

Ye have heard that it hath been said, An eye for an eye, and a tooth for a tooth:

But I say unto you, That ye resist not evil: but whosoever shall smite thee on thy right cheek, turn to him the other also.

And if any man will sue thee at the law, and take away thy coat, let him have thy cloke also.

And whosoever shall compel thee to go a mile, go with him twain.

Give to him that asketh thee, and from him that would borrow of thee turn not thou away.

"What does that mean?" he demanded. "If I have two suits, do I give one away?" The others resorted to the explanations and interpretations of this passage that have been repeated down the centuries. But Jim, the thinker who sought to draw every argument out to its logical conclusion, was not satisfied. He thought Jesus had meant what he said, and that therefore these precepts ought to be followed literally.

"We cannot escape the meaning of those words by interpreting them," he insisted. "The problem is with us, not with what Christ said. If I were really dedicated, I would give away my extra suit. I don't because I'm not dedicated enough," he concluded, pointing the finger not at the others but straight at himself. They all felt uncomfortable and let the argument drop. If anyone were to inspect the closets of the group, they reflected, they would find less clothing in Jim's than in any of the others. Besides that, he was about the most frugal fellow they knew. He was the only one among them who did his own laundry. That included ironing his own shirts. So far as anyone could see, he did it uncomplainingly and without self-consciousness. At the end of the year, they reflected, his efforts had resulted in a very considerable saving to his family. But for Jim it wasn't enough. In the light of Scripture, he felt guilty because he had two suits of clothes.

Jim conducted devotions for his corridor every morning and night. Attendance, though voluntary, was always good because they were thoughtfully prepared and the students found they got a lot out of these daily spiritual exercises. Each one related to something Jim had been thinking about. Generally they had to do with some problem the freshmen had been thinking about also. As the year went on he encouraged the students to lead the devotions themselves or to participate with him. At first they were self-conscious about it, but as time went on his efforts met with increasing success. Each night the group concluded its service with "Blest Be the Tie that Binds." They soon became famous if not notorious because they sang with such zest they could be heard all over the building and often out on the campus as well.

Jim was an active member of the Missionary Study Group, a very pietistic group even for a somewhat pietistic campus. They met Sunday mornings at 8:30 A.M. To be a member of it marked you as more than ordinarily religious. For this reason, among others, the group numbered a bare twenty. Jim attended faithfully. Following these meetings, the group adjourned and walked down the road to St. John's Lutheran Church in Northfield. Jim never missed. Sunday afternoons some of the students would go to the Odd Fellows Home for the Aged to pray with the old men there. Again, Jim always went. Evenings they attended the Lutheran Student Association meetings which usually drew some two hundred students.

There was also on campus a perfectionist group known as the Bethany Fellowship Forum. Jim seemed a natural for such a group and began attending their meetings in his first year. But to their dismay, although he remained in contact with them, he refused to join. Asked why, he said it was because they underestimated the persistence of sin. Their goal of perfection was a chimera, he thought. They seemed not to be aware that man is inevitably a victim of sin and that therefore the emphasis should be upon man's need of forgiveness, not on any process of self-perfection.

Much more to his taste was the Far Eastern Gospel Crusade, a missionary effort started by a group of G.I.s during World War II who had been in the Far East and felt there was a need of missions there. It seemed far more practical than most of the activities he was asked to engage in. During his second year he and his friends used to go out in threes and fours to neighboring churches, where they put on a program to generate support for the Crusade. The formula was usually the same. They began with a devotional service conducted by the students themselves. Special music followed: then one of them got up and talked about the Crusade. Jim was usually the one elected to do it because he was the best at it.

Even then he was clear in his own mind as to what a sermon ought to be. The preacher, he felt, should be so well informed that his address would not lack substance. There must always be plenty for him to say. Therefore careful preparation was necessary. But the actual occasion, he believed, would draw the address from the man when he faced the living audience. He always had notes but seldom consulted them. He never had a verbatim text. He felt he could only speak effectively when he was excited about the subject and was concerned to get it over to the people before him. He could be both impassioned and coldly rational. Yet he was never precise in his presentation. There was no point 1, 2, and 3. His talks had direction but they were never tight. As a result he often tended to ramble within a general train of thought. But everyone listened. Nobody was bored when he was the speaker. His fellow students themselves liked to listen to him: he seemed to care so much about what he was saying, and somehow what he said always had a deeply personal quality that was meaningful to each of them.

One Sunday as they drove toward a small town north of the college, they had a hilarious time laughing and joking with one another —all but Jim. He simply sat quietly, saying nothing. The jokes and the laughter went on without him. But that evening, for the first time, the service wasn't very successful. On the way back, Jim confided to Art Olsen, who was part of the group, his distress at their failure.

"We simply weren't prepared for what we had to do," he said. "Our mood was wrong. We weren't fit to save anybody. We were just

having fun." Everybody agreed. Thereafter, they still laughed and
had their fun on the Gospel Crusade—but on the way home after
their work was done.

Jim was as devout in his personal religious life as he was in its
more outward aspects. He believed in the strict observance of the
Sabbath, and, characteristically, carried out his belief to the letter. He
would not study on Sunday because that was work. He studied hard
all Saturday evening, but at midnight he would quit. Sundays he
devoted exclusively to church activities and Bible reading. Occasionally after a session with the Bible, he would tire of it and turn to one
of his roommates or wander into another student's room, hoping to
get him into a discussion. The student, however, would be busily
preparing his lessons for the next day and show little sympathy for
the rigid Sabbatarian who ought to have been working on his own
lessons. So Jim would wander off or turn back to his Bible, not hurt,
just bored. He understood. He always understood what others were
feeling and thinking even if they did not always understand him.

There came a day when Jim's Sabbatarianism was severely put to
the test. Somehow he had overlooked the fact that there was to be
an exam in Greek the next day. Sunday afternoon found him, as
usual, reading his Bible, the Greek grammar and all his other books
closed tight standing in a neat row at the back of his desk. Tiring of
his self-imposed discipline after a while, he got up, his Bible under his
arm as usual, and wandered into the room of one of his friends.
Normally tolerant and glad of a respite from study, the student on
this occasion was brusque.

"I've got to work," he said. "You may not have to study on Sunday, but I do if I'm to get any kind of grade on that test tomorrow."

"What test?" he asked.

"Don't tell me you've forgotten that Greek test tomorrow," said
the other. The truth was Jim had forgotten it, as good a student as he
was. And he always found Greek difficult. It was then four o'clock.
Before him stretched eight solid hours before midnight and the end of
the Sabbath, just about the time he needed.

"Somehow I overlooked it," Jim said, half to himself. Without
another word, his Bible still under his arm, he left the room, walked
back down the corridor, disappeared into his own room and didn't
come out again. Word of Jim's dilemma soon got around. What would

he do? As time went by and he did not reappear, the suspense became unbearable. One of the students was elected to go into his room on some pretext or other and see what he was doing. Walking in without knocking, he found Jim seated at his desk, the Bible before him. In the row of textbooks behind the desk light stood the Greek grammar, unopened.

Jim retired early that night, having set his alarm clock for 3:00 A.M. He passed the test and never overlooked another, but it was not the only time he set his alarm for an early hour Monday morning in an attempt to gain back some of the time he lost on Sunday. As a result of this practice, now and then he found himself tired for an exam. But he never compromised. He took a lower grade rather than break his Sabbath rule.

The rest of the week he followed a schedule of rising at 5:00 A.M. He would then wash, have his morning devotions. Sometimes he would wake Art Olsen, who reluctantly dragged himself out of bed to join him. Then he would begin his studies. For a while during his early morning study period he undertook to memorize the Gospel of John. There were few who emulated his schedule and practices. But all who knew him admired him. What was far more important to him, they liked him and enjoyed his company. They enjoyed his hearty laughter; they were stimulated by his constant flow of ideas and his constant readiness to discuss them, and they felt stronger to be associated with one who was so completely committed to the Christian way of life. But perhaps above all, they were glad to have a friend whose concern for each of them as persons was unfailing, and whose understanding of their feelings was so much greater than that of anyone else they knew.

Professor Harold H. Ditmanson, Jim's adviser in his first year, was also his favorite teacher, as he was of many of the students. They thought him the most intellectual. He did not preach at them as many of the other men tended to do. He had a basic interest in ideas, and they responded to his critical, hardheaded approach to religion. From the time he first heard of Jim, he also had a special interest in him about which Jim did not know. Like many, he was startled at the young man's last name—Rape.

When Jim, as a freshman, came around for his first interview before classes began, Ditmanson was relieved to find that the advisee

who presented himself under so unusual a name was an ordinary
American boy, a quiet but rather attractive one, he thought. He could
detect no self-consciousness whatever in him as to his name, and he
was relieved at that. When his class in the History of Christianity
assembled for the fall term, Jim was among its members. Ditmanson,
after a few preliminary remarks, called the roll.

When he called "Mr. Rape," he stumbled a little in spite of himself. As Jim responded "here" Ditmanson thought he caught a low
ripple of laughter in a row of ex-servicemen still in uniform seated at
the back of the room. In an attempt to cover it he hurried on to the
next name. He read it in a loud, strong voice as he saw the trap
into which he had fallen. "Miss Sexe," he called. A loud guffaw broke
from the group. Both Jim and the girl flushed and looked at the floor.
The rest of the class was embarrassed. Although the college required
attendance to be taken every day, Ditmanson never called the roll in
that class again.

During the year he took a strong liking to the young man with the
odd name. Among other things he learned that he was planning to
enter the ministry. A deeply religious man himself and a committed
churchman, he knew how hard a time many ministers have and how
easily they are made fun of. With a name like that, he reflected, Jim
will never have a chance, and what is worse, he will never know why
he can't seem to make his way. With his temperament he will seek the
flaw in himself.

But how do you tell a man he ought to have his name changed, he
asked himself. The next year Ditmanson found he had Jim as an
advisee again. The boy was already a junior. The next year he would
graduate. When in January Jim came to see him about applying for
admission to Princeton Theological Seminary, Ditmanson knew the
time had come. Now I've got to tell him, he thought. When Jim next
came into his office, Ditmanson said after a pause:

"I want to go a little beyond the bounds of my role as an adviser to
you as a student. I want to give you some advice that will affect your
life after you leave this school. Some names, like mine, have no
meaning at all: names like Jones, Hustvedt. But your name is one
that has meaning. It conjures up in the mind of a person who first
hears it an act that is utterly repulsive to everyone. It has nothing to
do with what you are. You stand for all that is opposite to such a

thing. You will have handicaps enough in the ministry. I think you ought to consider having your name changed."

"I have been thinking about that," Jim said. He then explained that the family name was in fact not Rape, but Reeb.

"Then I would have it changed back," Ditmanson said, "and I would do it before I entered theological school, and if I were you I'd get about it right away." Jim thanked him and left. When he returned home for the summer vacation he had a long talk about it with his father and mother.

"I've often thought of changing it back myself," his father said. "Don't know why I never got around to it." Legal proceedings were begun in due course and on October 19, 1949, by official court order Jim took back his ancestral family name and became James Joseph Reeb. Soon after, his father instituted similar proceedings on his own behalf.

As was true with the most important decisions in his life, the issue of what theological school to go to was settled at home after talking with his parents. Rev. G. Henry Green, at that time minister of the First Presbyterian Church, who was called in for consultation, strongly urged him to go to Princeton Theological Seminary, his own school. He should go to seminary in the East, Green argued, and of the Eastern schools, none was better than Princeton. Jim's father and mother were easily persuaded. Nothing was too good for their son. If Princeton was the best for him, to Princeton he should go.

The idea excited Jim greatly. He had never been east of Zelienople. The chance to live on the Eastern seaboard, to be able to see and visit New York and Philadelphia, not to speak of Washington and perhaps even Boston, was more than he had ever dared hope for. Then too, to be at a seminary near a great university like Princeton would be a great advantage. It all seemed to be too much, far more than he deserved, he thought. Princeton was more expensive than some schools he might have chosen, but by careful planning, he had used only two of the four years he was entitled to under the G.I. Bill. That meant the government would carry him through two of his three years at Princeton. His father assured him the third year could be managed, and in any case the catalogue spoke of work in nearby churches a student could get to earn a part of his way through.

During the Christmas holidays Jim went around to see older mem-

bers of the Casper community who had known him to ask whether he
might give their names for reference, and in January submitted his
application. He was duly accepted pending his completing the work
at St. Olaf. Not only was his B+ average at college more than adequate academically, but the references, when they came in, proved to
be outstanding. A chemist at an oil refining plant in Casper rated him
well above average in all the categories Princeton listed (religious
life, character, intelligence, studiousness, personality, leadership,
physical fitness, appearance). One of his teachers at Casper Junior
College thought him "much above average" in all but two categories;
in the other two, "above average." A local attorney also thought he
belonged generally in the "much above average" class and added:
"His zeal for the Kingdom work is boundless, stemming in large part,
I believe, from his excellent Christian background. I know of no
other young man I could recommend so highly." This was high
praise, but perhaps the most sweeping endorsement as well as the
most perceptive comment was made by C. R. Swanson, the Dean of
Men at St. Olaf. After rating Jim tops right down the line in all
categories, he said, "I am convinced [he] will go far and be a big
influence in the field of theology." Beside the "Leadership" category,
he wrote, "One of our best."

5 ℰ

The Dimensions of Life

WHILE Jim was at St. Olaf College he fell in love. It all came about very naturally. She was a Casper girl and her name was Marie Deason. Jim met her while he was a student at the Casper Junior College and she was a senior at the Natrona County High School. During that spring and summer they began going together. In the fall when he entered St. Olaf they began writing regularly, and when he was home on vacation he went to see her with increasing frequency. In the latter part of the summer following his freshman year, after Jim finished his six weeks of summer school at Boulder, Colorado, they saw a great deal of each other, and Jim returned to college with a large picture of Marie, hand-colored and framed in gold. It showed a very pretty girl with blond curly hair and a bright smile. No one looking at the picture could doubt that Marie Deason was a distinctly good-looking girl.

Jim placed the picture on his bureau. It was the first thing you saw as you walked into the room and always caused comment, an occasional wolf whistle, and, among his friends, remarks the strict Lutheran authorities of the college might not have approved but which Jim seemed greatly to enjoy. He wasn't saying anything publicly as yet, nor was Marie, but they had declared themselves to each other and hoped to marry when he graduated.

The following August, after Jim returned from summer school at the University of Wyoming at Laramie, he gave Marie a ring. No public announcement was made, but both families were very happy about the arrangement. The two seemed perfectly suited to each other. Where Jim was often fired by enthusiasm and sometimes deep in gloom, Marie was usually serene. Where Jim, though he could be very dignified, was often raucous, Marie never raised her voice and was always marked by calm self-possession. Where Jim was basically impatient (although he could be very patient with a particular person or problem), Marie's patience seemed never to wear thin. Both were exceptionally high principled, religiously devout, and fundamentalist in their beliefs. Yet both were basically joyous, and loved fun. For Marie, marrying a minister presented no problems. She was marrying Jim and was content to become his partner for the role in life that was most suitable for him. Each responded to the love of the other, which increasingly deepened and strengthened the bond between them.

Jim's father and mother, happy as they were with the engagement, were brought by it once again to the realization that little Jimmie Joe had grown up. He would never know, they reflected, until he had children of his own, to how great a degree he had been the center of their lives for more than twenty years. And unless he were to have but one child, he would never know ever how much their lives had been and would always be centered in his alone. When he entered the Army, the long separation of those months sometimes seemed to them to be more than they could bear. His homecoming and the brief time when he was at Casper Junior College and was around the house once more had been a kind of reprieve. But it was soon past. Then came St. Olaf, broken briefly by visits home at Christmas and Easter. Even in the summer he was away at summer school most of the time.

Now there was to be a new separation to add to those of distance and time: this would be a separation of the heart. Not that Jim would love them any the less after he was married, or they him. But it would be different. The emotional center of his life would shift, as it should. They might see as much of him as before—perhaps more—once he was married and settled. And there would be grandchildren. But with the sudden realization of the change that was upon them, they found themselves thinking not of the future that was to be, but of the past that would soon be gone forever, the past which had sometimes been difficult but would always remain precious to them.

After graduating from the Natrona County High School Marie had entered Casper Junior College and completed her work for the degree during Jim's first two years at St. Olaf. Now she was ready to transfer to a four-year college and take a regular A.B. degree. Then why not at St. Olaf? She applied and was admitted for the year 1949-1950,

Jim's last at the college. In September the two drove happily off to Northfield where they enjoyed five dreamlike months together. Their schedules permitted them to see each other often. Besides the usual social events and work with the various campus religious groups, they always had lunch together and Jim always walked her back to her dormitory after class whenever he could. Marie was delighted with St. Olaf as Jim had been, but it was all over too soon. By midyears Jim had completed his work for his degree, and when he returned to Casper, Marie went back with him.

They were married August 20, 1950, at the First Presbyterian Church on a Sunday afternoon. Art Olsen stood with Jim as his best man. Griff Williams played the organ; Mrs. Williams sang two numbers during the course of the ceremony; and Mrs. Edna Stowe Thomas, an old family friend, provided music during the reception in the church parlors. The wedding was a great event in the life of the church that year. After a brief wedding trip through some of the national parks, they returned to Casper to pack up before heading east for Princeton. The Reebs had given them the family car, a 1947 Nash, which they piled high with clothing and other necessities. On the long drive east they stopped in Zelienople and Ellwood City, where Jim proudly introduced his bride to all his relatives who had not been able to get out to Casper for the wedding. Then, dropping down to Pittsburgh to pick up the Pennsylvania Turnpike, they set off in high excitement for Princeton.

It was rainy and cold as they made their way through Philadelphia and northward along Route 1 toward Princeton. Expecting something like St. Olaf, perhaps, high on a hill with a wide expanse of country all around it, they were quite unprepared for Princeton Theological Seminary, modestly set back from Mercer Street with only Alexander Hall in view, and unprepared for Princeton University too. At first they could hardly tell where the seminary or the university began and the town of Princeton left off.

The next day, September 25, Jim registered officially, full of hope and anxiety. In this famous old school to which candidates for the Presbyterian ministry were drawn from all over the United States, he might not be able to keep up. He signed up for the courses regularly taken by first-year men—Hebrew, Introductory Bible Study, Introduction to Christian Philosophy, Introduction to Ecumenics, Church

Music, Christian Education, the City Church, Homiletics, and Speech. But he need not have been anxious, for again he proved to be a first-rate student. At the end of his first term he stood in Group I, the highest academic group in the class.

Expenses, happily, were not a problem. He registered under the G.I. Bill which would take care of his major financial needs for at least a year and a half. Marie got a secretary-bookkeeper job with a firm known as Princeton Municipal Improvement, Inc., owners of the Nassau Tavern, the local movie house, and various apartment buildings. "She would be discontented if she didn't have every minute occupied," Jim commented in a letter to his parents. A constant stream of gifts from home supplemented their resources.

Their rooms in Hodge Hall, a married students' dormitory, were sparsely furnished—a desk and two chairs in the living room; a bed and a bureau in the bedroom. That was all. Early in the fall, Jim wrote home:

"We spent the afternoon looking for some pieces of furniture to help furnish our two rooms. They were really bare. So after tramping in and out of many secondhand shops, visiting with some very characteristic second-class salesmen, being overcome by odd and unusual smells and sampling twenty different varieties of dust, we ended up in an antique shop. After some looking, we saw an old chest with a marble top set way back in the window. After some exchange of information we found out it was $10, solid oak, good condition, 'to anyone else $15, but I would like to give you a bargain . . .' We took it. Something to put our linens in."

Marie busied herself at once making their rooms homey as well as comfortable. She made drapes for the living room, refinished the oak chest, and recovered a lounging chair they bought. "The job she did on the chair was excellent," Jim wrote his parents. They found an antique love seat and bought some old rugs. Jim made some bookcases, and soon their quarters were not only comfortable but had a real "lived-in" look about them.

Slowly they adjusted to the Eastern seaboard. Jim wrote his father at the end of the second week:

"I think we like the town better now. First, the sun has finally pierced the gloom, all the people at the school are extremely friendly and helpful (much more so than even at college). Second, any place,

I suppose, upon becoming more familiar seems less foreboding than at first impression.

"I think it is one of the most inspiring experiences of a man's life when he first enters seminary. Here there are people from all over the world, you see God is still active and in all countries he is touching men in order to bring his purposes to a final fulfillment."

The old seminary campus, some thirty acres in all, had a certain mellowness only age can give that he liked. The school had been established by vote of the General Assembly of the Presbyterian Church in 1811. They had chosen the country town of Princeton, New Jersey, because "The College of New Jersey," now Princeton University, was located there. Then, as now, students in the theological school could take courses at the university and had access to the library. Of all the buildings on the campus, Jim liked the chapel best. Small and unpretentious, it stood adjacent to Alexander Hall and directly across from Hodge Hall. It was built in the period of classical revival in the United States. Its clear glass multipaned windows reflect the colonial period, while its portico of white Doric columns, supporting a clean cornice, invite the worshiper into an interior of classical simplicity and grace. No steeple mars this Grecian gem. The seminary has been wise enough to keep it in the form in which it was built well over a hundred years ago.

On their second weekend, Jim and Marie drove to Merchantville, just outside Trenton, to stay with his Uncle Chester and Aunt Hazel Cable. He had seen little of them since Kansas days when the Cables had lived with the Reebs for a year. But he had always been fond of them both. Aunt Hazel reminded him of his mother, and he liked to talk to his practical-minded Uncle Chet.

Except when asked, Uncle Chet tended to keep his religious views to himself. He knew how widely they differed from those of his nephew. Jim, however, liked to engage him in theological argument, questioning him as he questioned everyone who would talk with him, seeking to understand why he thought as he did and how he defended his position. Chester Cable noticed that Jim's three years at St. Olaf had had some effect. With a far wider knowledge of history and science, Jim was not nearly so certain any longer that all wisdom and all knowledge was confined to the Bible. His religion was still Bible-centered and it was still undiminished in fervor, Chet saw, but the intellectual structure through which he explained and defended it had greatly widened.

Early in the fall Jim wrote his father:

"I hope in the days ahead you will write more. In a very real way I feel that we didn't have as many long talks this last visit. [His parents had come east to see him in the fall.] I wish you were more open to speak of what you really think and feel, but then I haven't been either. . . . I was very interested in what you said about life in this past letter. It certainly is true. I only hope that by the grace of Jesus Christ I shall be able to make every minute count for Christ. Sometimes these days I feel like I'm believing in Christ for the first time. If there is anything you can do, I would have you pray for me and Marie and for yourself. Let nothing that has happened or may be happening keep you from this.

"I want to thank you for all you have done for me. There are so many things I can't name them. Most of all I want to thank you for being especially patient with me through some very difficult years."

But Jim grew restless during his first year at Princeton and increasingly so during the remainder of his stay there. He did not find the intellectual stimulation he had expected. The work was difficult enough. That was not it. And he was able to maintain his customary high averages. The problem was, the work was not very exciting. Much of what he was studying just did not seem very important. The school was so large and the professors so busy that many of the students, including Jim, found it all very impersonal. Only the most brilliant, the most aggressive, or the most troublesome were likely to make much of an impression on the faculty. Of all his teachers Paul Lehmann, Professor of Theology, made the greatest impression on him. Lehmann's interest in ethics and politics turned the attention of the students away from the strictly academic toward an area where their thoughts might be applied in concrete instances.

James Reeb achieved no prominence while at Princeton. Although his grades were consistently high (in his middle and senior years he hovered between Group I and Group II), he did not graduate with honors. None of his teachers and none of his fellow students marked him as one who would later distinguish himself. He impressed the faculty as quiet, almost retiring, competent and studious, but neither brilliant intellectually nor more committed spiritually than the rank and file of students who came before them. They set down several of his classmates as having great promise, but not Jim.

Donald Macleod, Professor of Preaching, had him as an advisee in his junior year. Like his advisers at St. Olaf, Macleod found that young Reeb seldom turned to him. He seemed to be a sober, sensible young man who knew what he was about and needed very little guidance. He was quiet, even-tempered, respectful, and obedient, and never got into trouble of any kind. Macleod noticed the same characteristics in him in class as in conference. Jim's sermons were uniformly thoughtful and well-prepared, but never exciting and never profound.

Elmer G. Homrighausen, Professor of Christian Education, who later became Dean of the school, was aware of another side of young Reeb. He could never escape the impression that Jim was somehow looking past him both when he was lecturing and in conversation. It was not that Jim's attention drifted, but that he seemed to be pondering some of the deeper aspects of what was being said while listening to the more obvious surface statement. Homrighausen also noticed a marked curiosity. No answer ever seemed quite to satisfy him. Always another question lay beyond it to which he sought an answer.

The one man who detected something of the unusual in James Reeb was Wilbur Beeners, Professor of Speech. Like the other faculty members, he found the young man neither brilliant nor dull. He was not the kind of academic sponge who easily scores high grades, but he was nevertheless exceptionally conscientious and attentive. Often he stayed after class when Beeners offered extra help. He was in no way aggressive, asked no sensational questions in class as some of the students obviously liked to do. Beener's method of teaching speech involved the concept that it is the whole man who speaks. As a result, he paid the closest attention to the personality of his students. To change speech patterns, he felt, one must also change personality patterns. With some students this is not easy to do. With James Reeb it proved very difficult, in fact impossible. But he noticed an intensity beneath the quiet Reeb exterior and he longed to show him how to release it in public utterance. Jim had the fire essential to good preaching, Beeners believed, but his practice sermons never stirred either the class or the professor or Jim himself.

He had another quality Beeners liked: a critical eye. Not a professional iconoclast, he simply examined closely whatever anybody said. This quality appeared in his sermons also, but unfortunately it gave them more of an intellectual than an emotional appeal. When he heard Jim's Senior Sermon, the student's final exercise in preaching before he graduates, Beeners knew he had not been able to accomplish what he hoped to do. He had not been able to release the potential he knew lay deep within Jim Reeb, for his throat muscles were still tight as he spoke. His voice was not resonant. It lacked the timbre Beeners knew was there, for he had heard it on more than one occasion when Jim was relaxed and at ease. Young Reeb is still afraid to let go, still afraid to get excited, he mused. Before an audience his voice thins out, and with it his ability to persuade.

But this did not happen when Jim came before a real congregation as he did from time to time during the summer when he and Marie were home on vacation in Wyoming. In July following his first year in seminary, Jim was invited to preach two sermons at the First Baptist Church in Casper. They were very well received. The first, which he called "Eyes of Faith," dealt with a problem long central in his thinking: assuming you are ready to do the right, how do you know what the right is? Sincerity is no guarantee of rightness, he observed. The Nazis were sincere in their belief in the rightness of their course. So are the communists. He then moved to the familiar problem of the churchgoer in whom the fires of faith have died, for whom religion has become a mere formality. These people were all-sufficient, he said, but self-sufficiency is not enough: we all have deep human needs that must be satisfied. "Jesus," he concluded, "met these needs with a love and compassion beyond anything the world had ever seen. We lose concern for self through Jesus and thus become concerned with our fellow men." What he was trying to say then became lost in the traditional theology in which he expressed it, but the answer he gave to the question he asked is clear. You can tell which the right course is because it is always the course where love of self yields to love of your fellow man.

This interpretation of his meaning is not exaggerated. A year later Jim revised the sermon and preached it at a church near Princeton. A week after that he revised it again and preached it at the Willow Grove Naval Air Base. In each succeeding revision, the original emphasis on the love of Christ gave way to increased emphasis on concern for one's fellow man.

The second sermon Jim preached at the Baptist Church that summer was better. He called it "Having the Mind of Christ." On this occasion he offered his congregation a test by which to find out whether they had the mind of Christ or not. "Our growth must fit the pattern of a forgiving spirit," he said. Forgiveness was one of the main concepts in his earlier sermons. It was central in his thought at the time. Once in a class in homiletics the students had been given a sermon by Peter Marshall to read and discuss. Its title was "Forgive . . . or Else!" In his sermon Dr. Marshall, dealing with the line in the Lord's Prayer "Forgive us our debts as we forgive our debtors," had asserted that a man must forgive his fellow man before he can experience the forgiveness of God. Jim took violent exception to Marshall's position. God, he asserted, is free to forgive anyone, no matter how unforgiving that person might remain. As he saw it, there could be no limitation upon God, no conditions set up against what he might choose to do, even to the forgiving of an unforgiving heart.

But Jim had a second problem on his mind that morning. He was concerned with the meaning of life itself: his own and all life. "A man's life is his most precious possession," he began. Then he asked, "What shall a man give for his life?" Without answering the question, he went on to observe that while we may use our lives unwisely or well, a Christian accepts his life as a trust. This was merely a statement of the philosophy by which he had always lived. Ever since he could remember he had felt the deepest sense of responsibility regarding his own life and what he was to do with it. But now the old question had suddenly taken on new meaning for him. For there was now a new life to think about, of which as yet only he and Marie knew. If all went well, their first child would be born the next February or March. That life, too, he knew he would take in trust as he had his own.

With a child coming, they could no longer remain in the dormitory. Returning in the fall, they began house hunting, and at last they settled on a rather poor suite of rooms on one of the main highways at seventy-five dollars a month, which was more than they wanted to pay. Then, still delaying, still not committed because they kept hoping for something better, they saw an ad in the paper for a barn apartment about two miles outside of Kingston, some eight miles from Princeton. The barn, painted a bright red, had a furnished apartment upstairs with a living room, bedroom, small dining room, and kitchen. Downstairs was a bathroom and another large room, which Jim could use as a study. It was heated with oil stoves and rented for only thirty-five dollars a month. The landlord provided nothing but a hot plate for cooking, so they bought a secondhand electric range and a refrigerator as well.

In February, when Marie's time drew near, Mr. and Mrs. Deason drove east to be with her. The birth was easy, the baby was a boy, and they named him John David. He was born March 4, 1952. Jim was overjoyed that both mother and baby were well, but most of all that the baby was a boy. Mrs. Deason said to Jim's mother later:

"You know, he asked the doctor three times if it really was a boy."

He proved to be a devoted father. When they brought John home from the hospital, Jim was ready to do whatever he could. Everyone was amazed at the ease and confidence with which he changed his diapers and generally looked after his needs. He seemed like an old hand at the job. Marie breastfed John. Even for the night feedings Jim got up to help out. It was exam time at school, but somehow he kept up his work too.

The wonder of the young life that had come into his home reached deep into the inner recesses of Jim's nature. It all seemed to him too great a privilege to be his. He would sit by the cradle for long periods of time watching the baby sleeping, completely absorbed in the experience. There were times when he found it hard to think about anything else.

At the end of the month, Marie's father and mother left for Casper. The day they were to go back Marie cried all day. She was scared. How could she ever handle a baby all by herself, she wondered. But she managed, as all new mothers do. Not long after, a new problem rose to plague her. She found herself beginning to be lonely. Jim was always home nights, but usually he was away from breakfast to supper. Now Marie experienced for the first time in their marriage the long wait so many wives know between the departure of the busy husband in the morning and his return in the evening.

During the same year, Jim's second at the seminary, there was yet another factor that tended to accentuate Marie's growing sense of loneliness. In the spring of his first year he had applied for, and been accepted as, one of six second-year students to do field work in hospital chaplaincy. It was an experimental program. The seminary, cooperating with the Philadelphia Presbytery, had set up a clinical training course at the Philadelphia General Hospital. It was to be under the direction of Rev. Robert Foulkes who graduated from the seminary in 1950 and had just been installed as full-time Presbyterian Chaplain. Previously there had been no full-time Protestant chaplain there except a retired Episcopal clergyman, although the Roman Catholic Church had long had a priest assigned to the hospital full time.

PGH, or Blockley as it is more familiarly known, was an ideal place to try out such a course for young theologues. It is the public hospital for the city of Philadelphia. The indigents of the great metropolis who can afford little or no medical care go there, and the city picks up the bill. Understaffed in the light of the work assigned to it, badly overcrowded because of the demands made upon it, PGH provides almost unlimited learning opportunities for the medical student. There he sees a wider spectrum of cases than he is apt to meet in a lifetime of private practice. The same advantages and disadvantages, and the same breadth of experience are open to the minister or student for the ministry.

With the program ready to go into effect in the fall of 1951, Chaplain Foulkes, a quiet man with a soft voice, gentle manner, and a kindly twinkle in his eye, came to the seminary in the spring to interview prospective students. They were drawn to him at once. At the same time, he began his studies for an S.T.D. in the field at Temple University, where he would teach the following year. All this further increased his stature in the eyes of the Princeton students.

He interviewed each with the greatest care. They must have certain characteristics, he felt: they must be personable, they must have a deep interest in human beings as individuals and a desire to understand people as a means of helping them. Since the program was new and was still in the experimental stage, it had a very strong appeal to the seminary men. Foulkes had no lack of applicants. He held his classes at the hospital each Saturday all day. Often there was extra work on Sunday, too.

In a group so small the men soon got to know their teacher very well and he them, and as time went on Foulkes began to see in James Reeb all that he had suspected was there in their brief interview the previous spring. Even then he had been impressed by the tall, earnest young man from Wyoming. It soon was clear to him that in this very select group Jim stood out. Far more than any of the others, he really seemed to care about people. He, more than anyone else, sought to get at them as persons. He, above all the others, in fact, tried to find out what the spiritual problems of the patients were and to help resolve them. Because of this, he more than any other student sought to master the psychological principles that underlay the clinical training course.

Jim also impressed his fellow students at the hospital. As they drove back and forth from Princeton to the hospital each week and came to know one another better, they began to see a different Jim Reeb from the man any of them or anyone else at the seminary knew existed. Slowly, the quiet student they saw around the campus grew boisterous. He had, they discovered to their surprise, a loud laugh which at first seemed to some of them a little forced but which they soon found infectious. In fact, he became downright jovial and very noisy. Each of the men felt that he himself was too serious. Jim's joviality helped them all to relax and laugh.

They had many a hot argument, much as Jim and Art Olsen and Howard Cole used to do at St. Olaf. On more than one occasion they discussed child rearing. Jim's first baby was on the way through much of this time, and it was more than a casual matter to him. Talking about Christmas one day, they moved to the commercialism steadily growing up around the festival. There would be no gift-giving in his home, Jim asserted.

"Come off it, Jim," one of them said. "Not even for the baby?"

"No, not even for the baby," he announced with finality. He would not deny his son the gifts he would ordinarily get at Christmas, he said. He would simply distribute them through the year, outside the context of Christmas commercialism.

"No Santa Claus either, then, eh?" they asked.

"No," he said with even greater emphasis. "It's just a myth. I can't teach my children lies. And there won't be any Christmas tree either," he said. "It isn't Christian, it's pagan."

"Come on, wise up," the others protested. "You don't have to carry things that far."

In life, Jim never did. By the time the next Christmas rolled around, John was nine months old, and in their living room stood a little tree with presents all around it, as in most American homes. This was not because Jim ever in his life said one thing and did another. It was because he had now thought the question all the way through. What his fellow students never quite understood about him was that with his hard, clear mind and his inner demand for integrity, he had to carry every argument as far as it would go. He had to be sure his position was sound. He could not deplore the commercialism of Christmas and then succumb to it. He could not recognize the possibility of deceit in the Santa Claus myth and then risk having his own children feel they had been deceived. Jim had long since realized that there are no absolutes in life. Now he saw that this principle applies to commercialism in the American Christmas. The harm does not come from Santa Claus or the tree, he concluded. It depends upon what you do with them.

Both the hot arguments and the unusual gaiety of those trips back and forth from the seminary to the hospital served as a necessary release for the six men who sometimes found their experiences at PGH more than they could take. Like Jim, they had all lived quite sheltered lives and had seen only the genteel side of American life. None of them had had any contact with the vice, the crime, the squalor, or the general social decay that lies at the heart of a great city. At the hospital, they saw for the first time the results of that decay.

All this they might have managed but for the fact that their experience put their religion to the severest test. Confronted by the misery as well as the cultural deprivation of the city's poor, they found the simple theological clichés of the seminary classroom and of Sunday School memory a little thin. Talk about God's love seemed to mean little to those who had known nothing but anxiety, hunger, and cold throughout their lives. The patients by no means always wanted their prayers, they discovered. It was not easy to fit their hospital experiences into the intellectual framework they had always taken for granted. For this reason their sessions together in the car were also often deadly serious, for their experiences at the hospital struck at the roots of the faith that had brought these men into the ministry in the first place.

Chaplain Foulkes proved an excellent teacher. But his method was to have his students learn by doing. He did not lay out all the techniques of Christian chaplaincy in a set of lectures and then send his charges into the wards to practice what he had taught them. He lectured and discussed chaplaincy problems each week. But then, meager as their knowledge might be, they went into the wards to serve the spiritual needs of the patients there as best they might. The following week they discussed together what they had done and what they had learned. They learned a great deal, lessons they never afterward forgot, but their lack of knowledge as to what they ought to be doing and how they ought to do it gave them a great sense of insecurity, particularly at the outset.

One of the six students in Chaplain Foulkes's class that year was Alex Nemeth. He too found the clinical course discouraging. The terrible suffering he saw there, the desperate poverty in which most of the patients lived, the neglect they had suffered before they came to the hospital—all this got him down now and then, as it did the others. But he began to notice that Jim's reaction to it all was different. There was something about the way Jim took it that he envied. Jim seemed to feel the suffering of the people more deeply than any of them, yet it did not upset him in the same way. Perhaps, Nemeth reflected, it is because he is able to reach them better than any of the rest of us. Why is that, he wondered, and why has he the capacity afterward to rise above these things, to laugh and sing and talk about something completely different in a way that I find it very hard to do? He wasn't sure why, but he wished it were true of himself. Doubtless it was, to a greater degree than he suspected, or he would not have noticed it in Jim.

The sensitivity that seemed to be second nature to Jim Reeb showed in many ways. Once when they were discussing their interviews in class with Chaplain Foulkes, a rather heavy-handed member of their little sextette told of a young girl who had a disease which affects the bones. She had already lost one arm. It was his task to give her spiritual comfort. Feeling utterly helpless, more ready to weep for the girl than to counsel her or pray with her, he felt he had to say something, and suggested:

"Well, at least you still have one arm left."

Jim was outraged, and his vehemence was such that the class still remembers it.

"That's a terrible way to comfort anybody," he exploded. "That would just make her feel all the worse."

"All right," said the other, "what would you say?"

"I don't know," he said slowly, "but I wouldn't say *that*. I guess I'd try to talk to her about herself, about her feelings toward the disease. She'd probably like to talk about it if anybody gave her a chance."

Chaplain Foulkes, listening closely to the discussion, was making careful mental notes. Jim was learning fast, he thought. Or maybe he would have said that anyway, even before he began the course. It is his nature. He just feels for people. He knows how they feel. At any rate, the course ought to help him to implement and channel his sensitivity.

Toward the end of Jim's senior year at the seminary, Chaplain Foulkes was offered the post of chaplain at the Presbyterian Hospital in Philadelphia. Because he had done so well at PGH and was continuing his work at Temple University, the Presbyterians wanted him at their own hospital. It was a promotion, so he accepted it and without hesitation recommended his star pupil, James Reeb, for the position of chaplain at Philadelphia General. Jim was delighted at the prospect, and accepted the offer immediately. The field work at PGH and a clinical training course he had taken at the New Jersey Neuro-Psychiatric Institute, better known as Skillman Village, was the only work he had done at Princeton that really excited him. All the Bible minutiae, the church history and theology courses, seemed tedious to him. Because he found them neither intellectually exciting nor practically important it had become increasingly clear in his mind that he would not take a church after graduation but would seek a chaplaincy post instead.

From his extensive involvement in church work before coming to Princeton he felt he knew what the parish ministry was like. Neither the administrative side—the Sunday School, money-raising, the routine parish calls—nor the weekly preparation of sermons appealed to him. But the continual and immediate confrontation with people who desperately needed him had a very strong appeal. This was what the chaplain's post at PGH offered. Here were people who needed him far more than those who filled the pews of most of the churches, who he felt did not need him very much at all.

Perhaps the controlling factor was never quite present in Jim's thinking, namely, his obvious skill in the work and his own personal need to be needed. He seemed to have a particular empathy with people who were not or could not be aggressive. He not only understood them, he found it a joy to help them. The world's castoffs whose only virtue was meekness responded to him in a way that was almost unique. They who had sought to solve the problems of life by submission because no other solution seemed possible, those who had made their way into the refuge of alcoholic insularity, those who had wound up in the neuropsychological wards of an urban hospital, found in James Reeb an unexpected and unbelievable friend.

His experience at PGH brought Jim's doctrine of forgiveness into full focus. By no means all of the people he dealt with there were forgiving. Some were marked by the deepest bitterness toward members of their family, toward society as a whole, and toward him. They met his talk about God's love and forgiveness with hostility or incomprehension. In the teeth of this experience, Jim reached the conclusion that no matter how they felt and how they harbored resentment against individuals or against a society that had wronged them, God in his infinite mercy could forgive them if he chose.

But his theological position was more an attempt to justify to the patients a change in their attitude than a solution to a theological problem. "God's love, expressed in his forgiveness, is his most potent weapon to change us," he wrote in a sermon preached for Professor Beeners in his senior year. It was the old sermon "The Eyes of Faith" he had preached two summers before at the Baptist Church in Casper and which he had subsequently revised twice. But this was not a new revision of the old text. It was a fresh attack upon a new and now very real aspect of man's concern for his fellow man: how do you reach the heart of a person whose life experiences have hardened him so that he is all hostility and hate? As before, Jim's solution of the problem was cast in the orthodox language. "When we know God is forgiving," he wrote, "we should become forgiving, not out of fear of what God may do but out of love for what he has done." But his real solution of the problem revealed by his own words was not theological but practical. You reach the heart of a man hardened by the injustices of life by persuading him that no matter how great the wrongs he has done, God has forgiven him even before he himself is ready to forgive.

As in high school and college, when Jim took his degree from Princeton Theological Seminary in June, 1953, he was quite different from the boy who had entered three years before. Life in its many dimensions had meanwhile greatly expanded for him. Then he was a bridegroom just beginning life as a married man. Now he was the father of a fifteen-month-old son. Then he looked forward to a career in the parish ministry. Now he felt he could be a better minister as chaplain of the Philadelphia General Hospital. Then he had believed unquestioningly in the "fundamentals" of the Christian faith: in short, his theology was strictly fundamentalist. Now the intellectual awakening that had begun at St. Olaf had gone much further. Theological questions that never seemed real to him before were steadily increasing in number and importance while the old answers no longer served. But the greatest change had come about through his clinical work at the hospital. It had opened to him a wholly new and exciting field of knowledge. He had always tried, with only modest success, to understand his fellow human beings. It was the same with his understanding of himself. Now suddenly a vast new area of knowledge was opening to him, and he looked forward with the greatest anticipation to giving his full time to it and to the service of his fellow man that it would make possible.

Upon his graduation from Princeton Seminary, a formal ceremony of ordination was held by the Casper Presbytery at the First Presbyterian Church. Jim had every qualification a minister needs for success, everyone agreed after the ceremony: dedication, personality, education, looks; he should go far. Rev. James Joseph Reeb, they said, was a young man of great promise. In the future they would hear from him.

6 ❧

Chaplain Reeb

ONE DAY in 1956, the Presbyterian churches of the Philadelphia area received a notice. It read:

PHILADELPHIA GENERAL HOSPITAL
Presbyterian Chaplain, James J. Reeb

SUNDAY WORSHIP SERVICES

1. Many patients are unable to walk. They must be brought to the Service in wheel chairs. We need a group of from 5 to 10 people each 3rd and 4th Sunday of the month to bring these people to the Service and return them to the Ward. Hours: 9:00 to 11:30.
2. We need individuals, small groups, or choirs who will come and provide special music for our Services. Hours: 10:00 to 10:30, 2:00 to 3:00.
3. We need individuals or groups who will provide flowers for our Sunday morning Worship Services.

VISITATION OF PATIENTS

1. We need both men and women who are interested in visiting patients. The Chaplain will provide a training program. The opportunities for service in this manner are unlimited. The type of service can be different with each individual. Some patients appreciate having someone to read to them. Others need someone to write letters. In every case the purpose of the visit is to help the patient feel he has not been deserted by God or His church in his moment of need.

SPECIAL PROJECTS

1. There are about 150 patients who are long-term residents in this hospital. We need groups who will provide special breakfasts, entertainment, and parties for these people.

2. Many of these patients have no friends remaining on the outside. We are trying to get people to adopt them. This means visiting them, remembering their birthdays, fulfilling requests or needs, etc.

3. There are many types of literature that could be given to patients. It woud be excellent if some individual or group would devote themselves to this type of ministry.

Seasoned in church work as he was, Jim knew better than to stop with a mimeographed announcement. He took his campaign to the churches themselves. Panel discussions were set up in local churches, where the need for hospital volunteers was explained and debated. His own sincerity and enthusiasm always created a great impression on these occasions. It was apparent to any audience to which he spoke that he really cared about the people under his charge. If only Prof. Beeners could have been present on one of those occasions he would have seen that his appraisal of this young man's potential had been accurate. When he participated in these panels, there was no lack of fire in him, no lack of timbre in his voice, no lack of power to persuade.

One of the projects that resulted was a plan to enlist volunteers to serve breakfast to the patients on Saturdays and holidays. The chronic cases, he explained to his audiences, never, in all the years they were in the hospital, had had a chance to choose what kind of eggs they wanted. Institutions, he reminded them, cannot offer the variety at breakfast that others take for granted. His sense of humor, always on hand when he was confident, came to his aid.

"How would you like boiled eggs every day for five years?" he asked. As a result, many church groups came to the hospital to cook breakfast to order for people who had forgotten what such a luxury was like. The program took some understanding of the hospital, and no little cooperation on the part of the staff. But the minor administrative difficulties were overcome because of the heightened morale of the patients. The program was so successful under his direction that some groups still do it to this day.

James Reeb, "Chaplain to Hospitals for the Philadelphia Presbytery," had begun his work as full-time chaplain at the Philadelphia General Hospital in September, 1953. He and Marie rented a second-floor apartment on South Sixtieth Street in Southwest Philadelphia.

The house was owned by Mr. and Mrs. Harry Mozenter, Harry and Sara, as they soon came to call them. Here Jim was himself again, always laughing, constantly making things joyous.

On a number of Friday evenings Jim went to the synagogue with them. To his surprise, he always found the service inspiring. Sometimes they went on outings together, but mostly they just sat around in the evening talking. On one memorable picnic, the Mozenters saw Jim really let go. At heart he is just an exuberant, uninhibited, unsophisticated boy, they thought as they watched him romping in the sand, racing into the water, wolfing down an amazing stack of sandwiches, pickles, olives, deviled eggs, and cake. This, they felt, was the real Jim; the real man was a boy who reacts to life spontaneously and without thought, as a boy does. And yet, they realized that the other side of Jim was no less real, the deadly serious young man who had chosen a hospital in which to begin his ministry rather than a church, the young man who had chosen life in the city, work among the city's poor, when he might easily have had a far more comfortable living pattern in some snug suburban church.

The Mozenters never ceased to be impressed by Jim's keen interest in everybody he came in contact with: themselves, the people next door, the children on the street, the man who ran the corner store. One day when he was on his way to the hospital, he asked Mrs. Mozenter if he could pick a few of the flowers she had growing in a border at the front of the house. There was a woman at the hospital, he explained, a Negro, who had just died. He had been visiting her, and now he was to have her funeral. She had no one. He alone would be at the service. Sara gave him the flowers and he went on his way.

Doubtless he never thought of the incident afterward, but Mrs. Mozenter never forgot it. As she stood looking after him she thought, in that simple act, you can see all of Jim's love for the poor and oppressed. No one will be there to see that he placed a bouquet of flowers beside that forgotten woman's coffin. No one but me will ever know he did it. The dead woman herself will not know. But that wasn't his reason. He did it for her, to lend dignity and a touch of beauty to her forlorn departure from the world.

The move to Philadelphia meant a far greater change in Marie's life than in Jim's. She had been very happy in their spacious barn quarters, in the beginning. But with Jim away all day every Saturday and sometimes on Sunday, as well as each day during the week, she was often left by herself for long hours at a time, often many days in succession. Now and then, when Jim had been picked up by one of the other students, she used the car to drive down to Merchantville and spend the day with Jim's Aunt Hazel. It meant company for her, somebody to talk to, somebody to be with. When they moved to the congested area of Philadelphia, Marie was happy again. Now there were people around her all the time. Sara Mozenter was away all day. Marie was busy too, but in the late afternoons, in the evenings and on weekends, whether or not Jim was at home, there was always somebody to talk to. And now that Jim did not have to study every evening, he had much more time for her and also for John, who was getting to be a very lively little boy.

The excitement and determination with which Jim took up his work as chaplain at PGH soon landed him in trouble. Neither the doctors nor the nurses, not to speak of the administration, at first appreciated his enthusiasm for his work, nor did they perceive his sense of dedication to it. During his student days he had seen enough of the hospital to understand how it worked. He knew what services were available, who got them and who didn't, and who had the authority. Seeing a need that ought to be met, he went to those who had that particular area of responsibility in their charge and demanded action. At first they looked at him with astonishment and gave him the brushoff. The hospital had managed to run and to look after the patients before he came on the scene to point up its shortcomings and generally disrupt things. Who did he think he was? Well, he would soon find out. And he did. He met with stony, impassive resistance wherever he turned. As his demands increased, resistance increased. He was at a loss to understand it.

Jim's honesty also got in his way. People misunderstood it. Where others would try to cover up their mistakes, Jim would speak of his readily. It took his associates nearly a year to learn to accept him at face value. Many, before they were willing to do so, had actually to see him do things to his own hurt for honesty's sake. Then they believed what others had told them, that here was a really dedicated man. As a result, Jim, after a while, began to get results. When he asked for medicines a patient needed but for some reason did not have, he got them; when he asked for a bed to replace one that was broken, he got it; whenever he asked for anything, people listened because they had learned through experience that he asked only when the need was dire, that his requests were always reasonable and they were never for himself

One of Jim's biggest frustrations during his early months at PGH was Miss Verna Schwalm, Supervisor of Obstetrics and Gynecology. He had not been there long before he began making demands upon her on behalf of certain patients he thought were being neglected. The first time, she heard him out, but informed him with unmistakable clarity, when he had finished, the limits of service the hospital could provide to the patients. The next time, she was shorter with him, and before long she would simply say, "I'm sorry, Chaplain, it simply can't be done," give him a stony stare, and go on about her work. That young man is not going to turn this hospital upside down, she said to herself as he walked off, not if I have anything to say about it.

Jim got the point, and thereafter his demands sharply decreased. But Miss Schwalm noticed that his attention to his job did not. He is not against me, she concluded one day, he is with me. He wants the things at this hospital I want to see. For Miss Schwalm was not without her own frustrations and resentments. As she reflected upon them, she realized they rose from the same concerns that animated Chaplain Reeb. She felt this in particular with regard to the Negroes with whom she worked. To the young Presbyterian chaplain, race seemed to make no difference. He served all alike with no apparent consciousness of color. This was Miss Schwalm's standard too. But there were a number of people on the staff who referred to them as "niggers" and who tended to treat them as something less than human. Whenever this happened, Miss Schwalm felt as if someone had struck her. Once a delegation of officials came to the hospital and made the rounds.

"Don't you have any *white* patients?" they asked her. She was infuriated.

"They are all people," she replied as politely as possible, but she felt they never got the point.

James Reeb had been chaplain at PGH for about six months when Miss Schwalm summoned him one day for a baptismal service. A newborn Protestant baby was dying, she informed him. Would he please perform a christening service before the baby breathed his last.

Jim complied, but later, in a lull during the day's activities, he asked her if a christening service under those circumstances was a hospital regulation. No, it was not, she said, but she supposed it to be a church regulation.

"What church? Yours?" Jim persisted.

"No, not mine," she said. "I belong to the Evangelical and United Brethren Church. We don't require it, but I assumed that most Protestant churches do." In the course of their conversation Miss Schwalm told him about an experience she had had as a student nurse. On that occasion a Catholic baby was dying. Not knowing Catholic regulations on the point, she had not called the priest, and had been soundly punished for the omission. She never forgot it, she said. Jim assured her that he felt as she did, and that the Presbyterian Church agreed with hers that a christening service was not a life-and-death matter. With that their friendship began. Thereafter, whenever Jim had a few minutes, he would stop by Miss Schwalm's desk for a chat, or, as was more often the case, to talk about some problem in the hospital.

Jim's greatest interest was in the charity patients, particularly the alcoholics. Many of these patients had been in the hospital for years. Neglected or altogether forgotten by their relatives, they were utterly alone and friendless. Once when he was on the way to the alcoholics' ward, Miss Schwalm handed him a list of patients to be operated on the next day. It was his task as chaplain to pray with or for each of them. He protested. Why should he go to see these people, he asked. Why should he not spend the time that remained that day with the alcoholics who needed him even more. Miss Schwalm represented the establishment, and Jim, who always respected authority, complied with her request. But as he went off to do her bidding, she found herself wondering: Why *shouldn't* he go to the alcoholics? It is true: they need him more than anyone here.

As Protestant Chaplain at the Philadelphia General Hospital, James Reeb was also a teacher. Like Robert Foulkes before him, he had a class in clinical training for six of the students at the Princeton Theological Seminary each of the years he served as chaplain.

"His course, which was not given for credit, was one of the richest experiences of my seminary years," said Rev. William Payne, later minister of the Presbyterian Church at Huntingdon, Pennsylvania. "Jim was not only a teacher, but a counselor and friend. He helped

me survive some severe storms during my seminary days. He helped
me by his compassion for others to see what the ministry really
meant. He helped me by his zest for life to be willing to invest my life
in something greater than my own concerns."

His students during those years are today outspoken regarding his
influence upon them. Rev. Truman D. Nabors, Jr., who grew up in
Selma, Alabama, said Jim meant more to him than anyone else he
came in contact with during his seminary years. "As my counselor
[in the clinical training program] and as a friend, he was a liberating
influence in my life. In particular he helped me to understand and
gradually to overcome the racial prejudice which lay so deep within
me I was unaware of it. He gave of himself in love and understanding
in a way that was unique in my experience."

As with Chaplain Foulkes, the men under Chaplain Reeb spent all
day Saturday at the hospital, often Sunday too. They first met in
the chaplain's office. There he explained to them how the hospital ran, what they were to do and not to do, and how they were to go
about their work. He then took them on a tour of the hospital,
showing them everything, the best and the worst—the indigents, the
alcoholics, the psychopaths, the insane, the out-and-out criminals.
There was a ward just for policemen and firemen injured in the course
of duty. None of the students had ever realized before the cost in
human suffering of a police force to maintain order and a fire department to prevent the city from burning down. He made some pastoral
calls while the students observed him, then assigned to each student a
ward or section of his own. Each student had to write up one interview a week. This was then discussed by the six with the chaplain
who emphasized the good points and pointed out the errors.

Misery, suffering, and tragedy such as few of the students had ever
witnessed or even dreamed of were thrust constantly before them. But
here Jim's ever-ready sense of humor sustained them. Trusted by his
students, in fact openly admired by most if not all, he was at his best
with them. The tragicomic was always present and Jim always made
the most of it, but always with charity, always with sympathy for
human suffering.

One of the most valuable experiences for the young students was
the psychiatric classes for medical students they were permitted to attend. There they saw shock treatments and were introduced to the

psychiatric aspects of hospital work from the doctor's point of view. They found their introduction to psychiatry in this manner the revelation of a whole new world. But they also found the attitude of some of the psychiatrists a little hard to take. A number of them showed little sympathy for religion. Often the cases they discussed in the amphitheater before the medical students involved religious fanaticism, and the psychiatrists seemed to the theologues to be blaming religion itself for such psychological disorders.

On the other hand, the theologues were forced to face the fact that many of the problems of the psychiatric patients did indeed involve religion. Moreover, the attitude of the doctors was in no small part caused by the tendency of the chaplains and students to go overboard on psychiatry. Introducing theological students to the psychiatric aspects of medicine was still quite new at that time. So also was the use of chaplains for anything but the more set forms of religious ceremonial such as baptism, communion, extreme unction, a Bible reading or prayer, administered to, more than participated in, by the patient.

The seminarians were also permitted to attend operations, autopsies, and the like right along with the medical students. It was grim sometimes, but after a few fainting spells they got used to it or dropped out of the course. Following these sessions, Jim made the students face up to themselves. They must confront their own feelings, he insisted. Sometimes he seemed cruel in his determination to do this, but afterward they were glad. It was a cleansing process, they learned, one they badly needed. He told them he had taken the course in an attempt to understand himself as much as for any other reason, and they all admitted they had done the same. But understanding yourself is one of the most difficult things to do, he reminded them, because it is so hard to face yourself, so hard to see what you really are.

The manner in which Chaplain Reeb conducted the course was so strenuous that not all students finished it. One year a member of the course, now highly placed in world ecclesiastical circles, dropped out after only two months. He would not expose himself to the self-revelation Jim thought necessary if a man was to be able successfully to counsel others. He had first to know himself, Jim argued. It was a principle he had accepted from Bob Foulkes because it seemed to him to be valid. He intended, if he could, to make it as real in the lives of his students as Bob had made it for him. Jim was unaware, however, that he was a far more dominant type of personality, when in the driver's seat, than Bob had ever been. He was far more ruthless in driving his students to face themselves. In this process his customary compassion was lacking. But once the students had found themselves, if they needed help, Jim did not fail them. To every member of the class he was both counselor and friend.

The next week after the student had dropped out of the course Jim asked the others what they had done about it. They admitted they had done nothing at all, among other reasons because they were glad. The man hadn't fitted very well into the class. His spirit was quite different from that of the rest of them. Nevertheless, by his question Jim had made them feel guilty. During the next week each of them stopped by to visit the dropout. They discovered that his reason was different from the one they would have given. Theologically he was quite conservative, he explained. Some of the ideas and concepts being bandied about in the course, in particular by the psychologists with whom they came in contact, he found very disturbing.

The students liked best the fact that their instructor was himself so much a part of the course. He did not sit back and manipulate the discussion while the students went at one another. He participated in the discussions with them and on their level. He put them completely at their ease. They held nothing back either from one another or from him. Often he would move out to the edge of his chair, lean forward, and pay the closest attention to whatever they had to say. Although some of the things that came out were a little odd, he never made fun of any of them. Thus no student ever felt threatened. This was the secret of the success of his teaching method. With no fear of humiliation, the students soon lost their fear of self-exposure. The course became an adventure in self-discovery.

The students got so much out of the course and talked about it so much around the campus that admission to it became a status symbol. Often after a session, they would gather in one another's rooms, discussing what they had seen and done, while other students listened in with envy. Some students took the clinical training course at no little financial sacrifice, as Jim himself had done. A student who took a weekend church, and many did, could earn most if not all of his keep while in seminary. The field work pay for the hospital chaplaincy course, however, was only five dollars a week, and out of that the student had to pay for his transportation and lunches. It amounted to hardly more than reimbursement for his out-of-pocket costs.

Their experiences were widely varied. One day one of them visited an unmarried sixteen-year-old girl in the maternity ward. She had just given birth to her fourth baby. What the student found most unbelieveable about it was her attitude. She was completely unconcerned. She had no fear, no anxiety, and no sense of guilt. It had happened before, she told him, and would probably happen again. When the student related the incident in class, Chaplain Reeb forced them to examine its meaning for them. He was in no sense callous: but he was eager that no aspect of the cross-section of life open to them at the hospital should escape their notice, and that none should be pushed aside. Each must be accepted on some basis or other and dealt with accordingly.

He told them of his own problems as he tried to face such experiences and determine his own attitude. He told them of his struggle with the doctrine of God's forgiveness. You can't just condemn the girl out of hand, he said. Of course she has done wrong: of course society cannot countenance such an attitude of irresponsibility. But that is not the end of the matter. When you have said that, you have to ask sociologically what is wrong with a society that produces a sixteen-year-old girl with such attitudes. You have to ask theologically whether God can forgive such sin, and if so why and how.

Jim developed this point in a sermon he preached in one of his regular Sunday morning chapel services during his first year as chaplain. He explained that we deal with the problem of sin in others by achieving a new understanding of each other. We have to remember that we usually approach a new situation with an old attitude derived from the past. He was thinking of himself, of course, and the uncompromising, unforgiving attitude he had had toward all immorality but a few years back. We must realize, he continued, that truth is not absolute. This gives us a basis upon which people of different economic, social, and racial backgrounds can draw together. The churches are to be critized for preaching a doctrine of absolute truth that divides people from one another when they ought to be drawn together. His conclusion was a plea for religious, social, and personal toleration and acceptance.

None but he could have been aware of the basic change in outlook which that sermon represented for him. His studies in psychiatry and counseling had shown him how judgmental he had once been in his moral attitudes. "When the moralist in you dies, then life begins," he wrote a little later on, as his thought became more clearly articulated. The contrast between this statement and a paper he had done while at Princeton on "The Wrath of God" was very great. Then he had carefully assembled all the evidence for God's wrath contained in Deuteronomy and had concluded: "We fail to see that God is a God of wrath to our destruction. Nations rise and fall. Inner decay receives its judgments." Giving him a straight A on the paper, his professor commented, "Excellent work! You have cited abundant evidence, drawn valid conclusions, and made timely applications."

Jim's method of teaching was to participate with the students in their work with the patients while watching both without seeming to. If, for example, they took a group from the psychiatric ward out in the yard for games, he might ask afterward: "Why didn't you talk to patient X instead of just throwing the ball with him?" If the student did talk, he would want to know what they talked about and what purpose the student had been pursuing. What Jim said was not critical. He was not hounding the students. He was trying to force them always to be aware of what they were doing. With him it wasn't enough for them to pass the time of day with a patient. They were charged as chaplains with helping them.

On one occasion when he was reviewing with the students their experiences of the previous Saturday, one of them told about a man living in a row house who had deep suspicions of his neighbor. The man next door, said the patient, had bored a hole through the wall and had been piping gas into the patient's apartment—at least he was planning to. What was worse, he said, the neighbor was now able to see through the wall and could watch the man's sister undress. At this, the student had asked him: "Do you have any sexual feelings toward your sister?"

That was the end of case reviewing for the day. Chaplain Reeb spent the remainder of the time explaining through this blunder how a counselor works.

"You don't throw your bits of knowledge about psychological principles at people," he said. "They will neither see their validity nor accept them. Instead, you get the patient to talk about himself. You get him to tell you what is bothering him. You don't tell them, they tell you. When the patient himself discovers what his problem is, he has already taken a long stride toward solving it.

"You never approach anyone with a formula," he continued. "You take each person as an individual. You respond to him as a person according to what he is. Then, you proceed from there, depending upon what your own resources are."

Such doctrine was a delight to the students, for it stood in sharp contrast to what most of the professors at the seminary were saying. The latter seemed to have everything worked out. With them the formula was complete. One of the professors, for example, insisted that successful pastoral calls had a fixed form: they were short, contained an appropriate Bible reading, a brief prayer, and that was it. Chaplain Reeb made no attempt to hide his disagreement with this approach.

"Some calls ought to be short," he said, "but some have to be long if you are going to get anywhere. It all depends on the person and his problems."

Dr. Edward Cooper, who was in residence at the time, was attracted on first meeting Jim by his eager friendliness and his ready smile. He found himself wondering whether it was forced. When he discovered that this was the real man, he was pleased. "Just the sort of chaplain we need," he commented to one of his colleagues. "Friendly as well as competent. How far all this psychiatric stuff goes I don't know, but I do know that he has the same effect on my patients he has on me. If I had to climb into one of these beds, he is one of the first people I'd like to see come into the room."

Sometimes Chaplain Reeb would be downright angry. When this happened it was always a relief to the students. They felt reassured to know that their teacher, who seemed to have unlimited self-control, was human after all. But here too there was a difference. He was never angry with them, and never angry with his fellow workers. He was most often angry at situations in which he was not personally involved at all: as for example, when a doctor, because of his superior authority, became abusive to a nurse for some trivial failing on her part, or when a supervisor would vent his anger on an orderly for no apparent reason.

One day, while the students looked on in amazement, he got into a rage as he watched a doctor go through one of the indigent wards followed by a flock of medical students. PGH was a teaching hospital for the University of Pennsylvania and this was a common occurrence. Often the doctors were rather impersonal about it. This particular doctor was utterly so. He talked to the students openly about the condition of the patients as if they were cadavers or wrecked automobiles. He unceremoniously exposed their bodies, their wounds, and their diseased parts as if they had been so many laboratory specimens. When later at a staff meeting Jim spoke of his sense of outrage at such conduct, everyone agreed with him.

Chaplain Reeb conducted Sunday morning services for the entire hospital and Sunday afternoon services in the psychiatric ward. There anything could happen, and it often did. Chaplain Reeb, unperturbed, went on with the service. It was at these services that his almost magical effect on people could be seen. He sang rolling gospel hymns with them with the verve of his college days at St. Olaf. His prayers, always extempore, were never directions to the Almighty to calm this one or cure that one. Rather, they were directed toward the patients' feelings about themselves, and were an effort to help them to bring their concerns before God. He tried to make the patients aware of God's love for them no matter how lowly they might be. He never asked God to make them well.

Always Jim seemed to be generating new ideas, which he then sought to implement. In the early part of the summer of 1956 he set up a program of instruction for students from the seminary designed to introduce them to the social problems of the city. They were to learn not through textbooks and lectures, but through firsthand contact with the city's life. Chaplain Foulkes agreed to cooperate with him on the program. The students lived at the hospital. Jim began by taking them about the city. They went to the Tenderloin section where the "winoes" are to be found; they sat in at trials in the civil courts, the criminal courts, and the juvenile courts. They went to the office of human relations, they visited industry and whatever else might show them how a great modern city runs. He organized it all on the basis of contacts he had developed through the hospital and his own ideas of what the students ought to see and know. A lengthy discussion period followed each of the field trips. Here again he forced the students to verbalize their feelings about what they had seen and to state and defend the attitudes they took in each instance.

In his enthusiasm for his new position, Jim sometimes went beyond bounds he himself would have set for others. On one occasion he had invited a young cleric who had just taken a degree in social work to address the students in the summer seminar. It was clear that the cleric thought very well of himself and was ready to rattle the teeth of the seminary students by his realistic, down-to-earth approach. When he was through, Chaplain Reeb began asking questions. Some were searching in character. It was obvious that the young minister lacked first-hand knowledge of some of the seamier sides of the city, in contrast to his wide fund of theoretical information. Chaplain Reeb went after him with question after question. Soon the man began to tremble. He fled from psychology and social work to the Gospel. The problems of the city were forgotten as he turned instead to defending the most orthodox theological views. Chaplain Reeb continued to pursue him, setting the demonstrated values of psychiatry over against the doctrines of theology. When it was over, the minister who had come as a heretical social worker intending to set straight a group of wide-eyed seminarians, ended as an apologist for the theological status quo, which is about where most seminarians are when they finish school.

Sometimes Jim would bring one or two students home with him on Saturday evening. But Marie usually saw little of them, for they arrived late after having visited store-front churches and other aspects of the inner city at night, and in the morning the students were off early to get back to the hospital. Sometimes they went to night court. This was of particular interest to them because the men who came before that court were so often drunks who later wound up in the alcoholic ward of Philadelphia General Hospital.

The tempo of Jim's work increased steadily while he was at the hospital, not because more was exacted of him—he was on his own —but because he exacted more of himself. As a result he experienced deep inner conflict because every additional hour at the hospital was an hour he could not spend at home with Marie and John, who was now past four years of age and in a very formative as well as delightful period of life.

Talking about the problem with the Mozenters one evening, he said:

"I would like never to have to work again. I'd like to give up the church and the chaplaincy entirely and just be with my family all the time. There is so much to do and see in the world!"

Occasionally Mrs. Mozenter would baby-sit for the Reebs when they wanted to go out, but this did not happen very often. They lived quietly, not only because there wasn't much time for going out, but also because their means were small. For the same reason they had few friends except the Mozenters. Sometimes Robert Foulkes would come for an evening, but that was about all. Reflecting on his feelings during this period, Jim wrote in 1957 in his diary:

"I also feel a deeper commitment to John. For a long time I have been in conflict between his demands on me and other things I felt I wanted to do or must do. Now I see that he is one of the persons I will most influence in life. The thing that carried me through PGH when nothing else seemed to have meaning was my slowly growing realization that the influence of one person upon another is one of the most significant aspects of life and one which the religion of the future is sure to see as the realm where it must experiment and guide people. My opportunity to influence John in the sense of doing those things that bring him happiness will not last forever."

He achieved each summer the life with his family he longed for. When the year's work was ended, he and Marie, with little John, drove back to Wyoming as soon as they could be off. Except for their customary visit at Zelienople and Ellwood City, they drove night and day, taking turns at the wheel, until they reached Casper. It was always a happy reunion, even though the visits were briefer now. Jim's work at the hospital did not give him the long vacation they enjoyed while he was still in school. As John grew older they noticed with delight that the Wyoming summers meant as much to him as to them. He seemed to respond to the wide-open spaces just as they did. They knew part of his obvious joy came from the fact that there they lived as a family in a way they never did in the East. But it was clear too that that was not quite all of it. John like his father loved to get out of Casper, out on the plains, up into the mountains away from the city into the natural wonderland that surrounds the city on all four sides.

Jim had begun to explore the region around Casper with his parents from the time they first arrived in the city more than ten years before. Even during the war years when gasoline was rationed, they carefully saved their coupons in order to make a few trips out into the country. He and his parents, with friends or with a group from the North Casper Boys Club, or the church, would go up Casper Mountain to the south of the city, eastward to Glenrock and Douglas, and north-ward to Teapot Dome. But they liked especially to go west and southward into the gently rolling flatlands where the remains of a petrified forest were still to be found, where artifacts of stone-age man still lay about, and where far more ancient fossils only awaited the sharp eye of the amateur paleontologist. Here their happiest holi-days were spent. Often they camped out. On these excursions, as soon as they arrived at their destination, the door of the car flew open and Jim was off across the plains with John on his back, or with John after him as soon as he was old enough to run.

Slowly, without planning to do so, Jim began collecting fossils. These remnants of life fifty million years old seemed to have the same curious effect upon him that new life had, like that of his first child, or abused life, as he saw it among Philadelphia's poor. To him it was a basic kind of experience that was somehow religious, part of life's miraculous continuity. Now he believed in evolution as he had not formerly. These evidences of the development of life on earth during vast ages of time were endowed in his eyes with a special character. His fossil discoveries in the Douglas area somehow sym-bolized the self-discovery then taking place within his own mind and heart.

The impact of his study of psychiatry, together with his firsthand contact with the stark realities of life, had wrought basic changes in him. Outwardly James Reeb was still the same as the seminary graduate who had accepted the chaplain's post at PGH. Inwardly he was not. Aware of his true feelings as always, and honest about them as well, he knew the time was soon coming when the inward changes must be given outward expression.

7

Integrity of the Mind and Heart

DURING Jim's first year at Princeton, a student named Benjamin Sheldon lived down the corridor from him in Hodge Hall. Sheldon liked to study Hebrew with Jim and used to drop by his room each day at noon. Jim always welcomed him warmly. He was alone, since Marie was away all day at her job. The two men would go through the paradigms together, then test each other on verbs, nouns, and other forms. Sheldon found these sessions a delight, and valuable as well. "It was Jim's high standard of excellence that encouraged me to pursue it, too," he said later. "Without his drive toward a near-perfect attainment of the given assignment, I would have easily been satisfied with a lesser achievement. Dr. Fritsch, our professor, told us that we were his two best students, but I know that the credit all belonged to Jim."

Often they moved from grammar to theology. In this area, Sheldon noticed, Jim also strove for the highest standard of excellence. He was eager to discuss the views of thinkers they read about, carefully comparing and distinguishing between them. Yet he was very reluctant to discuss his own views. If Sheldon pressed him, he would fall silent. Sheldon respected his friend's reticence because he was aware that Jim's attitude toward basic Christian doctrine was undergoing a change. But he never knew that Jim's views had so recently been even more fundamentalist than his own, for Jim never intimated the fact in any way.

By the time he entered Princeton, Jim was far from sure what his theological position was on many points. He was clear that now, as always, he sought the truth, full, complete, total, and unblemished by any other considerations. The difference was that he was no longer as sure as he had been when he entered St. Olaf that all basic truth was contained in Holy Scripture. His courses in history and science, though taught in a Christian frame of reference, had introduced him to wide areas of knowledge that were not to be found in Scripture at all. He had learned much that was obviously inconsistent with what was written there, and his studies as well as his midnight arguments with fellow students had gradually forced him to the conclusion that there were many points at which the Bible was inconsistent with itself. In short, he now realized that the fundamentalist position, once so clear and indisputable to him, was now no longer so.

However, the basic tenets of his traditional faith as yet remained unchanged. At the beginning of his middle year at the seminary Jim wrote a gentle, consoling letter to a family in Casper on the death of their son. "Most of all," he concluded, "we trust faithfully in Jesus Christ as a true picture of God. He said, God is our Father and a good shepherd. His resurrection and life with us now is the ground upon which we rest our hope of eternal life. The presence of Christ with our loved ones is one of the most comforting things upon which we may meditate."

Even more revealing is a letter to his parents written at about the same time. "I want to tell you about my experiences last Friday at the Board of Foreign Missions in New York," he wrote. "We were *particularly fortunate!* Because of the world situation the board had called in the field representatives from all over the world. They had gone to upstate New York and stayed for a week at some hotel. There they prayed and started trying to determine just what God's will was for the particular fields at this time. This necessitated mapping out what is called the *New Strategy.* In case you don't know, John Mackay from here is president of the Board of Foreign Missions. So he was in the thick of all this. As chairman of the board and running the office in New York is a man by the name of Leber [Charles Leber]. I believe he is a fine evangelical man and certainly on fire for mission work to extend the kingdom of God. Both of these men, I might add, certainly need our prayers." There follows an extended description of the day's activities. "You can imagine how thrilled I was at this meeting in New York. It was just like a shot in the arm," he concluded.

Yet it was during that year, his second at Princeton, that a basic change in his thought took place. As disturbing questions increasingly arose in his mind, he sought answers in his course work, but he did not find them there. His professors were well aware of the questions that troubled him. They often discussed them. Apparently his theological problems were quite standard. But to Jim, his professors seemed not so much to meet his questions as to turn them aside. This was one of the reasons his course work at Princeton was less than exciting. Without quite realizing it he had expected the seminary to re-establish on a firm intellectual basis the faith he had once held undisturbed by doubt. But the exact opposite happened. His boyhood faith was not strengthened and made secure by his work at the seminary: while he was there it melted quite away.

When he took his problem to his professors individually they tried to reassure him. He need not be concerned, they said. Religious doubt among middlers was the rule, not the exception. He was to be commended for his searching, inquiring, and questioning of the faith. It was a mark of his increasing maturity. But when he had finished his re-examination, they said, his former faith would return to him, larger, stronger, and more secure than ever. Prayer, trust, and hard work would soon enable him to surmount the problem of doubt as uncounted others had done before him.

After talking with one of his professors, Jim sat down and drafted a paper, "An Analysis of My Problem of Doubt." In it he attempted to resolve the problem for himself. But his answers were as orthodox as the theology he was questioning. He related his state of mind to the general erosion of faith resulting from the advance of science. Then he observed:

"The accomplishments of modern science breed a sense of optimism and self-sufficiency." This, he thought, had created in him "an atmosphere in which God is not particularly needed." The sin of pride is at the root of my trouble, he concluded, resorting to an orthodox formula as old as St. Augustine and given new currency in his day by Reinhold Niebuhr.

Having identified the villain, Jim proceeded to reconstruct his faith, as a thousand texts in apologetics had done before him. His argument was as standard as his analysis of the causes of his doubting.

1. Scientific naturalism does not meet my deepest needs. Therefore it cannot be the answer.

2. But the new knowledge that science offers requires that I re-

evaluate my long-held religious beliefs. This is particularly true of the impact of psychology on my faith.

3. I must seek a new synthesis of religious faith and scientific knowledge.

4. My problem is accentuated by the fact that I am now able to see both the shallowness and self-centeredness in my former religious beliefs.

5. Above all, my doubts show my need for God's strength. It is a mistake to doubt God because he happens to withhold from me the strength to believe. Doubt must not be permitted to coerce belief. "To hear God say 'My grace is sufficient for thee' is to be freed from myself and to love God," he concluded.

Often during this time he found himself remembering his own words at St. Olaf: "If you can't accept the whole Bible as literally true, then you cannot accept any of it as necessarily true." The second alternative had seemed to him so outrageous—even blasphemous —he had not considered it as a possibility then. So sure had he been that the Bible was literally God's word, he had used the second, utterly objectionable alternative as a means of establishing the validity of the first. But now the second alternative no longer seemed quite so repellent. Certainly, he reflected, if the Bible were not God's word in the literal sense, a vast number of other questions which had become a great burden to him could be resolved.

Jim might have been willing to wait for God's grace to enable him to believe as he had in the past had there been no other influence on him at Princeton than classroom lectures and midnight discussions with the students. But there was also his work in clinical psychology at the Philadelphia General Hospital. The theology by which Christianity was explained and defended in seminary lectures seemed to him to be ignored or forgotten in dealing with the broken bodies and minds of living men and women at the hospital. One solution of the problem would be to keep his theology and his psychiatry separate. But not for Jim. Always a truth-seeker, he had long known that truth is not be to be had when you put it in compartments. Truth is one, he believed, and has to go together in all its aspects. When it does not, beware. That is the surest sign you have made a mistake or that you have left out something important. To Jim's alert and ever-restless mind, it gradually became clear during his second year that there was no common ground between the premises of his seminary work and that of his work at the hospital.

When he raised these questions with his fellow students, some agreed with him; others felt he saw more conflict than there really was, and all felt that he took it too seriously. Most were inclined to agree with the professors that it was a phase they would soon pass through after which their faith would return to them stronger than ever. Meanwhile, they were not inclined to worry.

Jim, however, was not satisfied merely to wait and hope. One day he found himself wondering what Chaplain Foulkes thought about it all. His teacher he knew, would have faced any inconsistency in his intellectual position and resolved it. He was a clergyman of the Presbyterian Church and as such presumably subscribed to the Westminster Confession. Jim went back and read it again. Much of what he was learning in Foulkes's course at the hospital was clearly inconsistent with what was written there.

Jim began listening more carefully to what Chaplain Foulkes said, not merely to his treatment of psychology and human personality, but more particularly as to how his teaching related to the Westminster Confession. The more he listened the more troubled he became. For a while he said nothing to anyone. Then slowly there formed in his mind the decision to go to Bob, as he now called him, and tell him what he was thinking and feeling. It was a risk. He might lose his friendship, yet he felt Bob would understand. And he hoped Bob would be able to show him that he had misunderstood and that his teaching did, in fact, square with the official beliefs of the Presbyterian Church.

Chaplain Foulkes was not surprised when, one day in the spring of 1952, his prize student asked for an appointment to see him. He was already aware of the drift of his thinking.

"It will take some time," Jim said. "I'll need at least an hour."

Realizing that what Jim had on his mind might well take longer, Bob suggested that he stay overnight at the hospital. The next afternoon there would be ample opportunity, after the service in the neurological ward was completed.

They talked far into the evening, and Jim just caught the last train back to Princeton. The young man who returned to the seminary that night was not the one who had set out gaily in the car pool with his fellow students thirty-six hours before. Then he had looked on himself as a believing Christian beset by the problems that trouble any theological student in an orthodox seminary. Now he wondered who he was and what he believed.

Chaplain Foulkes, no less honest in his approach to things than Jim, answered his questions honestly, even bluntly. No, he did not believe everything in the Bible: but then, neither did anybody else. No, he did not believe everything in the Westminster Confession: and again, neither did anybody else. Both called for interpretation and understanding, he argued. They always had. There was no need to be too literal-minded about it. The basic teachings of Christianity still stood: love and justice, mercy and forgiveness. Christ was still the way, the truth, and the life. God's love was sure.

Jim nodded in seeming assent, but he suddenly felt all at sea. His anchor line had been cut. He thought again of his position in St. Olaf days: if the Bible is not *all* true, then none of it is *necessarily*. There is no place to stop the sorting process. Once you begin it, the principle by which you do the sorting replaces the Bible as your final authority. Bob's solution—interpretation—would not do for him. He was still a literalist. Either words meant what they said, whether in the Bible or the Westminster Confession, or they could be made to mean whatever you wanted them to, depending upon the principle you chose by which to interpret their meaning.

Jim had by no means worked these problems through when he was ordained a Presbyterian minister in Casper immediately after graduation. Had he thought his way through them and out the other side so that he knew he no longer believed the Westminster Confession, he would never have permitted himself to be ordained. But in June, 1953, he had reached no such conclusion. On the other hand, neither was he able to accept the solution of the problem many were recommending to him: admit that you no longer believe the old dogmas as they were set down originally and devote yourself to seeing what you can make out of them today. When he graduated Jim still believed it all could be put together and made into sense. He was never one to suppose that he had all the truth, and he still believed that through grace, as he had said in his student sermon, he would find a way to believe again without compromise and without saying formally that he believed one thing when he really believed something quite different.

But the old faith did not return "enlarged and expanded," or in any other form. When he came back to Philadelphia in the fall to take up his work as full-time Presbyterian Chaplain at the hospital, he brought his theological problems with him, larger, more persistent, and more urgent than ever.

Jim now began a thoroughgoing reconsideration of his theological position. One of the doctrines that troubled him was that of eternal damnation. He had decided some time before that it was a very unlikely teaching. In fact, as soon as he had begun to think about it, he realized that God's mercy and forgiveness were simply inconsistent with any idea of eternal damnation. At the hospital Jim concluded that this doctrine was not merely intellectually faulty, it was morally evil. As early as his high school days he had come to believe that the poor are the obligation of human society, and they are not to be forgotten. His intimate contact with Philadelphia's indigents at the hospital confirmed this belief and suggested a further extension of it. Society's delinquents, juvenile and adult, are its victims also. An evil society, quite as much as original sin, is the cause of the evil they do. At the theological level, he now saw, the delinquent who is to be helped rather than confirmed in his criminal ways must believe that God can and will forgive him, not that he is condemned to hell fire forever.

There was of course nothing either novel or revolutionary in this idea, but it was where he began. Later on he was troubled by the supernatural aspects of prayer. In a sermon preached after his hospital days, he said: "As a hospital chaplain I was called upon hourly to pray for someone in desperate physical circumstances. Few religious practices were more difficult for me. The sick wanted someone to pray for them. They believed in prayer. Many knew that prayers had at times played an important role in their lives. They wanted someone to pray because they were afraid, they were lonely, they were stripped of supports that normally support our self-assurance.

"I thought that in many instances prayer was a substitute for actions that could conceivably have more influence in the situation than the God who was prayed to. I was particularly impressed that the mortality rate for the newborn fell markedly when the *city fathers* appropriated money for more personnel and better equipment for the maternity wards. I never remember an unexpected change occurring after prayers of the *church fathers.*" You cannot verify the fact that

God heals in answer to prayer, he saw. On the contrary, you can show statistically that he does not.

Another question that bothered Jim was the role of a creed in the religion of men, quite apart from the truth or falsity of its tenets. If you give your loyalty to a creed, he argued, you inhibit the free action of the spirit. To this he attached the greatest importance. He had always deeply believed that the spirit is the channel through which God speaks to men. Therefore nothing must be permitted to impede it. Of this he was still very sure. But he began to doubt the worth of the church as an institution. The churches seemed to him as remote from the real concerns of men as the theological school. In his paper on "Doubt," he had written: "My own inherited tendencies to have shallow or unrealistic views of certain groups in our social and economic relationships has made me doubt the value of organized religion to meet the needs of today's world." He cited in support of his view the failure of the church to participate in the labor movement and other movements seeking the reconstruction of society. This feeling too grew in him at the hospital.

Another aspect of the impact of psychiatry on Jim's religion was personal rather than intellectual. Watching the doctors working with patients, he was impressed by the fact that their sole aim seemed to be to help them with their problems. He was impressed too by the fact that they so often succeeded. They made it their aim to understand people and to help them by helping them to help themselves. Jim had always believed that God was the agency through which such help came. The teachers at the seminary said the same thing. It was man's task to pray to God for help with his problems. A kindly person would ask God to help others with their problems, too. Yet here were the psychiatrists, most of them openly professing disbelief in God, performing the same service the theologians said God was to be asked to perform. Measured simply in terms of effectiveness, theirs was a far greater service, Jim thought, than that of the clergy who came in and prayed over the patients.

Through his work at the hospital, Jim discovered how many things people do without knowing why they do them: irrational, hurtful things. No amount of prayer, he found, could help them. But psychiatry could. Psychiatry could discover the deep-lying forgotten causes of their behavior, help them to see what was happening, to face it, understand it, and so to be rid of it. In fact, he concluded, Bob Foulkes was more effective, and he himself was more effective, when they dealt with the patients in terms of psychiatry rather than theology.

To Jim's honest mind this was a deeply disturbing conclusion. As a result he came to believe that missions, which he had once thought to be among the most important aspects of Christianity, were harmful. They ought to be given up, he concluded, for they were based on a theology that convicts people of sin when they really need most to understand themselves. You help people, he now knew, not when you try to change their theology, but when you accept them as they are. This acceptance, in turn, enables you to help them because they trust you. But if you begin by trying to change them, to show them that they have been wrong all along, then you alienate them and render yourself powerless to help them.

Placing theology and psychiatry in juxtaposition as Jim found himself forced to do, he was brought to an extraordinary question. The theological presuppositions he had been asked to accept showed little or no understanding of human problems: psychiatry, however, readily understood those problems. Could it be, he found himself asking, that God is less understanding than many doctors are? What the theologians call the love of God, he observed, works in many ways, and not only through the clergy. Sometimes it does not work through them at all. On the other hand, very often it works through people who insist that they have no religion whatever.

As Jim's friendship with Bob Foulkes deepened, he turned increasingly to Bob with his problems, and Bob understood. They talked long hours together. They often played ping-pong and that helped. They were evenly matched and played with fierce determination in their effort to best each other. As students of psychology they were aware that they were taking out their aggression on each other. But this only made the game the more enjoyable. They would slash and hew and wham away until both were wet and tired. But when the game was over, both felt refreshed and ready to go back to work again.

After Jim graduated from Princeton and became chaplain at PGH, he continued his studies in psychiatry at the Conwell School of Theology at Temple University in Philadelphia. Bob was now teaching there in a program set up at the Medical School by Dr. O. Spurgeon English, head of the Department of Psychiatry. It was a unique program in which Dr. English was making psychological insights available to theological students. Foulkes's role was that of "Theological Consultant" at the Medical School, a post for which he received no pay, but in which he learned a great deal and was able to assist the doctors in understanding the role of religion in both physical and mental illness.

As Jim's enthusiasm for psychiatry mounted, Bob became concerned. He carried it too far, Foulkes felt. He was too eager to understand himself and too eager to get others to explain themselves to him. But then, he reflected, that was Jim. He always took up whatever he did with the greatest enthusiasm. Also he was an activist by nature, Bob realized, and therein lay part of the problem. Bob, who was much more contemplative, often wished that Jim would sit down for a while and talk or just rest. He found himself constantly in the position of throwing cold water on Jim's enthusiasms, for he always seemed ready to tackle something ten men might ordinarily be needed to do.

The depths of Jim's feelings during these years is revealed in an entry in his diary. "I have a feeling that I am doubting everything," he wrote in the fall of 1954. "I have many problems and no solutions. However, intellectually I tell myself this is a period of temporary turmoil in which my concept of the faith is being enlarged and expanded. In time I will come to a more well-worked-out faith even if it be an essentially agnostic position."

Jim was both right and wrong in his guess as to what would happen to his faith. It was indeed "enlarged and expanded" while he was at the hospital, but it was not the old faith which underwent such dramatic development. During these years *the* faith, by which he meant the traditional Christian faith, the validity of which he had always taken for granted, disintegrated, and as a new faith slowly took its place. In a formal statement made in retrospect, Jim described the change in his thinking which occurred at that time, as follows:

"As long as I can remember, I have been concerned about religious matters. As I neared the end of my high school education, I recognized that nothing in life was nearly as important to me as growing in my devotion to God and aiding other people to do the same. About the same time I came to a conviction that God had called me to serve Him as a minister. In due course of time, I did enter the Presbyterian ministry. I found ministering to people as a hospital chaplain a challenging and gratifying work.

"Today many of the convictions that earlier played an important part in my decision to enter the ministry are no longer meaningful. My understanding of religion has changed, but my desire to pursue the quest for the full depth of the meaning and purpose of life and to give it expression in my day-to-day living has not.

"I want to participate in the continuous creation of a vision that will inspire people to noble and courageous living. I want to share actively in the adventure of trying to forge the spiritual ties that will bind mankind together in brotherhood and peace.

"In the realm of human relationships in all of their individual and social aspects are to be found the spiritual frontiers of our age."

The basic shift that had taken place in his thinking is here made explicit. He had come to the point where he no longer thought in terms of doubt. He was no longer troubled by the fact that he did not believe the doctrines set forth in the Westminster Confession. He had become aware that the shift in his religious beliefs no longer concerned the details of that Confession. He had not departed from any of its particular doctrines and teachings. He had instead abandoned the premises on which the Confession itself rested. His goal was no longer to support and defend the one true faith. It was now "to participate in the continuous creation of a vision." The words were carefully chosen. He did not say what the vision was. He couldn't, for it did not yet exist. In fact, it would never exist as the Westminster Confession existed, clear, precise, and concrete. His faith was no longer centered in a Confession by which his faith could be tested. It was centered in a set of goals that were to be continuously created. The purpose of those goals—the vision—was explicit: to "inspire people to noble and courageous living." This was the test: not a theological formulation, but human life as people live it, qualitatively tested.

To face the fact that his basic religious beliefs had changed was probably the most difficult thing Jim Reeb ever did. In his exact mind it meant that his whole life direction must be changed—that he must leave the church and give up his chosen career. In January, 1956, he wrote in his diary: "Through a series of events that have occurred recently I have reached the decision to leave the ministry. I have clearly progressed in my views until I am much more of a humanist than a deist or theist. After visiting with Bob I have decided that it will make more sense to insure that my exit is as quiet as possible. The Presbytery is about to add another chaplain and I don't want to arouse opposition in the Presbytery to this plan or to subsequent developments in this field."

Despite the pain and anguish such a decision meant for him, Jim might have reached it much sooner had it not been for the fact that everyone to whom he turned for help and counsel urged him against it. Bob Foulkes, who was in a sense an agent of Jim's theological evolution, very strongly urged him not to do it. Bob had thought that through their work together in psychiatry he had been helping his friend to a wider understanding of the role of Christian theology and a deeper understanding of himself. He had not dreamed that the result would be Jim's leaving the ministry. He had supposed that it would be with Jim as it has been with himself: the traditional beliefs would drop away; he would no longer believe them in the old literal sense, but the heart of the matter would remain.

"Stay in the church," Bob urged him. "There are many who believe as you do. I myself am one. You are not expected to take the Confession literally. Few of us do. The winds of change are sweeping through the church today. Stay and help us change it. The church will be forever bogged down in its ancient theology if all who outgrow it abandon it."

Jim sought help in this period from numbers of different people. He had several talks with Rev. Robert Tignor of the Yeadon Presbyterian Church. The whole basis of his thinking had changed, he explained. He no longer believed that creeds should be imposed on people. They should find their own beliefs. For this reason he could no longer affirm the tenets of the Westminster Confession. Tignor listened patiently for a long time.

"Never mind what you don't believe," he said at last. "Accentuate the positive. Preach what you do believe. That is what we all do. There cannot be any rigorous application of the doctrinal teachings of our church. If there were, many of us would be out on our ear." Jim said he would think about it and come back again. They had two more sessions together, but their only effect was to drive him more completely to the conclusion that he couldn't just preach what he believed and leave out the rest. He had been a believer when he subscribed to the Westminster Confession. But it affirmed many beliefs he could not now affirm. Surely, he argued, his silence would be taken by his congregation for assent.

He also went to talk to his Uncle Chester Cable and plied him with a thousand questions. Uncle Chet answered them all as best he could. Still he was far from satisfied.

Jim next went to see a psychiatrist. They had four sessions together. Knowing what he did about psychiatry, Jim was well aware that unconscious motives for changing his religion might be much more powerful than the ones with which he was struggling consciously. The psychiatrist was very reassuring. He found no unconscious motivation for the change. It was, he said, due to two deeply-lying characteristics of Jim's that had been his since boyhood.

The first was his passion for intellectual consistency—his desire to establish a principle and then to line everything else up in accordance with it. The same demand that once made him accept everything in the Bible as literally true now required him to believe literally whatever his church professed. Again it was all or nothing.

A second and closely related factor was Jim's honesty. Honesty was so deeply ingrained in his nature that he could only use words to mean what they actually said. Why this was true was a complex matter. But that it was true no one could doubt. Jim understood very well the need to ascertain and state the true meaning of ancient words written in another language and in a very different cultural context. But he strongly objected to giving ancient words meanings they never had at all in order to make them useful in the modern age. He found the practice, so widespread in contemporary religion, no less objectionable when applied to the Westminster Confession than when used on Bible texts.

Why give so much effort to stretching old language into modern meanings? he asked. Why not let the Bible and the creeds say what they said for their own purposes and in their own time? Then, in new words designed for the purpose, let men set forth new religious concepts as they emerged in their minds. To him things had to feel right to be right. And it didn't feel right to him when, for pious purposes, words which patently meant one thing were made to mean something else. Since it did not feel right he could not bring himself to do it.

Jim also went to talk to one or two denominational officials in the Presbyterian Church. They were the least help to him. They understood that the change in Jim's theological views was a result of the impact of human misery upon his sensitive nature. It had been a mistake, they felt, to introduce students for the ministry to this sort of thing, and it had been a worse mistake to ask a student right out of school to live with it day in and day out as Jim had done at the hospital. That it should have proved too much for a deeply religious, idealistic lad from Wyoming was to be expected, they concluded.

One of the men he went to see really jolted him. Jim approached the man in his characteristic searching vein. But this was a practical, hardheaded man lacking in all sentimentality. Finally he said:

"Then I take it you don't believe in God."

Jim, in his reply, spoke of his changing concepts of the ways men think about matters of all kinds, including the most basic theological ideas.

"Well, if you don't believe in God," said the man simply, "I don't see how you can be a minister, and I think you had better get out."

Another of the men Jim went to see was his supervisor, Dr. Frank H. Stroup, Director of Urban Work for the Presbytery. They knew each other well. Jim had often been a guest in Stroup's home. When he said he had decided he must give up his post as chaplain, Stroup was not surprised. He had known of Jim's changing views.

"But you won't find what you are looking for in any other church," he told him. "It is life that has got you down, not your faith. Life is like that everywhere. It will always get you down."

No part of the transition process was as difficult for Jim as that with his parents. As they slowly became aware of the change that was taking place within him, they became increasingly distressed. Jim had not shared his doubts with them. He saw no need to. To do so would only upset them, he thought. Now, when he tried to talk about the change with them, it was no use—no more use than it would have been had he by some magic been able to talk with the boy he had been ten years before. The education they had made possible for him had widened the horizons of his thought far beyond anything that had been possible for them. They could not know the human suffering and

degradation he had seen and tried to deal with at the hospital. He had
tried to explain himself to them, and, having failed utterly, gave up.
Because he loved them deeply and so well knew their love for him
and the hopes they centered in him, he could not bring himself to
continue the effort. It caused too much pain to them and to him. As
with Sheldon at the seminary, when he was with his parents he simply
fell silent if the conversation turned to matters of theology.

In January, 1957, Jim wrote in his private diary: "Suddenly I feel
as if I have been betrayed—I have betrayed my own best interests.
Why have I made my decision to get out of the Presbyterian ministry?
Recently I have reduced the job of chaplain to manageable propor-
tions. I felt relaxed for the first time in my whole life. I didn't need to
get anywhere or know everything about something. I could enjoy
Marie and John."

Then he asked himself why he must make so difficult and painful a
decision. Why couldn't he do as almost everyone advised him to do:
relax, remain where he was, preach what he believed, forget what he
didn't, meanwhile doing his best to reform the church, making its
stated beliefs accord with the real beliefs its members hold. He wrote:
"Why do I always have to do the noble thing? Why can't I be imper-
fect and stop pounding my guts to bits—why can't I consciously
accept the idea of sinning—do it—enjoy what I'm doing—take advantage of it and live? No, I have to leave the ministry because of my
changed convictions. They may change again tomorrow for all I
know. However—possibly in the midst of this change, having caught
an awareness of what I really want from life and being dimly conscious of how to get it, I can proceed to learn how to live."

But it was an idle wish. Jim's character had been formed long
since. He was what he was, and though he might sometimes muse
over it, he really did not want to change. He worked out the rationale
for his position in a sermon on the subject preached at about this
time. In it he said:

"True faith may not appear to us as faith. It may very well appear
as the ridiculous, the strange, the unusual, as a threat to the established order, the recognized opinion, common sense, previously determined policies, deep-seated traditions." The sermon was really
autobiographical. What was now his true faith—that true religion
must be centered in man rather than in God—would have seemed

ridiculous to him but a few years before. What was now his true faith, his basic belief, had originally come to him as doubt, as unbelief, as a threat to religion.

He gave as an example the artist who starves in his garret only to become famous long after he is dead. But he was not thinking of the artist in his garret. He was thinking of himself, of his own integrity of heart and mind. He could not do other than he was doing and be true to himself. At about this time he wrote, in the same vein although in another connection: "The hallmark of persons with deep religious convictions has always been their unswerving dedication to their own vision of truth. Of all the facts of religious experience, this one has been the most difficult for religious leaders to absorb. Religions should above all else honor the need of each man to be faithful to his own vision of truth."

That was why Jim felt he must give up the ministry: in order to be faithful to the vision of truth that was now his.

8

Unitarianism

DURING the fall of 1956, someone gave Jim a copy of *Today's Children and Yesterday's Heritage* by Sophia Fahs. In it the author explains the philosophy behind the Unitarian program of education in the church school. Jim was enthralled. If this is how the Unitarians approach religion, he thought, I guess I must be a Unitarian. The book was written from the point of view of the child who was to be taught. Mrs. Fahs insisted that traditional methods of religious education are based upon ideas of child training we have given up. Her logic was simple. We must give up our traditional methods in religious education too. She wrote:

"The depths of human experience are emotional, and vital religion will always fathom those depths. Nor is it the adult alone who has such possible depths. Children also feel deeply. But 'each must plumb vastness and infinity. Let him call it what he will—fire, water, death, God, worlds, stars.' This the child must do *for* himself, but he cannot do it always *by* himself. He needs the feeling of honest and intimate togetherness with a group of his own kind. To encourage such a fellowship is goal enough for any leader in church or synagogue or family."*

Here was something James Reeb had never expected to find, a statement of religious philosophy by a church that would square with the religious philosophy he was evolving through the study of psychiatry. Here were his own thoughts duplicated almost exactly: the depths of human experience are emotional; it is the task of religion to fathom those depths; each individual must plumb the vastness of experience for himself, yet in community, for there we do it more effectively. He would like John to be learning such a religion, he thought. He himself would like to worship in such a church. Perhaps, he thought, he could

* Sophia Lyon Fahs, *Today's Children and Yesterday's Heritage* (Boston: The Beacon Press, 1952), p. 218.

be the minister of a church like that.

Not long afterward, Jim went to see Dr. Harry Scholefield, then minister of the First Unitarian Church of Philadelphia. Ushered into the minister's study of the old stone church on downtown Chestnut Street, he found himself facing a redheaded, good-natured, kindly man, perhaps ten years older than himself. He was surprised and delighted to be able to discuss his problem with a virtual contemporary. Jim explained that he had as yet reached no decision. He was exploring. But it was clear in his mind that Presbyterian theological concepts, and the general atmosphere of the Presbyterian Church, no longer permitted his full growth as an individual. When he mentioned Sophia Fahs's book, Dr. Scholefield immediately responded. He knew the volume well. Like most Unitarian ministers, he used it as the basis of his own church-school curriculum. After discussing the matter for some time, Scholefield suggested that Jim think further about the problem and come back and talk again. He made no suggestion that Jim seek to transfer into the Unitarian ministry.

A few weeks later, Jim returned to see Dr. Scholefield. His mind was made up. He knew it was the Unitarian Church for him, if they would have him. But would they? This time the interview was less casual. Scholefield wanted to know whether this man was really qualified and whether he was really interested, whether his supposed theological shift was genuine. Jim on his part wanted to know if he would be acceptable and what he must do to qualify as a Unitarian minister.

The interview went very well. When it was over Dr. Scholefield promised to write to Unitarian headquarters in Boston on Jim's behalf, and he urged Jim to write to the director of the Department of the Ministry. "My impression of him," Scholefield said in his letter, "is that he is stable, thoughtful, and probably a hard worker who is well motivated toward our ministry. He looks to me like the kind of man we are definitely interested in." In a concluding paragraph, he added: "Jim Reeb's problem becomes somewhat acute in June when he terminates his service with the Presbytery."

Two months later (March 23, 1957), Jim himself wrote to Unitarian headquarters in Boston regarding the possibility of transferring to the Unitarian ministry. It was no impulsive gesture. Not only had he thought about it for months, turning the matter over and over in his mind to test his own motives; he had in the meanwhile been attending Unitarian churches. He liked what he saw and heard. He also attended meetings of the Ethical Culture Society and the Society of Friends in order to be sure that the Unitarian ministry was really his choice. Now he was *sure*. He had told Bob Foulkes of his intention and Bob at last encouraged him to go ahead. His Uncle Chet urged him to go ahead. His doctor friends urged him to go ahead.

But not his associates in the Presbyterian ministry and not his parents. His father and mother were greatly upset at what he proposed to do. They wrote to remonstrate with him. They reminded him of the depths of his faith as a boy and a young man. His father sent him a letter he (Jim) had written in St. Olaf days cast in strongly evangelical terms. Across the top he wrote: "Please read this through and then I would like it if you would return it. I shall always pray that yet somehow you again will find the way to happiness and peace in the Lord." His mother wrote to her sister and brother-in-law, Hazel and Chet Cable, to ask them to try to talk some sense into Jim. Chet answered her as follows:

"We received your letter and there is absolutely no use in your being concerned about Jim. He has an excellent education, a very level head and a keen interest in his fellow man. He is somewhat of an idealist and does not quite understand the frailties that human flesh is heir to, such as the dismal failure of our leaders to have the interest of the people at heart. As for my discouraging his present interest in Unitarianism, I would have about as much chance of doing that as I would have in convincing you that you should vote for Harry Truman.

"While it is true that Unitarians constitute a small minority of the religious people in the United States, it is also true that Presbyterians are a very, very small minority in relation to the hundreds of millions of Buddhists, Mohammedans and Hindus. There are many paths to God and all religions have their good points. The fact that any person does not believe in the many inconsequential details of a particular religion does not, I believe, give you or me the right to criticize his beliefs.

"Religion is like politics—you either believe certain things or you don't. If you had been born in China of Chinese parents and raised to be a Buddhist, it is extremely doubtful that you would ever become a Presbyterian—or a Unitarian.

"Don't worry about Jim; he is exceptionally intelligent—has very high moral standards—and a level head. I'm sure that good Chinamen will be in heaven, too."

Jim, aware that he had made a momentous decision, was at the office each day to meet the postman. A favorable response from the Unitarians would mean so much. In a few days he heard. But the letter was routine. They must have many such letters, he thought. How could they know how long he had pondered the decision to write his, how many people he had talked to, the problem with his father and mother? The letter contained a few pamphlets on Unitarianism which he really did not need. He was persuaded already. The one that interested him most told of the procedures to be followed if he wished to transfer. It all seemed very elaborate and time-consuming. But he could see the reasons for it. He didn't want to join a church that would, without further question, welcome whoever might apply for membership.

Now he was faced with an immediate decision. Should he resign his post at the hospital before he was sure there was a place for him in the Unitarian Church? As the weeks went by and he heard nothing more, it began to look to him as if there was not. And he could not afford to be out of a job entirely, with a wife and child to support. Of course, they could always go back to Wyoming. His parents or hers would gladly take them in. But that was unthinkable. He might have been a little more encouraged had he known that Dr. Scholefield, true to his word, had written a letter recommending him. He would have been even more encouraged had he known how commendatory it had been and that Scholefield had stressed the fact that time was of the essence. Not knowing, Jim decided that he must take the risk nevertheless, and accordingly submitted his resignation as chaplain at the Philadelphia General Hospital to take effect July 31, 1957.

Many of his colleagues in the Presbyterian Church attributed his action to a rebellion against his parents. It was the well-worn formula. Naturally, they argued, in his breakaway he did the thing that would hurt them most. He rejected their religion and took the one that would be most abhorrent to them—Unitarianism. Nothing could have been further from the truth. Through this very trying period for all three, Jim never felt rejected by them. They on their part never felt rejected by him. Throughout the period of his transition, they felt and never doubted the warmth of his love even though they were quite unable to understand his religious point of view.

The days dragged on as Jim anxiously waited for word from Unitarian headquarters. Meanwhile, he began to consider various other lines of employment. He went to Pittsburgh to be interviewed for a possible personnel post with U.S. Steel. He looked into selling insurace and being a drug salesman. He also considered selling an encyclopedia.

His Uncle Chet encouraged him in this. "You'd make a good salesman," he told him. But after reviewing the training course, Jim gave up that idea. He was sickened and outraged by the methods the salesmen were trained to use. As far as he could see, although they were selling an established encyclopedia, they were not to make their approach on the merits of the publication. Instead they were to use every device of trickery and deceit in an attempt to get a hearing.

During this period Marie was less anxious about Jim's job than he was. Her concern was that whatever post he took should be right for him. Should such a job not come along by August 1, she stood ready to go back to work until it did. Above all she wanted him to find himself and put an end to his restless discontent. If the Unitarian Church was where he belonged, then that was what she wanted for him. She knew very little about the Unitarians but felt no urge to look down on them or condemn them because their beliefs were different from hers. There was a wives' lecture at the seminary at about this time at which a Unitarian woman spoke on her beliefs. Marie went to hear her and felt ashamed at the way she was treated. It seemed to her that the group did not look upon the lecture as an opportunity to learn, but rather as an opportunity to show the poor woman how wrong she was.

A far greater problem for her was the fact that Jim was just never home now. She seldom crossed him, seldom chided him, seldom argued with him. But during the winter of 1956-1957 she began increasingly to object to his almost total absorption in his work. Whenever he talked of the needs of the people at the hospital and the demands of the program he had developed, she began to set over against them the need of John for a father. Sometimes she spoke of her own loneliness, but not very often.

It had been bad enough back in seminary days. But after his graduation, when they moved to South 60th Street and he began his work as chaplain at PGH, things got steadily worse. Now, it seemed to her, Jim was gone day and night every day, Saturdays and Sundays included. The longer he continued as hospital chaplain, the worse it got.

As the weeks wore on during that spring and no word of any kind, either encouraging or discouraging, came from the Unitarians, Marie more and more was set on edge. Jim had romanticized the business world. It was, he had thought, cruel but honest. Now he found that whatever it was, there was apparently no place in it for him. Bob Foulkes was aware of the problem and would like to have helped, but he was powerless to do so. Jim had become so withdrawn that Bob could not get through to him. But this was in character, and Bob understood. Jim had always been very open and free with him on almost everything, but never regarding his relationship to Marie. He almost never spoke of her to him, and Bob did not try to intrude.

It was their family doctor who discovered that a physiological factor was aggravating the complex psychological situation in which Jim and Marie found themselves. His diagnosis: Marie had an over-active thyroid which made her fretful, although normally she was of a very even disposition. He prescribed surgery for the first week in June. Jim's mother came on to care for John. By the time Marie came home from the hospital, Jim was on vacation and there followed one of the happiest periods in their life together. Marie was her relaxed, serene self once more, while Jim was home most of the time.

By now Jim's personal theological problems had also been largely resolved. If all of his questions were not answered, at least the major ones were. At any rate, he knew where he stood. He knew what he did and did not believe. He knew what his approach to basic theological questions was to be. There was no longer to be any conflict between his true beliefs and a Confession promulgated by his church which he supposedly accepted. Now he was prepared to tell anyone who asked him that he no longer believed much of the Westminster Confession.

Bob Foulkes assumed that he would resign from the Presbytery when he gave up his post at the hospital. Thereupon, according to the rules, the Presbytery would "divest him of his office and erase his name from the roll." But this was more than James Reeb could bring himself to do. The church might throw him out if it wished, but he did not want to get out. He still believed deeply in the church. If others no less heretical than he could remain, why couldn't he? The difference was, he felt he could no longer be active, in his case as a chaplain, without being deceitful. But he saw no reason why this should make him more objectionable than those who remained active, yet believed as he did.

Accordingly, he did not resign, although his problem with the Presbyterian Church was perfectly clear to him. "I discovered my integrity was being undermined by the very confessional nature of the [Presbyterian] Church," he said in a letter written later to a colleague who wanted to know why he had left the Presbyterian Church. "When considering the validity of the doctrines of the church I was aware of external and internal pressures that made me desire to make my ideas continue to conform to those of the church. Thus I could not even begin to objectively consider new concepts arising as a result of scientific discoveries, insights of other religions, or ideas developed by various schools of philosophy until I determined to stand by what I really thought even if it meant I had to leave the church.

"A church based on a confession cannot in the final analysis be devoted to seeking truth. It must be devoted to upholding the ideas set forth in the creed. These ideas may be true. It is just that, to my mind, the confessional church does not provide a setting within which to test whether they are true or not. Any man considering the validity of the essentials of the confession realizes what conclusions he must reach if he is going to be able to remain within the church."

But to leave a post in a church because it was doctrine-centered was not, in Jim's mind, to give up allegiance to the church. Too much remained in which he still believed and thought to be of fundamental importance. The letter went on:

"Through the religious training in my home, a continuing study of the Bible, the nurture of the church and my theological education I have received much for which I am grateful. Part of what I received, a deep respect for truth and a sense of the importance of integrity—indeed I hold truth sacred above all else—has now brought me to act in such a manner that you suggest the Presbytery will possibly excommunicate me. I can, of course, understand why this may be necessary in light of the present laws of the church. I regret, however, that a loyalty to truth and an unwillingness to say more or less than one really believes and to join with other men of a similar frame of mind still constitutes, even in this present time, heretical actions from the point of view of the church.

"I regret this because a reading of church history has convinced me that those who have judged men or groups to be heretical have themselves been judged heretical by other men. Such judgments do not contribute to the growth of religion nor to respect for truth and therefore in a sense undermine the foundations of our society. In our time when we are engaged in a desperate struggle with authoritarian societies determined to mold the minds of men according to their own preconceived patterns our society needs to strengthen the foundations upon which our democracy is built. When I remember the deep commitment of the Protestant churches to our democratic way of life, it seems incongruous that the Presbyterian Church should still retain a practice so typical of those used by various authoritarian movements of our time."

Meanwhile, the denominational machinery by which Jim's application for admission to the Unitarian ministry was being processed had at last begun to move. The head of the Department of the Ministry had retired and a new man, Rev. Leon Fay, had come to take his place. Finding a huge backlog of work before him, he set to work to process it and also to get further staff assistance. But all this took time. In January, 1958, he asked Rev. John MacKinnon of the Wilmington Church to interview James Reeb. MacKinnon, in his role as field man to screen candidates for the Unitarian ministry, took Jim out to lunch, and after talking with him, reached the same conclusion as Harry Scholefield had fourteen months before.

"I would recommend Mr. Reeb highly for consideration as a Unitarian minister," he wrote the Department of the Ministry. "I talked with him for an hour and a half. He is sincere, earnest, intelligent and extremely attractive and personable. I think this man is top flight. He has a very sound concept of the ministry and I think a good feel for the sort of life he will have as a Unitarian minister. He almost leans over backward in his view of the importance of the congregation in running its affairs, and seems to want to work for a complete involvement of as many people as possible. If he operates as he thinks he will have an active and self-reliant church—no spoon-feeding of people by the minister."

Realizing that he had an unusual man before him who had already been kept waiting too long, MacKinnon soon afterward arranged for Jim to meet Dr. Dale DeWitt, Regional Director of the Unitarian Association for the Middle Atlantic States area. DeWitt too was attracted by him and arranged to have Jim meet the Regional Fellowship Committee, another step in the screening process. It was June before the report of that interview was sent to Mr. Fay in Boston, and it was now almost a year and a half since Jim first inquired about making the transfer.

DeWitt, never one to go overboard with enthusiasm, wrote: "The committee was quite favorably impressed. They felt that there was integrity of depth, sincerity and understanding of the requirements of liberal religion and a sense of commitment which would stand him in good stead. He has come to the decision to enter the Unitarian ministry at some cost to his family relationship. While the committee felt that he might not seem immediately impressive as a public speaker and the first impression was not too good, before the interview was over there was a deepening respect for him and his capacity to express himself."

His reaction was typical. On a one-to-one relationship Jim was at his best. Before a committee, where he knew he was being watched, he was always quiet, almost diffident at the beginning, but after a while as the committee warmed to him and as he in turn gained confidence and began to talk about the things that interested him, his manner changed markedly. It was this quality in his preaching, too, that people liked—his ability to overtake a reluctant congregation, so to speak.

In the meantime, a second child, Karen Ruth, was born to Jim and Marie, March 18, 1958. For Jim, the event was by no means routine, but there was none of the ecstasy he had known with the birth of his first child; none of the wonder at new life coming into the world. By now he had seen too much of life in all its many phases. Marie's mother came to look after John. Then just at that time, Jim's Grandmother Fox died at Ellwood City. Leaving Marie's mother in charge, he drove out for the funeral and to be with his mother. She came back with him for a brief visit and to see the new baby, then flew back to Casper. On the long drive and while she was there, she and Jim talked earnestly about the change in his religious convictions. She tried as hard as she could to dissuade him from becoming a Unitarian, and he on his part tried as hard as he could to explain his feelings to her. But it was no use: she just could not understand.

After she got back to Casper, she and Harry talked the question over with each other yet again. Perhaps, she thought, she had not really got over what she really intended to say, so she wrote Jim a letter, explaining once more what she believed and why.

Jim wrote back a brief note about the weather and how much Karen looked like John when he was a baby. Then he said:

"I received your letter yesterday, Mom. I read it carefully and thought about what you said. I hope you will always feel free to write me about your thoughts and ideas about what I should do. I was very pleased to receive the box of shirts that you sent. They will really come in handy as the hot weather arrives. Thank you so much."

His heart was heavy as he sealed the letter and dropped it in the mailbox. He must be true to himself. He had long since determined that. It was, he knew too, one of the basic principles by which his parents had taught him to live. He would always be grateful to them for it. How tragic, he thought, that that principle should now be a source of division between them. How tragic that they could not see he was most true to them, and most their son, when, like Job, he held fast to his own integrity as they had taught him to do.

After he gave up the hospital chaplaincy, Jim began visiting various churches. When he could he took Marie and the children with him in the car. They went first to the new Unitarian Society recently formed in nearby Springfield, Pennsylvania. Jim found it an exciting group, altogether to his liking. It was a lay-led "fellowship," as the Unitarians call such a group: new, active, but still too small to support a minister and to organize as a church. They also visited the Main Line Fellowship at Devon, the First Unitarian Church in Philadelphia, the church at Wilmington, Delaware, and the South Jersey Fellowship near Merchantville. Some of them they went to more than once.

They were warmly welcomed by all the Unitarian groups they visited, particularly the smaller "fellowships." Before long they began to ask Jim to preach for them, which he was glad to do. By that time most of them knew he was trying to enter the Unitarian ministry. There was always a good turnout the Sunday he preached.

Soon the Springfield "fellowship" became a "church" and called a minister of its own, Rev. Herbert Vetter. When he asked Jim to preach for him one Sunday, Jim accepted eagerly. It proved to be a memorable occasion. The people were greatly impressed with the obvious sincerity of the man as well as with his competence. Here, they felt, was an ideal candidate for the Unitarian ministry, a man of superior mentality, devoted to the way of freedom in religion, and completely committed to the welfare of his fellow man. When Vetter asked Jim to preach for him a second time, the enthusiasm of the people for him was increased. The Vetters on their part formed a very high opinion of Jim. One Sunday evening they invited the entire Reeb family to dinner, which enabled them to see another dimension of Jim's character. He had, they saw, remarkable ability to relate to their children.

Later Jim went to talk with Vetter. He was, he revealed, deeply distressed at the attitude his parents had taken toward his leaving the Presbyterian Church. As he talked he grew increasingly emotional. Vetter encouraged him to talk on. Soon Jim's eyes filled with tears, and before long it was difficult for him to speak.

This is true grief, Vetter reflected. There is an irreparable loss here—loss of the understanding of his parents for whom his feelings are very deep, and to some extent loss of rapport with his wife whose views have not changed as his have. He feels he cannot meet the expectations of those who love him.

Jim's grief was real, and it was not for himself. Above all it was for his mother. She had a virtual breakdown soon after returning to Wyoming after the birth of Karen. She seemed to be unable to do anything. She wouldn't drive the car, wouldn't even go out, and invited nobody in. It was a strange pattern for one who had always wanted people around her, one who had always entertained a great deal. She, who had not been sick for years and never complained, began going to the doctor constantly. The once-empty medicine cabinet was now filled with pills and concoctions of various sorts. It was a hard time for Jim's father, who found his son's religious shift hard to understand, and who, on top of that, now found himself married to a virtual stranger.

At last, in the summer of 1958, Jim received a blank on which to apply for preliminary fellowship as a Unitarian minister. In answer to the question, "Why do you want to be a Unitarian minister," he wrote:

"During the years that have passed since leaving Seminary my understanding of the nature of the religious life has changed. The traditional Protestant theology that was at one time most meaningful and helpful to me gradually became so no longer. Through the Protestant church I caught a vision of the importance of truth, righteousness, and mercy, the very pursuit of which has now led me beyond the bounds of that church.

"This is why I want to be a Unitarian minister. I believe the Unitarian Church emphasizes certain values that to me represent the enduring contribution of Christianity to mankind. In addition, I believe that it envisions an approach to the religious quest that can make it possible for religion to continue to be a vital, creative, and integrative factor in the life of any person or group both in this day and in the days to come.

"Because the members of the Unitarian Church are not bound to a creed or to certain conceptions held to be absolute truths, except that the pursuit of truth is always of ultimate importance, they can respond to new ideas and truths no matter what their source nor how evidently they contradict previously held beliefs.

"Since there is a recognition that there will always be people at different stages in their search for meaning and purpose in life, and differences of opinion among sincere and dedicated people as to the nature of life and the good life, the responsibility and freedom of each individual to proceed along the pathways that are most helpful and productive for him are emphasized.

"Finally, the development of people so that they may approach ever nearer to full fruition is accepted as the primary task of religion.

"I want to be a Unitarian minister because the church does not prescribe for people what the ultimate outcome of their religious quest must be; rather it attempts to create a fellowship that will strengthen and encourage each member in his desire and determination to live the truth as he sees it.

"Many men and women have labored long and arduously to help develop the Unitarian Church as a liberal religious fellowship. I believe the history of our country and other countries would certainly be different had there been no such group. I am grateful that through the devotion of these men and women in the past and present there is such a church which I can join. Now I want to share in the continuing labor of building this church."

Letters of inquiry went to all the references he gave in his application, and the answers were invariably flattering. Dr. Frank H. Stroup assured the department that Jim had "an unusually fine capacity for the ministry." Jerome E. Jungreis, Chief Psychiatric Social Worker in the Neuro-Psychiatric Division of PGH, gave him fulsome praise. His old friend Bob Foulkes wrote:

"I have a very high regard and deep affection for Jim." Then, after speaking of their long and close association, he continued:

"Many of our fellow Presbyterian ministers have registered their concern to me over Jim's leaving the ministry. I could never share their apprehension because I know how long Jim had struggled over the decision and how deeply it was a part of him, and in my opinion right for him. . . . Jim is an inveterate pastor. He has an abiding and most sincere interest in people, and what has always impressed me most from the earliest hospital days, he can raise questions of belief and attitude with people without making them feel criticized or on the defensive.

"Another quality in Jim that I think will make him a particularly good Unitarian minister is his insatiable thirst for ideas and knowledge. He loves ideas and struggling with values the way some people love baseball. A creedal denomination will always hamper this yen if it goes far enough.

"One or two Presbyterian ministers, who have their own theological misgivings, have criticized Jim for not being mature, meaning that he doesn't bend or make concessions, the implications being he should keep quiet about some of his disbeliefs, knowing that other men in the denomination have them too. I see this as a strength. But in any case Jim is the kind of person who will act on his convictions, once they are established, even though they seem foolish or unnecessary to others.

"I believe Jim is a superior person and recommend him highly. I have found him to be a sincere and loyal friend and feel any congregation he goes to will find him the same."

But with this flurry of letters the denominational machinery again ground to a complete stop. To earn a living in the meanwhile Jim had turned to quite a different kind of work, which like everything else he did proved to be one more step in the development through which he ultimately found his mission in life.

9

The Lay Ministry

ONE HOT July afternoon, when Marie was still recuperating from her thyroidectomy and Jim had not yet found a job to replace the hospital chaplaincy he had given up, he stopped by the West Branch YMCA in Philadelphia. They were having summer swimming classes, he had heard; John was the right age; it was just the thing he needed; would they be willing to accept him? Jim already knew the Executive Secretary, Charles Groesbeck. They were both members of the West Philadelphia Ministers Association. Jim didn't attend the meetings very often. He was too busy. But he liked them, especially because of their ecumenical spirit. And he liked Groesbeck, a congenial older man, now soon to retire. He liked also what he had heard about that particular Y. They were making real progress with integration there, and it was an experience he coveted for John. At PGH, while ministering to both Negroes and whites, he had formed some decided opinions on the economic, social, and cultural deprivation to which the American Negro is subject. The West Branch Y was, for this reason, one he was glad to support.

Groesbeck received him warmly, and John was forthwith entered in the swimming class. During their conversation, the fact emerged that the Y had not had a Youth Director on the staff for two years. The previous fall they had added James H. Robinson, a Negro. This was considered a great step forward, but they had made him Associate Youth Director rather than Director. The timid on the Board of Managers thought it important that the Director be white lest all the white members of the Y leave.

Would they consider him for the post, Jim asked. He explained that he was giving up the hospital chaplaincy, among other reasons because he found it no longer satisfying merely to pray with the sick and the dying. He wanted to get behind the results to the causes of the human misery he faced in the hospital. In the Y he would be dealing with young people and thus be working at the end of the problem where he now knew he wanted to be. He told Groesbeck of his work with the Boys Club in Casper. Perhaps that experience would be useful to him, he suggested.

Jim's feeling of restlessness at the hospital was not news to Charles Groesbeck. He had known Bob Foulkes ever since he became Chaplain at PGH several years before. They were now good friends. As chaplain at the Presbyterian Hospital, Bob was still a member of the West Philadelphia Ministers Association and was far more regular in attendance than Jim. They had talked about Jim at some length one day after one of the meetings. Bob had told him that Jim now questioned his former theological position; that he had begun to wonder if he should be in the ministry at all.

As Jim talked, Groesbeck became very much interested. This was just the sort of man he was looking for. While he lacked the formal training the Y usually required, James Reeb was highly trained in the general areas needed for Y work. Obviously he had the right motivation coupled with an eagerness to learn. Groesbeck would see, he said. He would consult with the Board of Managers while Jim thought it over and discussed it with Marie. The salary was modest. He would be earning less at the Y than at the hospital. It was pretty hard to get along on what they now had. Still, under the circumstances, Jim thought the Y salary would be acceptable.

That night on the way home, Groesbeck found himself strangely excited. I would be fortunate to get that remarkable young man on my staff, he thought. He may not have all the technical qualifications but he has everything else. His experience in seminary had been like that of many students for the ministry today, Groesbeck reflected. They are still getting the old stuff, and it is disappointing to them. They find it irrelevant to present-day concerns. Obviously Chaplain Reeb is just such a man.

But W. Byron Lukens, Chairman of the Board at the time, thought Jim a most unlikely candidate for the post of Youth Director. Tall, thin, and very idealistic, he hardly seemed the type, he was so much the opposite of the muscle-man Lukens supposed the Y would eventually secure. Besides, he seemed too much of an introvert. He'll never make it, Lukens thought to himself on first seeing him. But he knew about Jim's record at the hospital through his two sisters who worked there and were impressed with his likable, somewhat mercurial temperament. He might make up in friendliness and dedication what he lacks in muscle and special Y training, Lukens thought.

Since no suitable candidate had come along in two years, the Board of Managers, with some misgivings, appointed Jim Youth Director of the West Branch Y. Jim was delighted. Not only did it mean that he could now provide for his material wants, he could do so at a task that seemed to him completely worthwhile. He wrote in his diary the day he took the Y job:

"I have decided to stay in the field of religion. Here all my deepest loyalties are found. I have surveyed the business realm and nowhere have I found an adequate outlet for my interests. The ideas of freedom, justice, growth of the individual, sincerity, and love and service to others are very important to me. Their application to life is even more important. I have found a wealth of spirit in the YMCA that is refreshing and stimulating."

Marie too was delighted at the choice. All the other openings he had looked into would just have been a job—a means of making a living. She knew that for Jim such an arrangement would be misery. For her it would mean more anxiety. She knew he would not last long at any such post. He had always found it difficult enough to cope with the necessary routine connected with anything he had undertaken. Jim cared so deeply about things that he could do well only what he really cared about. But when he got excited about something, he could work at it with energy that seemed superhuman. The job at the Y, Marie felt, was one to which he could give his all.

On Friday, July 26, 1957, former Chaplain James Reeb began his work as Youth Director of the Philadelphia West Branch YMCA. His quarters were anything but attractive. He was given a small office down the corridor on the second floor with hardly room enough in it for a desk and a file. Adjacent to it was a small counter where game supplies—ping-pong balls, and the like—were handed out to the boys. The Y itself was badly run-down. Built in 1914 at the intersection of 52nd and Sansom Streets in what was then one of the better neighborhoods of the city, the Y had been ideally designed for the program of that day. But the depression told heavily on the budget, and the spacious rooms on the front of the building were converted into stores to provide rent. The side entrance on Sansom Street became the only entrance. Thereafter there was never budget enough to keep the building up to its earlier standard of light, air, and roominess.

But quarters made no difference whatever to the new Youth Director. He flung himself into his work with characteristic vigor. So energetic and so eager to get on with the work was he that Jim Robinson, his associate, found him a little hard to take at the outset. So did some of the other members of the staff. He seemed even harder to get at, for he had a reserve about himself and his own life that was quite at variance with his intense desire to get to know his associates.

Nevertheless, it was clear that he had a deep concern for people as people, and that race made no difference to him whatever. In his exuberance, he seemed to the staff like a boy let out of school. "He is like a pack of firecrackers," Lukens told Groesbeck once. "He has more new ideas in a day than most of us get in a year. You sometimes get the impression that he is going off in all directions at once. But if you watch him, you see that everything he does is designed to advance the main program."

The members of the Y staff were not the only ones who found Jim's enthusiasm and deep interest in them as persons a little trying at the outset. Alex Wood, a member of the Youth Cabinet, had much the same impression. He got the feeling that Jim was picking at him because of Jim's constant attempts to develop rapport with him. Wood was at that time Jim's counterpart at the Parkside YMCA. He was a Negro who had been born in the South. This seemed to arouse in Jim a very strong desire to get to know him well and to understand how he felt. In his very direct manner, he often asked Wood about race questions. The latter was reluctant to discuss these things, but Jim would keep at him.

One day, in an effort to get Alex talking, Jim said he thought he knew how Negroes felt.

"You can't," retorted Alex with some heat. "Until it has happened to you, you can't imagine what it is like to be spat on, called obscene names, or told to sit in the back of the bus. Perhaps you can imagine it," he said. "But you can't feel it. And until you *feel* it, you don't know what it is really like."

To his surprise, Jim replied: "But I do feel it. I feel the pain inside me—physical pain. I have worked among Negroes for several years now. I have seen them in their deepest misery, and I think I understand. But I must agree with you that few people do."

Alex let the matter drop. He did not think then that any white man could feel or even understand the humiliation that was the daily lot of the Negro in the South, and to no small degree in the North as well.

But if *any* white man can, this one can, he thought. His desire to help was plain, and his complete freedom from bias was plainer. He could see that Jim was a truth seeker as well, in religion, in racial matters, in everything, and he liked that in him too. As Alex came to understand the full scope of the man, and as Jim discontinued what had seemed to Alex to be almost an assault on his personality, they became fast friends. They also found that they shared the same hobby, that of American Indian lore. It had long been an interest of Alex's. On learning that Jim was from Wyoming, he asked him about Indians and Indian relics there. That loosed a torrent in Jim, whose excursions into Indian lore in Wyoming increased each summer as he went back. Jim told him about Independence Rock near Casper on the old Oregon Trail on which the settlers on their western trek carved their names. He told him there were places out on the prairie where you could still see the ruts of the pioneer wagon wheels. He told him he had seen the plains Indians in their native dress.

When the Philadelphia Museum opened an Indian exhibit, Jim phoned Alex and proposed that they go to it together. Families too, he said, and it was agreed. Jim came by for the Woods in his station wagon with Marie and John, and off they went together to the exhibition. It was a memorable day for them all. By this time, Alex Wood had begun to realize that part of his problem with Jim Reeb was his own. As a Southern Negro, he had his mind made up about whites. He knew that no matter how kind they were to you they would never accept you as an equal. With them you were always less than a man. Jim forced him to change his mind. Here, he found, was at least one white man who would accept him as an equal. When the day at the museum was over, Alex Wood realized that he was happier than he had ever been in his life before. Through the open, unreserved friendship of a white man and his family, he saw for the first time that the Negro dream of racial equality might one day come true.

After that it seemed to Alex Wood that Jim would pursue him following each meeting of the Youth Directors to ask him what he thought about questions that had been discussed in the meeting. Alex, the old habits still strong in him, would put Jim off. But it was not to be done.

"Come on," Jim would say in his broadest bantering manner. "Tell me what you *really* think." And in the end, Alex would. He is one of the few men I would trust, he thought. I really can talk to him about anything. He would, if he could, make Philadelphia the most integrated city in the nation. As time went on, he found this opinion increasingly easy to hold, because so many other people he respected, both Negro and white, thought so, too.

Jim's earliest impact on the Y program was in the area of integration. When he became Youth Director, the West Branch was striving desperately to maintain a balance between Negroes and whites. In an attempt to do this, they had adopted a quota system. Jim supported the idea of maintaining integration—that is to say, of keeping the whites coming—but he was quick to point out that to limit the number of Negroes who could come to the Y by the number of whites who would, was to defeat the purpose of the program. "Let them all come," he argued, "and let us get more whites to come too." To do this he set up a bussing program and constantly used his own station wagon for this purpose also.

Concern for the plight of the Negro in American life was now far more vivid and much nearer to the center of Jim's consciousness than ever before, but the origins of his concern lay far back in his childhood and in fact could easily be traced back into his ancestry. This particular characteristic descended to him from his mother's side of the family. The reasons, as is usually true in such cases, were many. To begin with, Ellwood City, to which the Fox family moved from the little town of Wurtemburg, was a racial melting pot. A steel town established by Andrew Carnegie as a fabricating center for steel products, it had attracted at the outset not merely the Germans and Alsatians who were already living in the area, but Poles and French Canadians, Irish and Italians. At Ellwood City, as the children of these and other ethnic groups grew up together in the public schools, the racial exclusivism that characterized their parents broke down. The town was not completely free of racial animosities, but it suffered from them far less than most communities.

The Negro, of course, only recently released from the bonds of slavery, as always suffered most from racial discrimination. However, there were few in Ellwood City, and their sufferings were due much more to their ignorance and their consequent abject poverty than to their color. It is not without significance that Jim's Grandmother Fox died of pneumonia she caught while nursing a destitute Negro in Ellwood City. She had found the old woman (nobody now remembers how) in a little shack down by the railroad tracks nearly dead of pneumonia. Each day she went down to the shack to look after her and while doing so contracted the disease herself. This occurred during Jim's second year at the Y. It is also probably not entirely coincidental that Jim's grandmother, Mary Majors Fox, whom he both loved and admired, was a nurse, intimately associated with the Ellwood City Hospital all her life, and that when Jim chose his first post as minister, it was to the hospital rather than to a parish church that he turned.

As early as his high school days we find Jim aware of the fact of racial discrimination and eager to do something about it. In his work with the Boys Club he learned that a boy of Mexican origin had less chance to make a place for himself in American society than other boys did. Hence the pressures on him toward delinquency and crime were greater. In August, 1945, while undergoing basic training at Camp Roberts in California, Jim wrote Bob Reed: "There is a great challenge in Paso Robles, especially in the Mexican and Negro district."

At St. Olaf the problem did not exist for him, but it came forcibly to his attention again in his first year at Princeton. During the spring term, as a part of his course on the City Church, he went to New York to visit the East Harlem Protestant Parish, a church established in 1949 by students from Union Theological Seminary in an effort to take the Gospel to people who might not otherwise have a chance to hear it. The Parish increasingly became an attempt to assist the city's poor in social rehabilitation. Jim was greatly excited by the work he saw being carried on there, but he was appalled by the conditions he observed in Harlem. It was the first time this young man from the western plains had ever had an opportunity really to see urban decay as it exists at the heart of America's cities. It was the first time he had ever seen Negroes in large numbers. It was his first introduction to mass misery as our American mass society has produced it. For the first time he became aware of the economic deprivation to which the American Negro has been subject. As a result, New York, the miracle city of skyscrapers and subways, of great bridges and huge ocean-going steamers, was quite lost on him. He returned to Princeton thinking only of the squalor of Harlem.

It was not until he began his work at the Philadelphia General Hospital, however, that Jim really came to understand the deprivation the American Negro suffers because he is a Negro. There every day he saw the poor, the downtrodden, the neglected and forgotten, diseased in body and often in mind, the social refuse of a great city whose potential no one knew because few of them had ever had a chance. Most of them were Negroes. Appalled by what he saw, Jim first supposed, as many Americans do, that the condition of the Negro is somehow related to his nature. But gradually, as he came to know them as people, as he discovered the social, cultural, and economic deprivation under which they had lived, he began to wonder.

Negroes, he found, were people with aspirations, like anybody else. They were warm, loving, kindly, thoughtful people, despite all the privation to which they had been subject. What would he have been like if his opportunities had been as limited as theirs? If he had been as involved in the bare struggle to survive as they, would he be so moral in his attitude toward others? Would he be so scrupulous about property rights if he had never had anything of his own but the clothes on his back?

Jim soon established himself as counselor and friend to the boys. Among these was a lad of ten named George Pearson. One day he broke the rule of the Y against throwing water. When Jim Reeb exacted the penalty against him which the rule required, he took offense and asked to transfer his membership to another Y. With a different director, the request might have been summarily granted and there the matter might have ended. But the request, as it came through the Y office, caught the eye of the Youth Director.

Jim called George in for a talk. First he explained what rules in general were for, illustrating the point not with the rule against throwing water, but rules in basketball, which George loved to play. They moved from that to traffic rules, and then to the laws by which human society is governed, including the Constitution of the United States. Finally they got to talking about the West Branch YMCA and the rules that were necessary there. Again George understood. When they were through, he said he would like to stay on at West Branch. Deep inside he knew it was not because he quite understood why society has rules. It was because he had found a friend. He had found an older man who cared about him, who didn't want to catch him in wrongdoing as he had supposed all white men did. No, this man seemed to want to help him.

"He was like a father to me," George said later. Jim was just that to a great many of the boys at West Branch, some of whom had no fathers of their own. On outings, he played with them as if he were one of them. Under his leadership, the youth department began to grow. They liked that, too. It was more fun when there were lots of kids around and something was always going on. As he had been with George Pearson, Jim was hard on them whenever they did not come up to standard. What he asked was always right and they respected him for demanding it of them. He kept the place in order, for which they were really glad. Boylike, they would always leave things around if they could get away with it. "No swim until the game stuff is picked up," he used to say. It was a rule he was able to enforce that few others could because he never relaxed it and because of his practice of talking to the boys. Any boy who slipped downstairs without first putting away the things he had been using had to face the Youth Director alone in his office the next day.

They followed the rules because they knew that Mr. Reeb did not care about their enforcement but about how the Y looked, how it ran, and whether everybody had a good time. He cared about how they thought and felt toward one another. He wanted to know what kind of men they were going to become. This they slowly learned. And because he cared, they cared too.

For serious offenses, suspension was the standard punishment at the Y, but Jim seldom invoked it and never at the first offense, no

James Reeb
about three years old,
Wichita, Kansas.

The Rev. James Reeb,
Washington, D.C.

At work in his study, All Souls Church, Washington, D.C.

It was this scene on TV of Alabama state troopers' brutal attack on civil rights marchers at Edmund Pettus Bridge at Selma that sent Jim Reeb south. (*Wide World Photos*)

Marie Reeb, Jim's wife, at a press conference at University Hospital, Birmingham, March 10. (*The Birmingham News*)

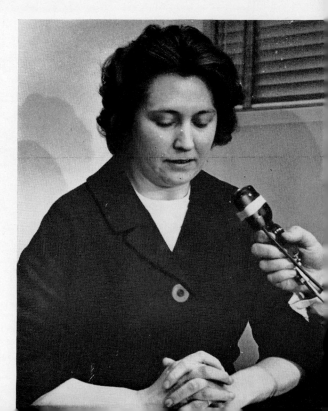

A.D. 1965

JAMES J. REEB
—
SELMA, ALABAMA

©1965 HERBLOCK
THE WASHINGTON POST

Herblock in
The Washington Post

Memorial service for James Reeb, Lafayette Park, Washington, D.C.,
March 14. (*Washington Evening Star*)

matter how serious it was. Always a talk with the offender in the office came before any disciplinary action. A second chance followed. If there was a second offense, there came a second and longer talk, with a visit to the parents, if possible. Suspension was used only as a last resort. "The boy who is suspended is the boy who needs the Y most," he always said.

Youth Director Reeb took great interest in the aspect of the Y program designed to draw in the parents. He not only visited the parents of troubled boys himself, he got the Youth Committee to undertake systematic visitation of all parents. He developed a list of their church affiliations, if any, and got the committee members to urge attendance. If there was no church affiliation, the committee member was to help establish one.

Clifford Trent, the first Negro board member, was Chairman of the Youth Committee at the time. Realizing how completely Jim was dedicated to the welfare of the boys without regard to the question of race, he backed him in every proposal he made. It was easy to do, among other reasons because Jim was always thoroughly prepared to defend whatever he asked for. He was, for example, eager to lower the fee schedule in order to enable more boys to use the Y. To back up this proposal he made a demographic study of the West Branch area, showing the degree to which it had become Negro and hence lower class. Only working-class Negroes were moving into the area, he argued. Unless the fees were lowered, many of the newcomers might not be able to use the Y.

Sometimes, however, he let his enthusiasms run away with him. There was a part of Jim, lying deep within him, that liked to argue. Now and then, particularly in preparing written statements, he would argue with a committee to the point of exasperation. There was a time when the Cabinet, at one of its monthly meetings, sought to adopt a formula by which to implement a part of its program. A statement, drafted for consideration at the meeting, was generally satisfactory to most of the Cabinet, but when it seemed on the point of adoption, Jim raised a question. "Will this program as stated here really achieve its purpose?" he asked. They thought the question valid, and discussed it a while. Again they were ready to vote, but again Jim had questions. Harry Strothers, a member of the Cabinet, wanted to get on with the work, and said so. Finally, after some time, they adopted the statement over Jim's protest. They did so with some annoyance, feeling that they had given time discussing the statement that might better have gone into implementing the program.

Although ordinarily keenly sensitive to the feelings of others, he sometimes seemed quite oblivious to the impression he was making. He had developed the habit of smoking cheap, crooked cigars and this bothered more than one of his associates. Chided about it, he just laughed it off. Apparently he never realized that anybody found his cigars offensive.

The instance most often discussed, laughed at, and argued over among his friends, concerned his beard. Having had no vacation in 1957, the following summer he and Marie took John and Karen back to Wyoming for his month's vacation. While he was there, Jim went on a camping trip. As often happens on such expeditions, the entire party came back with beards. Jim, to his surprise and delight, found his beard a great source of amusement. Why not keep it till we get back East, he thought. We'll have some fun with it there too.

But when he reported for work at the Y, beard and all, nobody seemed to think it very funny. They joked with him about it, but he was a little nettled by the fact that everybody expected him to shave it off that night. He felt coerced. It was irrational, he knew, but he felt coerced just the same, and decided to keep it a while longer. When he came in the next day, he felt a distinct chill in the air. Now there were no jokes. Nobody said anything at all. When after a few days the beard was still there, he found himself the butt of an occasional dig or outright "When are you going to get that spinach off your face?" Mr. Groesbeck was inclined to be indulgent. His own son had returned from a camping trip with a beard which he soon shaved off. Jim, he felt, would do the same. But when a week had gone by and the beard was still there, now larger and bushier, Groesbeck called him into the office.

"I'd like to have you shave the beard off, Jim," he said.

"Are you telling me I have to?" Jim demanded.

"No," said Groesbeck slowly. "But I wish you would."

"Why?"

"Because it makes you look like a beatnik. It gives the Y a bad name." Jim couldn't agree.

"It's a private matter," he asserted, and the beard stayed on. By now Jim was troubled, and he went to talk the matter over with Bob Foulkes, feeling that he would understand. But he didn't.

"What difference does it make?" Bob asked, "whether you have it or don't?"

"An individual has a right to make his own decisions about his own person," Jim retorted. "This is no concern of anyone but me."

Bob again expressed his feeling that it was a trivial matter, having nothing to do with one's rights as a person, but rather with the prejudices of the people of the Y. He did not try to argue or persuade, but he did what Jim asked him to do. He told him what he thought, frankly, as he always had. To Bob's amazement, Jim was hurt. It was one of the few times in their long friendship. Jim felt let down by his friend. He had turned to him for support, but got from him only what he got from everyone else.

Charles Groesbeck, meanwhile, also sought outside advice. He went to his Board Chairman, W. Byron Lukens. He also talked to one of the committee members. Both gave him short shrift.

"Tell him to shave it off," they said. "You have the authority. Let that be the end of it."

Groesbeck did so as gently and persuasively as he could. But Jim was angry. This was as unexpected as it was rare. He left the room without saying anything. But when he came to work the next day, the beard was gone, and no one ever spoke of it again.

After six months Jim Robinson resigned as Associate Youth Director to take another post. He and Jim had gotten on most amicably, but soon after Jim's coming it was clear to him that both of them were not needed on the staff. This factor was by itself reason enough for leaving, but Jim Robinson had also to admit to himself that there was a supporting reason. He found Jim Reeb easy to get along with but hard to understand because of his habit of reaching into the deepest levels of Robinson's consciousness, but never permitting Robinson to reach into his.

"I used to get the feeling sometimes," Jim Robinson said later, "that he was trying to psychoanalyze me. He wanted me to tell him how I felt about things, but I could never get him to tell me how he felt about things at the deepest levels of consciousness. Sometimes when I would ask him questions about himself, he seemed to be deep in thought and way off somewhere. It was, in fact, not always easy to communicate with him."

Sara Mozenter had had the same feeling. After the Reebs had left South 60th Street and moved to Yeadon, as they did in 1957, she realized one night while talking with Harry that she knew almost nothing about Jim. His conversation was always in the present. He talked about what he was then doing, but never about the past, about where he had been, what he had seen and done. Nobody really knows him, they concluded. The same thing was true with regard to his problems. They never knew what he was thinking about. He might discuss personal matters with an intimate like Bob Foulkes, but with no one else. And even with Bob there were questions he would not deal with, his relationship with Marie, for example, as there were things he would not take up with her. Once there had been a time when he discussed everything with his father and mother, but not now. He would no longer discuss religion with them. On that point, since leaving the hospital, he had pulled down the curtain and had simply stopped talking.

But James Reeb's associates were never concerned very long about his reticence about himself. They knew that he cared for each of them in a way that few of them could do. Because he seemed to care so much for them, they cared for him. They took him as they found him and were grateful as they plunged together into the work of the Y. For this reason, he was very successful in gathering lay volunteers for the many and varied projects he developed.

An example was his Pre-Delinquent Program. Any boy he thought likely to get into trouble, or any boy who already was in trouble with the police, got his special attention. Jim would talk with such a boy as long as he would listen, trying to get through to him, trying to give him some notion of the future that lay ahead. More than one boy, then on his way into a life of crime, was given a different vision of himself by the program James Reeb developed and the assistants he enlisted in the project.

To bring in as many boys as possible from every kind of background, he went to the churches to enlist their help, spoke at PTA meetings, and organized a Gra Y program for grammar school boys to match the Hi-Y program long in existence. These activities were always fully integrated.

He also organized a Mothers Club in order to maintain closer contact with the parents. Thus, when he spotted a pre-delinquent, he knew to whom to turn for help at home. Among the mothers was Mrs. Alberta Cole, a Roman Catholic, who eventually became Assistant Youth Director for him. She found him as free of bias religiously as he was racially. He always knew who the pre-delinquents were, but he never revealed this knowledge to the boys themselves in any way.

Working among boys, many of whom came from backgrounds marked by deprivation of almost every kind, Jim's concept of forgiveness and human understanding underwent further development. While he was at the Y a group of teenage Negro boys killed a Korean student near the University of Pennsylvania where he was studying. The city was outraged. To satisfy the public clamor, the District Attorney announced his intention to seek the death penalty for the boys. At this, Jim got permission from his Youth Cabinet to circulate a statement of "Concern." Deploring the murder of the Korean student and all crime, Jim addressed himself to the question as to what should be done about it. He proposed that all Y Youth Committees seek more directly to allay the conditions that breed crime. He called for a foundation to study the disease of delinquency just as polio, arthritis, and muscular distrophy are studied, backed by funds from a foundation set up for the purpose. He asked that the attitude of groups such as his be communicated to public officials so that they would know such a body of opinion existed.

"Justice will not be more firmly established by the execution of these teen-agers," he concluded. "For mere justice to be done, all those responsible for the conditions that influenced these boys must also be put on trial. To execute them will only encourage the community to ignore its share of responsibility."

Then he came to the point he really wanted to make. "We have a share in that responsibility. Their lives most certainly have been influenced and in a sense determined by the system of slavery and prejudice under which they have lived. Prejudice predestines the majority of Negroes to live in the most deteriorated neighborhoods of our city.

Selfishness that feeds on money received by cutting up once fine homes into dirty, rotting barracks to house as many families as possible undoubtedly influenced their lives.

"We must ask: will the public be safer if these boys are executed? My answer is no. The vindictiveness given expression in such an action can only arouse further violence. The children of our city will only lose confidence in the compassion of the adults of this City of Brotherly Love."

Back in the seminary, Jim had written: "We must see the sin of no man as greater than our own." Now the unfolding thought of an idealistic theologue was being applied in practice, when the lives of teenage boys were at stake, and the philosophy of a great city regarding teenage crime was being determined. It was out of this statement that his pre-delinquent program had come.

Jim's ever-increasing activity at the Y created the old problems at home, however. As time went on he was out more frequently in the evenings at committee meetings and often for entire weekends as well, as he took groups off camping or on various excursions. It was the same old pattern. To see a need was for Jim to attempt to fill it, and with someone of his alert mind, there were ten programs that might be designed for every need. As at the hospital, his energy was inexhaustible. He tired everyone who was associated with him; they all gave out before he did. But his programs all took time, time Marie often would have liked to have, time to which she thought John and Karen were entitled. Perhaps the most poignant letter Jim ever wrote, judged by what it reveals about the conflicting demands of his family and his work, is dated Christmas Eve, 1958. It is a Christmas note to his parents, thanking them for the gifts they have sent him and the love the gifts express. He comments that the Y is quiet, as if expecting the holiday. On the afternoon of Christmas Eve he was still on the job.

From the beginning, Jim had been frank with Groesbeck regarding his efforts to enter the Unitarian ministry. This made the Executive Secretary a little uneasy because he never knew when his able, hard-driving Youth Director might hand him a letter of resignation. In August, after Jim had been with him a year, Groesbeck stopped him in the corridor one day.

"There is a conference early in September I'd like to have you go to," he said, "but only if you are going to remain with us. If not, I ought to be looking for a replacement and send him in your stead."

Jim was embarrassed. "I'll be glad to go," he said. "I thought things were coming to a head in June or July, but lately I have heard nothing at all."

"Then I'll have to ask you to agree to stay another six months," Groesbeck said.

"Agreed," said Jim.

He went to the conference and came back. And still there was no word from Boston. Patient, but no less persistent, he wrote again in October, reminding the Department of the Ministry that he was eager to talk with them about getting a church. In November he got a bundle of books from them and a blank to fill out "For Minister Seeking New Church."

Meanwhile, time was inexorably marching on. Shortly after November 1, Groesbeck stopped him again. Was March 1 the final date or did he plan to stay after that? Jim frankly said he didn't know, and was even more embarrassed.

"I'll write to Boston and see if I can't get some word from them," he said.

A very long, patient letter followed in which he carefully explained his situation. With the letter he sent a blank, duly filled out. The last question read: "Any additional comments," and Jim wrote:

"I would like the opportunity to serve in a large urban area and preferably in the inner-city area rather than in the surrounding suburbs. I believe in light of my particualr experience and interests that it would be in such a setting that I could make my best contribution to the Unitarian Church." It was the first time that he clearly formulated a concept that had gradually become central for him—large urban area, the inner city.

Still there was no word from Boston. Ever patient, but ever persistent, Jim sent yet another reminder just before the holidays, wishing the director a merry Christmas as well. This time he received a reply by return mail. But it was hardly encouraging. It read:

"The best answer I can give at this end for your immediate problem is to suggest that you continue at your present position at the

YMCA until next fall. Settlement in our churches is at best a slow business, and while we are endeavoring to get your name around as open pulpits occur, it does take time since pulpit committees are lay committees in our denomination and work slowly."

"Slowly," sighed Jim to himself, *"slowly* is it." But ever patient and ever understanding, he wrote back during the holidays:

"Thank you for your letter of December 22, 1958. I understand the process involved in settling a minister in a church and appreciate the fact that it takes a considerable period of time. I am sure your suggestion that I plan to stay at the Y until next fall is a wise one."

During the winter months the only church that made contact with him was a Unitarian church in suburban New York. They were in need of a Director of Religious Education and thought him a likely person for the post. It was by no means what he wanted, but Jim was willing to consider it.

"You can't expect very much when you transfer in from another denomination," Mr. Fay had written from headquarters. "You have to start where you can." Jim was by no means as impressed with the church as the people of the church were impressed by him. They offered him a salary of $5,600, which was not enough to live on in a well-to-do suburb. When they told him he could take a summer job to supplement his salary if he wished, his mind was made up. The whole flavor, he felt, was that of exploiting a man. The minister of the church, who did not take part in the negotiations, was outraged when he heard about the summer job proposal, and telephoned to apologize. He had met Jim and had formed a very high opinion of him. Jim was grateful but not encouraged. He would wait a little longer.

That winter and spring, All Souls Church in Washington, D.C. of which the writer is minister, had been trying to find someone for the post of Assistant Minister. There had been several candidates, but none seemed quite up to the job. Then by chance I heard about Jim Reeb. Three men from the Philadelphia area stayed overnight at my home March 30 in connection with a ministers meeting. They were Rev. Herbert Vetter, Rev. John MacKinnon, and Rev. Edwin Lane of the South Jersey Fellowship. At breakfast the next day I mentioned in passing the difficulty we were having in trying to locate an Assistant Minister who would really be up to the job. At this they all laughed.

"We have the opposite of your problem in the Philadelphia area," they said. "There is a fellow up there, a Presbyterian, working in a YMCA, who has been trying for over two years to get into our ministry."

"How is he?" I asked.

"Great," they said. "He's tops. He can handle the job for you." They then told me about Jim's work at the hospital, why he quit, and the outstanding job he was doing at the Y.

"How can I get in touch with him?" I asked.

"I'll telephone him for you when I get back this afternoon," Ed Lane volunteered. "I think he'll be interested." Late that afternoon Jim phoned me. The men had been right. He was very much interested. So was I. The voice seemed to tally with what the group at breakfast had said. He sounded friendly, warm, eager, well-spoken.

The following Saturday, the first day Jim could get away, he drove to Washington to see me. I was taken with him at once. The Chairman of the Board of Trustees, Howard Wahrenbrock, dropped by. He was equally impressed with the young man. Jim was then recommended to the Board for official action. Two weeks later, the Board interviewed him at a special meeting held after church. He was enthusiastically received by every member. Marie came with him and made an equally good impression. James Reeb was duly appointed Assistant Minister of All Souls Church before the meeting adjourned, his duties to begin as soon as possible.

Jim set July 1 as the probable date. It was, he said, the earliest time he could get away and give the Y not merely the required notice but also adequate time in which to seek a replacement. His resignation would come as no surprise, he assured us.

But it occasioned the deepest regret at the West Branch Y. In June, a banquet was held in his honor. No one hesitated to say that his contribution to the Y, and through it to the youth of the West Branch area, had been outstanding. The climax of the evening was the presentation of a plaque by W. Byron Lukens. When he finished reading the words inscribed upon it and handed the plaque to Jim, the assembly rose in a body. They clapped their hands until they were tired in an attempt to show how they felt. Jim, looking down at the plaque he held in his hands, read:

In grateful appreciation of his unswerving devotion to the youth
of our community, and in recognition of his inspirational leadership, this citation is made to

JAMES REEB

with the best wishes for continued success and happiness in
service to his fellow-men.

June 16, 1959   *W. Byron Lukens*
                                                               Chairman

10 ❦

Noble Leader

THE congregation of All Souls Church was as taken with Rev. James Reeb as the Trustees had been. As they came in contact with him, one by one, they too were captivated by his open friendliness and by his capacity to relate to them as individuals.

Benjamin Ostergren, at the time Executive Director of the American Road Builders Association, and with wide knowledge of men, formed an excellent opinion of Jim which was strengthened when later as Chairman of the Board of Trustees of the Church he worked more closely with him. Ostergren was Chairman of the House and Grounds Committee at the time, and to him fell the task of finding a second parsonage to the liking of the Assistant Minister. It did not prove difficult. He located a two-story brick house in the Chevy Chase area of the District of Columbia, about four miles from the Church, but was apologetic in showing it to Jim because it was badly in need of redecorating and minor repairs. But Jim replied: "It is better than we have been accustomed to. My family and I will be delighted with it." He described the house to Marie and John when he got back to Yeadon, giving them all the details he could remember, which were, in fact, a great many. "It is one of the nicest houses we will ever live in," he told them.

They moved in July, 1959. The house was so much more spacious than the Mozenters' apartment or their place in Yeadon, that their furniture seemed lost at first. But they enjoyed the new roominess even if it was an invitation to John to make a race course from the living room through the dining room, out into the kitchen, into the hall leading to the front door, and back into the living room again. They were soon settled. Their third child was to be born to them in October, but Marie, unhampered by her pregnancy, got the house in order with Jim's help. Anne Elizabeth duly arrived on October 7.

With his customary enthusiasm he began his work at the Church. It was decided that he should have no official duties in July. It was to be a learning period for him. He was to take over the work of Dr. Laurence Staples, for forty years Executive Director of the Church, who was soon to retire. He was to be on vacation in August at which time Jim would assume the full responsibility for the management of the Church's program. This, however, was not too difficult an assignment, since the summer schedule of the Church was less arduous. When things really opened up in September, Dr. Staples would be back to help Jim as the program swung into high gear.

Dr. Staples found Jim eager and thought he showed unusual ability to grasp the complexities of operation. He also found Jim a delightful personal companion. Jim was utterly reliable, he saw, if anything too conscientious. "He will handle the job very well indeed," Dr. Staples told the Trustees. "Now I can retire with full confidence that the administration of the Church is in truly competent hands."

Jim on his part was no less pleased with his new job and his new associates. In September when the activities moved back up to their normal level, it was obvious that the new Assistant Minister was taking up his duties with relish as well as with skill. His energy was noticeable and his dedication to the task beyond question. For this we were all grateful. But it was his unfailing friendliness and human sympathy that really made the difference. This characteristic, added to his first-rate performance, established him in the minds and hearts of the congregation in a very short time. All Souls Church had neither hoped nor expected to find a man who could bring so much to the post of Assistant Minister.

Coupled with his other qualities he soon showed a very genuine skill at reconciling differences between people. A case that arose early in his ministry established at the outset his reputation as a mediator who cared more about the dignity of the parties to a quarrel than its resolution. There was a dispute between the two co-sponsors of a weekly square dance program, the Wayfarers Club of the Church and the local council of the American Youth Hostelers. Attendance had been lagging. The two groups had sharply divided over the promotional methods to be used in attracting new members. As the differences between the two groups sharpened, recriminations rose.

The situation had become quite tense when it landed on Jim's desk in the fall of 1959. Jean Wells, one of the participants, describes what he did as follows:

"He called a special meeting of the officers of both clubs and others immediately concerned. He set the tone for the meeting with his dignified and reflective manner, asking for a factual and objective review of the dispute. Each one was given a respectful hearing on his viewpoint, with Jim discouraging a few attempts to interrupt. After a long session of presentations and orderly rebuttals, he named a small sub-committee to meet with him further and then adjourned the meeting. Actually, the meeting itself had resolved much of the controversy, as it had revealed that many of the differences had more of an emotional than factual basis. And Jim's smooth and fair aproach to the situation had provided a sound basis for the sub-committee's subsequent and reasonable settlement of the hassle."

His rapport with young people was also noticeable from the outset. The high school youth group (Charmian Club) annual fall outing comes each year on the Labor Day weekend. It was the tradition of the Club to go to Dunbrack Inn in the Catoctin Mountains near Gettysburg. It was also the tradition that the young people stay up all night for the two nights they were away. That did not seem sensible to Jim, but he argued with the leaders in vain. They were adamant, and in the end he went along with them. He and they stayed up all night both nights.

For this reason and some others besides he got off to a slow start with the group. "We didn't like him much at first," Sara Dulaney, later President of the Club, recalled, "probably because his predecessor (whose name at this point I can't even remember) had been very popular, and because Charmian, like most teen-age organizations, was a close-knit group with a good deal of informal ritual, and was therefore reluctant to accept any newcomer immediately. Jim seemed meek and rather ineffectual, with his slight build, glasses and soft voice."

Jim did not completely win over the Church high schoolers during their brief forty-eight hours together at Dunbrack. But they came back to Washington with quite a different impression of him from the one they had formed at the outset. They were surprised that he entered with such enthusiasm into every one of their activities and that despite his attempt to break their tradition of staying up all night, he was not authoritarian in temperament. Throughout the two days and nights, he strove to have them reach by common consent whatever decision they made affecting their program and discipline. He respected them as individuals, they found; he respected their opinions and he relied on them to reach decisions that were both wise and in accordance with standards of good conduct. During the outing he made friends with several of them. This too surprised them. It pleased them that he should care that much. In short, they began to see that Jim Reeb could level with them and that he was good fun besides.

During the fall as he began his weekly meetings with the Club in his official role as their adviser, they dubbed him "Noble Leader" because of the ideals he persistently kept before them and because he continued to force them to decide for themselves how far they would adhere to high principles in the Club and in their personal lives. It was a title he cherished far beyond some of the more formal accolades he received in the course of his work.

Often he met with the Executive Committee on a weekday. "At first he did not seem very energetic," Sara Dulaney observed later, "and he did seem picky, discussing the tiniest details at great length. But what was worse still, he challenged some of Charmian's time-honored routine. We began to be afraid that he was going to try to run our Club himself.

"Our fears were unfounded and our annoyance gradually disappeared. Jim never stopped being 'picky,' but we soon became grateful for it; he never stopped speaking softly and lengthily, but we eventually saw that he was only trying, in this way, to make *us* see a problem and solve it; he never stopped challenging our customs and our ideas, but soon we began to be less defensive and more open to accept his challenge; and he certainly never lacked energy."

The high schoolers found that despite his permissive manner of handling the Club and the patience with which he sought the expression of every opinion, he was neither meek nor ineffectual, and could direct their affairs in a perceptive and practical if not always thoroughly democratic manner. Sara Dulaney, as President of Charmian, would find Jim saying to her quietly after an Executive Committee meeting: "That topic that X wants, don't have that for a meeting. He is the only one interested and nobody else would come"; or "You don't seriously plan to put Y in charge of that committee, do you? He hardly knows his own name"; or "Go out of your way to talk to Z. She may annoy you but she has problems and we should try to help her." Discreetly one always followed his directions because they always made such good sense.

His praises sounded around the Church because of his work as a pastor, the sort of thing you hear in any church fortunate enough to have a minister who is sensitive to the needs of people and who takes the trouble to attend to them, the thousand thoughtful things he does, the thousand comforting words spoken at the right time and in the right way, the thousand treasured memories such a man leaves behind when he dies or moves on to another post. These too were Jim's. He treated the lowliest beggar who came in off the street with the same friendliness and consideration he showed to the president of the Women's Alliance. He pitched in and worked with the sextons when the occasion demanded it, and would do chores for an elderly parishioner in sudden need of help but unable to get it. He seemed to know just how to handle grief and was equally good at marital problems. His premarital counseling sessions invariably left an impression both deep and lasting upon those who came to him to arrange a marriage.

He was by no means always sweetness and light. One day a member of the congregation, the sort that always has a new project on hand, marched into Jim's office and outlined the venture he had in mind. Jim heard him out. It would require quite a number of volunteers.

"Will you be the first to volunteer?" Jim asked.

Early in his ministry at All Souls he chided his old friend Bob Foulkes in a letter regarding a former colleague who was in trouble with the Presbytery. "The defense of such a person as X," he wrote, "should be of as much concern to you, though you violently disagree with him, as it would be to those who agree with him. It seems to me it would be good for the church if in this instance the liberals defended a conservative in the hope that some day conservatives might defend the liberals."

The administrative detail to which Jim had to attend was enormous. Besides overseeing the clubs and organizations in the church, and his work with the young people of both junior and senior high school ages, he was in charge of editing the church publications, not including sermons; supervising the church office, the janitorial staff, the building and grounds, including the scheduling of all uses of the building. There were many of these because the church facilities were widely used for neighborhood and community activities. The church building was open seven days a week from 9:00 A.M. to 11:00 P.M. Jim also was expected to provide staff assistance for the annual fund drive, an operation which consumed an enormous amount of time in the spring of each year. One of his headaches was the church parking lot, located about two blocks away. "If ever I find myself teaching in a theological school," he used to say, "I am going to tell them to replace their course in Old Testament with one in Parking Lot Management."

In the spring of his first year, Jim found that a "Blind Artists Concert" had been scheduled at the Church. His dealings with the group in arranging the concert made him uneasy. On looking into the organization he found it was not the charitable effort it purported to be but a commercial enterprise whose artists were indeed blind and who were duly paid for performing but the proceeds of whose concerts went to the promoters, not to the blind. Backed by the Trustees, Jim took the position that the concert could not be held at the Church because of its deceptive character. The sponsors proved very wily and difficult opponents, but Jim fought the question through to a showdown with the thoroughness and attention to detail so characteristic of him, and the concert was not held.

Of all the mental pictures of Jim Reeb held by the people of All Souls Church, the most familiar is that of him at his desk near the entrance of the parish house, both doors to his office open, talking on the telephone while waving to someone going down the corridor, or directing into a nearby chair someone who wanted to see him. As likely as not he would have a cigar in his mouth. He was never happier than when the church was abustle with activities. One stormy day as I met him in the corridor, he said:

"I don't like it around here today."

"What's the matter?" I asked.

"Too quiet," he said. "I like it best with the telephone ringing, the mimeograph running, people at the desk, somebody waiting in the office to see me, and meetings going on all over the place." The busier the church got the harder he worked to keep up to it. He usually managed to get home to supper, but he went back again, and night after night would not return until ten or eleven o'clock.

Jim was not only very happy in his new job, he was equally so with his move to Unitarianism. On coming to All Souls Church in the summer of 1959, he applied for and was granted a Preliminary Certificate of Fellowship as a Unitarian minister. The Final Certificate making him a minister in full standing was issued in July, 1962. In his letter applying for it, he wrote: "The Unitarian ministry from the inside has been all I hoped it would be from the outside. A Unitarian minister has the freedom to nourish his own integrity as well as that of the members of his congregation. If progress in the ministry can be measured by the degree of satisfaction a person achieves in it through this profession, then my progress has been substantial. I am content to leave it to others to measure my progress by other standards."

In June, 1960, the Philadelphia Presbytery deposed him because he "had renounced the jurisdiction of the United Presbyterian Church and joined an heretical body." A Presbyterian spokesman told the newspapers it was believed Reeb was connected with a Unitarian church in Florida. This action hurt Jim deeply. Nevertheless, realistic and charitable as always, he understood the reasons for it. After all, he had refused to resign as they expected and wanted him to do.

All Souls Church had no problem measuring Jim's progress by any standard. We counted ourselves very fortunate to have a man with so many skills, with such complete dedication to the task, and with such boundless energy to serve as our Assistant Minister. To me, as to many others, he became a close and trusted friend. We had little time to go about together, for our work at the church was very demanding. But we saw a great deal of each other in connection with our work. Ours was a partnership marked by harmony and mutual support. Occasionally, Jim would come into my office to discuss a problem or I would go into his, but for the most part we did it over the lunch table. During Jim's first year while Dr. Staples was still with us, we three would go to lunch together and Dr. Staples, out of his forty years' experience, would help us with the complexities of a church and its people still new to us both.

The one insoluble problem with which we had to deal was that of time. The demands upon us both were such that we were seldom able to talk about anything but the work of the church and never able to do together the things we might like to have done. People turn to their minister for every kind of human need. A church does what it can to meet these needs, but there has to be a limit. Human needs are endless. Two or three times the staff of a well-run church could not do all that might reasonably be asked of it, measured by the expectations people have of the church. That means setting up priorities. It is logical to do so, but by no means always possible. Someone who finds his way into your office or gets you on the telephone, but who has no real claim on your time in conscience or common sense, can rob you of half an hour or an hour you desperately need for something that is really urgent.

Jim and I by no means always agreed. One of the things that I liked best about him was his readiness to express his opinion whenever we disagreed. He never held back out of a sense of deference or for reasons of tact. I could always count on him to say just what he thought, and I learned to rely heavily on his judgment. He was particularly keen at appraising human qualities. Whenever he and I agreed on a potential staff person or committee member, there was no need to hesitate longer. The chances were the performance would match our estimate. When we didn't agree, on personnel or policy or anything else, we usually kept at it until we reached common ground.

But that was not always possible. Early in his ministry at All Souls Church we sharply divided with each other on the use of the building by outside groups. Almost from the beginning Jim was distressed by the fact that All Souls Church would not let whoever wished to use its premises. Ours was a free church, he argued. Since it was private property, we could refuse all use of it to outside groups, but if we opened it to one we ought to open it to all. It took some arguing to show him that this principle did not work out in practice. If the church were to allow groups whose aims were contrary to its own to use its premises, people would become confused. They knew us as a liberal church. To take an extreme example, should it be stated in the paper that the Ku Klux Klan held a meeting at the church, the average person would assume that we must approve of the KKK in some way. We could explain all we liked that we were only permitting them to use our premises, but the paper would never bother to print it. There was nothing to do but tell them they couldn't have it.

Jim and I fought that one out again and again during his early years with us. Unfortunately, the cases were not usually as clear as with the KKK. Some of them were very hard to decide, but we were often helped by the very determination of a particular group to get permission to use our building and the methods to which they resorted to achieve their goal.

On one occasion when we attempted to check out the program a particular group had in mind, we became lost in a maze of double talk which infuriated Jim and also disillusioned him as to the high-mindedness of the group. He soon learned through experience that not all groups fostering supposedly good causes are trustworthy. Some proved to be actually deceitful. On the other hand, I found it exhilarating to have my principles constantly tested by Jim's vigorous challenge to their application. He was as cooperative a fellow minister as a man might hope to have.

The fact that Jim drew almost all who came in contact with him into a warm human relationship might have been supposed to drain off the warmth and intimacy that would otherwise have existed with his family. Just the opposite was true. Jim's loveliest relationship was with Marie and his children. There were, however, times when his growing involvement in the life of the church and the wider community gave Marie some cause for concern. She was never bored: her children kept her too busy for that, but now, as in Philadelphia, sometimes she was lonely. She felt the need to get out of the house, to be with young men and women her own age. She and Jim went out together only occasionally. And in between there were long stretches when she sat by herself evening after evening after the children had been put to bed, waiting for a husband who often did not return until after she had given up and gone to bed herself.

Yet her feelings during the Washington phase of their lives were never like those she had known in Yeadon before her thyroidectomy. In the first place, that dreadful experience was already behind them and they would always profit by it. But in the second place, a new set of circumstances had intervened which placed the marriage in a new light for Jim and allowed him to see Marie as he had never seen her before. In the fall of 1960, a little over a year after their move to Washington, it became clear that they were to have another child the following summer. They decided that the birth should take place in Casper rather than in Washington. Casper had a good hospital. Besides, Washington was desperately hot in the summer, and it would be a shame in any case to pass up their vacation in Wyoming unless it was absolutely necessary. Marie would fly to Casper June 1; Jim would follow about mid-July when his vacation officially began. That left him alone without Marie for only the second time in their married life. They had been separated briefly the year before when she had gone back to Wyoming early.

Jim was no letter writer. Ever since Princeton days his letters to his parents had been brief and very matter of fact. But now there began with Marie the most intensive correspondence of his life. Marie had said before she left that she hoped he would write as often as he could. But knowing his habits and how busy he was, she didn't expect much. Nevertheless, she hoped. She had been gone but a few days when he not only wrote; he went straight to the heart of the problem of their relationship.

"It would be funny if it weren't so tragic," he wrote, "but once you are several thousand miles away I can say things on paper I cannot otherwise say. When you asked me about whether I would write, all I could manage was 'If I get time.' This is not really what I meant in my deepest feelings. But to have said more would have somehow been at that point some sign of weakness. The people you want to love you, you must keep at arm's length, then you can't be hurt by their lack of love. Of course, this is a very destructive emotional pattern. I feel bad now that you didn't call but I have no one to blame but myself. (Of course you may have tried as it was after 12:00 when I got home from Dave's). [Rev. David Osborn, minister of a suburban Washington Unitarian Church.] But I rather think my outward indifference may have wounded you as indeed it would me if you were to treat me in such a fashion. Usually I keep almost all my thoughts and feelings to myself. This is a quite unsatisfactory way of life, and yet I find there is little I can do about it under ordinary circumstances. I reveal very little of myself and as a consequence you don't reveal much of yourself. This is a penalty I pay."

The letter closed, "It's Sat. morning and I'm off to the Youth Conference."

A second letter followed only two days later. It concluded: "I wish you were here tonight. I am filled with longing for you." To the third, written two days after that, he added before his signature the line "Good Night, my love." The letters continued in a steady procession every two or three days for the next five weeks. He told Marie what he was doing, what his hopes and anxieties were, advised her with regard to the children, tried to console and support her in the disciplinary problems she was having, particularly with John. When Marie had been gone about two weeks, he wrote one night:

"It has been almost up to tonight before I could really feel how much I miss you. I think one of the ways I handle being on the go so much is by really shutting out all feeling for you and the children. This is one way of deadening the pain and anger that is generated by a job that takes so much of my time. . . . So far, all the time we have been married I have been struggling to get ahead, but I'm not any happier now . . . and certainly not necessarily a better person. I have to earn enough money to support us but then it shouldn't take all of my time. . . . I am getting older—I increasingly feel that life is passing me by. I want to live fully in the time I have. But one can't live fully and be on the run all the time or even most of it for that matter."

Some time later Marie wrote again to say what a hard time she was having with the children. She wished she had not gone ahead to Wyoming without him. Jim replied: "There are many times I wish that you had not gone. These separations are very difficult for me. I know that many times I talk to you very little. This is because at least in part that when things don't go well I get depressed and when so I retreat in myself and have little to say to anyone. When things are easier as they are now I really miss you for there are so many things I would like to talk with you about. I think this is an aspect of our marriage we should work at much more than we have in the past and I know that it is something which is up to me in a large part. If I only do, I know you would, for I know you would be happy to hear what it is that I think about and what concerns me, for I also realize that what concerns me concerns you."

Three days later he finally got into words what he had always felt but never really said before:

"You know, the closer the time comes the more anxious I am to see the new baby. I love each of our children and I wouldn't have missed one of them. They are a terrible pain in the neck lots of times, but you and they are the most important things in life to me and really in one sense the only ones who make life worthwhile. If it were not for you life would be very grim for me. I know that when I am here alone. Loneliness is a most destructive and devastating emotion."

As the correspondence drew to a close just before he flew out to Wyoming to join Marie, his letters began "Dearest Marie," and they concluded with such lines as "I love you, hugs and kisses for you and the children."

On Sunday, July 16, Jim flew to Casper to rejoin his beloved Marie, the children, his parents, and to see for the first time their fourth child, Steven, born only a week before. Jim had never been happier. He had never felt so close to Marie and the children, and in his new relaxation and self-confidence he was more at ease with his own parents.

One thing that helped was the fact that emissaries from his mother had visited him during the preceding winter, Rev. Griffith Williams and Rev. James Guyer. Each was an overnight guest in his home and each talked with him earnestly about his becoming a Unitarian. He talked at length with them. Each had left fully satisfied that Jim was doing the Lord's work as he understood it and that he was very happy in it. Each felt that Jim's work was important and both tried to reassure his parents in Casper as a result of their visits.

That summer again the family all went fossil and artifact hunting. They went to the backwaters of the Pathfinder Dam hunting arrowheads and to the Badlands south of Douglas for fossils. Jim seemed to be almost ecstatic on these trips. His passion for the prairie was as limitless as the sky over their heads. He was like a boy as he ran about looking here, digging there, with John close at his heels. On these occasions it was clear to all who saw him that Jim's love of the open and in particular of his home state of Wyoming, was a very basic part of the total man. And yet, observing him in repose on the way home, they often saw upon his face the lines of a great sorrow that lay equally deep. There was a faraway look in his eyes sometimes, and then they knew he was thinking about the city which he had left behind, the metropolis with misery, suffering, hopelessness, and human degradation at its worst.

11 ❦

Taking the Church into the
Community

AT THE end of his fourth year at All Souls, Rev. James Reeb was promoted by a grateful church to the office of Associate Minister, and given a raise of $1,000. This was accomplished at a little ceremony held after church on a Sunday late in May, 1963. It was intended to symbolize the fact that Jim and I were not so much junior and senior Ministers of the church, as we were partners in its ministry, having different emphases but joint responsibility. There was always a tendency on the part of those not close to the operation to think of Jim as literally my assistant. Now that he had more than proved himself I felt it was important to make the real situation clear. The new title did not change Jim's role in the church nor our relationship to each other one whit. It recognized formally what we had already achieved in fact. Jim was pleased. Shortly before the ceremony he wrote to his father and mother:

"I have decided to stay on here at All Souls. Our finances have improved so the raise will be retroactive to the beginning of our last fiscal year. That means I get $1,000 at the end of the month. We will pay the car off and be in the clear for the moment at least.

"The Board has voted that at the Annual Meeting there will be an announcement of my being named the Associate Minister of the Church. I wonder if you realize what an honor this is."

There were, however, two problems that seriously concerned us with regard to Jim, each closely related to the other. One had to do with the very heavy work load he was carrying; the other was related to his ever-expanding community concerns. From the start, Jim gave unstintingly of his time and energy to the work of the Church. But after he had been with us only a year and presumably had his work well in hand, we became concerned when there was no let-up in his activity. If anything, the hours he spent at the Church were increasing. I urged him to take a little time off now and then, but to no avail. The Chairman of the Board, Howard Wahrenbrock, spoke to him, trying to assure him that the Church would approve of his letting up a little. We would back him up, we told him, in any schedule of leisure time he cared to work out. The Church would too, we said, even if it meant that some things didn't get done. He was working too hard, and we feared he might break under the strain. He always listened politely; he never complained; never demanded to know how the work was to be done if he didn't do it; but you always got the feeling that while he agreed with what you said, he would never find the time to do it.

One reason was Jim's intense concern for the individual which in turn overflowed into a desire to be completely involved in the life of the Church. He would have found it very hard to reverse the roles he and I occupied. As senior minister of the church, it would have been very difficult for him to say to me, as I had said to him, "You have the administrative side of things in your charge. It's your responsibility. Do what you think best. I'll back you up even when I think you are wrong. Anybody is entitled to make an honest mistake. You can come to me anytime but don't feel you need to keep checking." There is a great personal loss in this kind of delegation of duties, but it is necessary if the work is to be done. It involves complete trust, which I was able to put in Jim as soon as I had a chance to see how good his judgment was and how utterly reliable he was. But he would not have been willing to pay the price in isolation such an arrangement involves. With him it would not have been a matter of trust or lack of it. He would not have been willing to be outside of—in fact literally ignorant of—so many of the details of our corporate church life. He would not have been willing to go without the large number of immediate continuing personal contacts that were his in the administrator's role.

Jim's basic motivation was now clearer than it had ever been before. He wanted more than anything else to serve his fellow man in his need. It was this that took him into hospital chaplaincy rather than into the church, he now realized, and this that took him into Y work among Philadelphia's poor and dispossessed. He came to All Souls because he wanted to be a minister, but once there, he found he responded most easily and quickly to those who came to him for help. In none of his sermons did he admonish the congregation to give themselves in service to their fellow men. He did not need to. By the life he lived he preached it to them dramatically every day.

Rev. James Wilkes, minister of a neighboring Unitarian church, on watching Jim at work at All Souls Church, made virtually the same observation in regard to him as Bob Foulkes had made at Philadelphia General Hospital.

"He's got fire in his belly," Wilkes said once. "It is more than wanting to help people, more than wanting to serve his fellow man in his need. There is some kind of compulsion that seems to be driving him on. He seems to be bound to take on more than he can do in an effort to provide yet more help to people who need it."

To lighten Jim's administrative load and to give him more time for the sort of thing he really liked to do, we added an Administrative Assistant to the Church staff. We did this at the time that Jim was made Associate Minister. Mrs. Mildred Reynolds, who took the post, very soon lifted from Jim's shoulders the management of the building, scheduling of meetings, replacing of staff members, and dealing with the great number of people who came to the church with their problems. The office operation became much smoother as a result, not only because Mrs. Reynolds could give more time to this aspect of the church's work, but because she was willing to say "No" to church members and others who would make requests of the office that could not be met. Jim's approach was the opposite. Just about any request was to be handled somehow, he felt.

A classic exchange took place between the Associate Minister and the new Administrative Assistant one day after she had been on the job about six months and felt she had things fairly well in hand. A request for mimeographing had come in from one of the organizations in the church at a time when the office was carrying a peak load. Mrs. Reynolds had politely told the organization that at the moment its request couldn't be handled. The organization appealed to Jim. He went to see Mrs. Reynolds. "It has to be done," he said to her.

"But it can't be done," said Mrs. Reynolds.

"Well, it has to be," Jim insisted.

"Mr. Reeb," said Mrs. Reynolds, "it *doesn't* have to be done. If necessary, they can take it to a commercial house."

Jim acceded reluctantly. But it was not his way. Six months before the job would have been done somehow, even if he and all of the girls stayed until seven or eight o'clock to do it, as in fact often happened.

But no administrative improvements and no staff enlargement affected Jim's pattern of life. As he had been doing since his days with the Westminster Fellowship in Casper, at All Souls Church he was always generating new ideas, starting new projects, establishing new groups, and organizing new activities. To release Jim from one set of obligations was only to provide him with the opportunity to generate some new enterprise. Among the activities he organized while at the Church was the Colloquium, a couples club at the outset, which he used as a sort of testing ground for his ideas. Here each individual was to be supreme. There were to be no outside speakers. The members were to lead the discussion and all were to participate fully at each meeting. They were to enjoy close interpersonal relationships with one another. Here thought and expression were not to be vicarious, as he felt they sometimes were elsewhere in the Church. Here each person was to be his own minister.

From the beginning Jim was careful to see that the Colloquium was racially integrated in the numerical sense in order that it might in time become integrated in a far deeper sense. And here, as much as anywhere in the Church, integration was in fact real. The members were without racial self-consciousness. They did not avoid racial topics. When they came up, they were discussed as freely and naturally as any other issue, yet nobody made a special point of it.

By Jim's third or fourth year at All Souls Church, the Charmian Club began to feel the effects of his taking on an ever-increasing load of community responsibility. His problem was further complicated by the fact that under his leadership it had grown considerably. It was now impossible for him to establish the close person-to-person relationship with individual members he had enjoyed formerly. This in turn meant that his technique of running the Club no longer worked. As a result, problems developed in the Club which had not existed before. In the early years he had won support for serious programs and discussions because the members knew that when they were over and the recreation hour came, he would be one of them, as much of a kid as any. Thus they were perfectly relaxed and felt completely free to express themselves in the discussions when he was present.

Another reason for the change in Jim's relationship to the Charmian Club was the coming of J. Ronald Engel to All Souls Church as ministerial intern in the fall of 1962. That relieved Jim of the major responsibility for the Club. Engel had spent two years at the Meadville Theological School, and under their internship program was to spend his third year in a church, returning to take his degree in the fourth year.

Arriving at the beginning of the Labor Day weekend, his baptism of fire was the annual outing of the Club at Dunbrack. Thus his first introduction to James Reeb, under whose direction he was to work, was to see an aspect of the man the Church never saw, a man who could without difficulty or self-consciousness become a teenager among teenagers. Ron watched him with astonishment. He was no less astonished at his ability to relate to the individual members of the Club at their level. He was obviously one of them without effort or contrivance.

For this reason the Charmian weekend got Ron and Jim off to a bad start with each other. Ron had no desire to spend a year under the direction of a grownup teenager. He knew he could not function in that irrational, impulsive framework. He had to admit that Jim was always in control of the situation, however. The spirit of the weekend was uninhibited freedom. Yet it was always kept within bounds. Nothing untoward occurred or even threatened to occur. Ron came home in a daze, feeling ten years older than Jim, who was ten years his senior. Jim, he realized, was free in a way he, Ron, could never be.

But as the year began at All Souls Church, Ronald Engel began to see an entirely different James Reeb. He saw the competent church administrator at work, handling a vast number of interrelated problems and many that were quite separate all at the same time. He saw how successfully he dealt with the members of the staff as well as with the members of the church and Board of Trustees. He saw how well he handled the college student group at American University. He saw him as counselor to those in trouble and a friend to all. He saw him as a preacher, speaker at various gatherings, and as community organizer. Gradually, as they came to know one another, they became fast friends.

Jim, in turn, found in Ron all he ever asked for in a friend. As the year went on, Ron increasingly saw Jim's ministry as close to his own. A sense of spiritual kinship grew up between them which further deepened their friendship. Jim made the church credible to Ron. Here, he thought, is a doer, living out in his life the central ethical teachings of Christianity. One day they were talking about inner-city work, and Ron, who was a great woodsman, said:

"I will go to the city and do my work there for the sake of my great moments alone in the northern forest. When a man experiences beauty, a claim is laid upon him. He cannot enjoy it forever. The only way he can perpetuate that experience is to extend beauty to those who have never known it at all."

"I understand," said Jim. "When I am in the inner city, there is a sense in which I feel I am still on the Wyoming prairie." He paused, and then he asked:

"Do you ever feel you have to suffer for this?"

"No," said Ron. "Why?"

"Because," he said, "the people in the inner city are beginning to discover what we have deprived them of. They will try to seize it before we can get the white community to give it to them. I think it is a deep-seated wrong for which we are going to suffer before it can be righted."

Jim's fourth year at All Souls Church, 1962-1963, proved to be crucial, for it was during that year that a change was taking place within him of which he himself was not quite aware. During that year his center of gravity slowly shifted from the church to the community. The process began as early as his second year as a result of his deep and abiding concern for the dispossessed and the fact that many such people lived in the area in which All Souls Church found itself. At that particular moment in its history All Souls Church stood in the midst of a rapidly changing neighborhood. Built at the end of World War I on Sixteenth Street at what was then almost the edge of the city, All Souls Church had been a part of what was at that time called "embassy row." But beginning with the New Deal, a change had taken place in the city. New and better apartment buildings appeared on Connecticut Avenue and the embassy area shifted to Massachusetts Avenue. As a part of the same trend the "better class" of government workers increasingly moved to the residential areas of Maryland or across the Potomac to Virginia.

Meanwhile, there had been a vast influx of Negroes into the

Nation's capital from the farms of the South, in particular North Carolina. At first they were confined to an area largely south of the Capitol. As their numbers increased, they spread both northward and westward. By 1960 the "Negro Section," although intermixed with a number of "white" sections, lay north, south, east, and west of the Church. As the whites fled to the suburbs, blockbusting prospered throughout the area. First, genteel Negroes moved. Then the block was "busted" again, and as the middle-class Negroes fled to better sections of the city, the poor and dispossessed moved in, crowded sometimes six to ten to a room, victims of the rent gougers, loan sharks, and all the other members of respectable society who prey upon them.

With the second turnover in the neighborhood came crime, one of the means of livelihood of the dispossessed. It began with pocketbook snatching. But as women learned to hold their pocketbooks tightly, with the straps wound about their arms, the snatching operation became more vicious. Young boys, twelve, fourteen, sixteen, shod in sneakers, thought nothing of running up behind an elderly lady, leaping upon her back, throwing her to the sidewalk, wresting her bag from her and fleeing before anyone might see. The women of All Souls Church had been fortunate or perhaps more cautious, or both. None of them had been attacked. But early in Jim's ministry we learned of two women in the neighboring Baptist Church who had been attacked and injured.

What should we do? What could we do? Jim suggested we could at least get the churches together to talk about the problem. Shortly afterward we gathered the ministers of nearby churches for lunch in our dining room. Various joint projects were discussed. Two that aroused the most enthusiasm were: a car pool to transport children of working mothers to dental appointments, eye examinations, and the like; and a clothing center. The latter proved the more practical in the long run. It was set up in the basement of All Souls Church because we had the space for it, and was at first manned by volunteers from the participating churches. Eventually it became the responsibility of our people and the staff of the Columbia Heights Boys Club, another of the service organizations established by and still associated with the Church.

But Jim was not satisfied. The Clothing Center was but a tiny start

on a very large problem. The deteriorating neighborhood was breed-
ing many social ills. Could we not go further, Jim asked. We agreed
that we could and should. But the going was not easy. Most of the
senior ministers of the neighboring churches did not come to our
meetings after the first time. Some never came at all. The assistants
did not feel that they had sufficient authority to commit their churches.
Nothing daunted, Jim was ready to work with whoever would work
with him. Soon there was a small nucleus of us who were determined
to go ahead.

Our next approach was to Howard University, only eight blocks
to the east of us. We had heard something of their program of neighborhood rehabilitation. Could we not join forces with them, we
asked. A meeting was arranged with representatives of the University
in the office of Vice President William Stuart Nelson, who had such
programs in his charge. The meeting generated much enthusiasm and
more meetings followed. Dr. Nelson knew that certain foundations,
Ford in particular, were interested in such neighborhood projects, and
shortly afterward the Ford man attended one of our meetings. The
Foundation subsequently provided funds for teams from our group to
visit similar projects that had been developed in other parts of the
country.

Out of these meetings came the University Neighborhoods Council.
Jim was made chairman of a steering committee set up in January,
1962, to launch the project, and Howard University offered to provide a full-time social scientist to direct it. The first public meeting was held in March, and a second in April. By fall the Council had
a director in the person of J. Allen Young, a highly qualified man
who was at that time working for the Baltimore Urban Renewal and
Housing Agency. Membership included an impressive list of
churches, thirty in all; thirteen school principals; fifteen parent-
teacher associations; five civic associations; five neighborhood associations; and others. Plans and projects for community development
and rehabilitation virtually exploded as these community leaders
found release for their common purposes in the strength they drew
from one another.

The visiting program under the Ford grant was launched in November. By January, 1963, the Council was in high gear. A folder explaining its work was published in February. Projects continued to

expand, a newsletter was established, and commissions with special responsibilities such as education and youth activities were set up.

Gradually the Council began to develop various programs and services designed to meet the most pressing needs of the community. Funds were badly needed but hard to raise. All Souls Church gave $1,000 to the Council in addition to the thousands it was already spending in its own service projects. Other churches, community organizations, business associations, and the like, also contributed. The need was urgent.

A year later the Washington Agency for Youth (WAY), and the United Planning Organization (UPO), government agencies operating under the Government Juvenile Delinquency and Poverty Programs, adopted the general area of the University Neighborhoods Council for its crash program. Jim was delighted—at first. Now he felt sufficient financial resources to do the work would at last be available. But he was discouraged and angered by the agencies' treatment of him.

"They were disrespectful," he told the Council Board, describing his interview with their leaders. "They were not even reasonable in their approach to what we have been doing. They apparently want to sweep us out of the way and begin all over again as if we had never been here at all." To Jim their attitude was both unwise and immoral. They were, he felt, both by the terms of their monetary grants and by simple common sense, required to work with agencies already in the area, who knew at first hand what the needs were. He had no patience with the political complexities of such a program, and his feelings of hostility were so aroused by them that he felt himself incompetent to negotiate with UPO and WAY and deliberately left it for others to do.

As the work of the University Neighborhoods Council proliferated, Jim was faced with a serious inner conflict. He knew that in creating the Council and giving a large amount of time to its development, he was carrying out the philosophy of All Souls Church on its behalf as its minister. He knew that I had not only worked with him in founding the project but that I wholeheartedly backed his participation in it. He knew that I had defended his work with the Council before the Board of Trustees—on one occasion in a very tense session when an attempt had been made to pay part of his salary out of welfare funds on the ground that much of his time was now going into welfare work.

Yet he knew too that some of the members of the Church, people whom he respected and cared about, were beginning to criticize him, not for spending time with the Council, but because he was no longer giving the necessary time and attention to his work at the church. This hurt him deeply because of his great conscientiousness and because he never lost his love for the people of the Church or his desire to serve them. But it only accentuated what was already a grave problem for him. In his fourth and particularly in his fifth year, what was really exciting to him was no longer All Souls Church. It was the University Neighborhoods Council. As always, Jim's response was the greatest where human need was the greatest. No matter how hard he worked nor how late he stayed up at night, he could not meet all his obligations both to the Council and to the Church. There was simply not enough time.

Jim thus found himself wrestling with an old question in a new guise. How far was the Church justified in spending its substance to meet human needs generally? Should it neglect its own people in order to serve those whose needs were far more grave? It was like the question he put to Miss Schwalm at the Philadelphia General Hospital the day she handed him the list of preoperative patients with whom to pray. Why couldn't he go to the alcoholics who needed him more, he had asked then. Now, as the demands of the University Neighborhoods Council increased, he asked himself the same question once more. Why could he not attend to the poor and the deprived of the University Neighborhoods Council area even though to do so meant neglecting matters of importance at All Souls Church?

Another aspect of the question, one that had been with him since St. Olaf days, also came home to him. Then it had been theoretical; now it was so no longer. When he preached at the First Baptist Church in Casper back in July, 1951, he had centered his message in Jesus' parable of the publican who went up to the temple and loudly thanked God that he, unlike other men, was righteous, while nearby stood a publican who beat his breast and cried, "God be merciful to me, a sinner." If we concern ourselves only with the formalities of religion, he had said on that occasion, we think only of our own superiority. On that point he had never changed. But the question had never been resolved. Where does formal religion end and true religion begin?

Jim had tackled the question in a sermon at All Souls Church preached in July, 1960, which he titled "The Danger of Being Religious." We are all beset by inner conflicts, he said on that occasion, and "to the extent that religion helps us to resolve these conflicts it is a constructive function in our lives." But he added, there is "danger in being religious because religion is quite often used as a means of delaying the resolution of these conflicts." He then listed four needs and the way in which religion may be made falsely to satisfy them.

1. We need to be certain: religion offers us certainty when often no real certainty exists.

2. We need to be right: religion tells us dogmatically what the right is.

3. We need to be identified with noble ideas: religion does this for us too.

4. We need a cloak of righteousness to hide the fact of our neutral if not unrighteous lives: religion easily fills this role for us.

Now Jim had to decide the question for himself. Religion for him could never be a sham or a prop or a cloak of righteousness. He was not worried about that. His question lay at a deeper level. In effect, he was seeking a kind of hierarchy of values for himself. How was he to choose between the demands made upon him by his job as Associate Minister of All Souls Church and his responsibilities as head of the University Neighborhoods Council. His question, he saw, concerned the nature of the church itself. What was the proper role of the church as an institution in society?

At about this time Jim began talking about a tent-making ministry. The reference was to Paul, who earned his living making tents while traveling about the Mediterranean organizing Christian churches. Why should a minister be paid, Jim wanted to know. Yet he had answered the question by entering the ministry as a profession and accepting in return the house his church had bought for him and the salary they gave him to enable him to clothe, feed, and rear his family. But was that the right answer?

Professionalism itself Jim readily accepted. He knew, for example, that he had special competence in the field of counseling. He also knew something of the professional standards that prevailed within it. He himself filled the role of expert in this area with outstanding success. When it was proposed to add a counselor to the staff of All Souls Church to lighten his and my load, he insisted that only a person with the highest technical training and competence be employed. Because of its other commitments in service projects, however, the Church was unable to find the funds to pay the salary of such a person and no professional counselor was therefore added to the staff while Jim was at All Souls Church.

Yet he feared professionalism among the clergy, as many men do, because it so often degenerates into the exercise of empty forms and the pronouncement of empty words backed by neither action nor belief. He feared churchiness in churches even more. He knew the tendency of human institutions dedicated to high purposes to become lost in the problems of self-maintenance and to become dedicated only to their own perpetuation. He was not sure that any church could escape entanglement in such problems, even a church that spent its resources in social service to the extent that All Souls Church did.

For these reasons, when Rolf Hochhuth's play *The Deputy* was first reported in the American press, Jim became very much interested in it. Produced in Germany on February 20, 1963, *The Deputy* concerned the failure of Pope Pius XII to condemn the Nazis for the slaughter of the Jews. The play was widely discussed in the American press before it was produced in New York a year later, February 26, 1964. On the opening night, a hundred policemen were on duty outside the theater and ten plainclothesmen circulated on the inside. Some one hundred and fifty Catholic, Protestant, and Jewish laymen picketed the performance with signs. Some fifteen members of the American Nazi party, who also showed up, were consigned by the police to the other side of the street and kept behind wooden barriers. There were no incidents.

Besides the question of the self-serving church, the play concerned another old interest of Jim's, also dating back to St. Olaf days, the role of the churches in Germany under Hitler. He had never lost interest in the question. At Princeton he had taken a course on the subject. For his term paper Jim had written about the capitulation of both the Catholic and Protestant churches in Germany under the pressure of the National Socialists. It was a very mature analysis of the complexities facing the church under such circumstances, and his professor commended him on it.

Ever charitable and ever the realist as well as the idealist, the conclusion Jim had reached in his seminary paper was more sympathetic to, than critical of, the churches. "Consideration should be given to the complexities of the relationships in which the church found itself," he had written.

Early in April, 1964, Jim was due to preach a sermon at All Souls. As the time neared, it became increasingly clear to him that Hochhuth's play was to be his topic. He had not seen it. Nor was he able to get a copy of the book to read until the final week of his sermon. But he knew what he wanted to do. He wanted to deal with the basic issue the play raises: When does a church modify its stated policy in the interest of its own survival? *The Deputy* suggests that Pope Pius XII should have spoken out against the Nazi mass murder of Jews. In the play the decision of the Pope not to do so is defended on the ground that the church has to get along in a real world and cannot risk its power to act in the total scene by assuming what might be called an heroic posture in a particular instance. This had been Jim's own question again and again. In attempting to deal with it for the congregation through the play, he was really trying to resolve it for himself.

We can get no clearer insight into the man James Reeb than by following his thought as he worked it out in this sermon. "The moral issues raised by this play," he says, "far transcend the question of whether Pope Pius XII had a major responsibility for the slaughter of the Jews. I do not say this to minimize the importance of his decision on the fate of the Jews, but rather to emphasize that the questions raised by the play are broader than the evaluation of the responsibility of a single individual."

Jim then takes up the question whether Hochhuth's indictment of the Pope is justified. He is clear that the playwright had every right to deal with the issue, but he is not clear on the facts—who can be? He leans toward the view that the Pope not only could have spoken without unduly jeopardizing the church, but that he should have because of the impact his speaking would have had on Nazi policy. Perhaps the most telling bit of evidence he cites is a line of testimony from Adolf Eichman at his trial in Jerusalem. " 'Nobody came to me and reproached me for anything in the performance of my duties.' He could say that without contradiction," Jim commented.

In the light of Jim's constant insistence that the church live up to its own highest ideals, everyone expected him to conclude with a thumping endorsement of Hochhuth's position: that the Pope should have condemned the Nazi slaughter of the Jews. But he did not. He spent the last quarter of the sermon defending the position the Pope had taken. In the early part of the sermon his sympathies had been clearly with the young priest Ricardo in the play who had dared to challenge the policy of the Pope. He had quoted the lines in which the priest shows himself ready to assume on the Pope's behalf the role he believes the Pope should have assumed. "You must see," the priest says, "that the silence of the Pope in the face of the murders imposes a guilt upon the Church for which we must atone, and since the Pope, though only a man, can actually represent God on earth, I, a poor priest, if need be can also represent the Pope—there where the Pope ought to be standing."*

But Jim would not hold the Pope to blame personally as Hochhuth does in the play. "The Deputy's indictment is misdirected," he said, "in the sense that it focuses on one man when what we need is to have the light focused on all of us everywhere who indulge in the evil of racial persecution.

"Before you indict the Pope, ask yourself whether you are willing to be a part of a fellowship, namely a church, that promises not peace, but constant war with evil—not security, but constant sacrifice for righteousness—not pleasant adjustments to current morals, but harsh confrontation with every current waywardness.

"Great evils are possible only because little evils are indulged from day to day.

"Ask yourself not what you would have done had you been the Pope. Ask yourself, rather—have I done enough about the evil I see before me?"

As the people listened to the concluding portion of the sermon, they had the curious feeling that they were listening to two voices at the same time: one, the voice of Jim Reeb leaning over backward to be fair to his opponent and understand his position as he tried to do with everyone; the other, Jim Reeb for whom the church could never lift people to ideals that were too high, who, since his youth, had trembled lest the church be concerned more with its own pros-

* *The Deputy* by Rolf Hochhuth, tr. by R. and C. Winston (New York: Grove Press, Inc., 1964), p. 156.

perity than with the society it was intended to serve, who believed in his heart that the church or any of its servants must be ready to destroy themselves, if necessary, in order to support a high principle. "Was the existence of the Church protected at too high a price?" he asked. "Did not silence mean violating the essential purpose of the church? I think the answer is yes."

Jim's plea on behalf of the Pope was not merely a self-conscious exercise in fairmindedness. There was more to it than that. Jim respected, understood, and loved the church. He had ever since he could remember. He knew its importance as an institution for the cultivation of ideals in human society. He had made a far more explicit statement of his doctrine of the church two months before in an informal talk to church-school parents on the Unitarian Universalist program of religious education. "Religion concerns that which is of ultimate significance," he had said on that occasion. Then he asked: "What do we think is of ultimate significance?" He answered his own question: "The supreme worth and dignity of every human being. This is our faith, and the religious education program should be developed in accordance with it."

"Let there be elementary courses on the idea of human dignity for the first grade," he went on. "Let there be a class in our present understanding of human dignity for the senior high school student. Let the first grade study our concepts of justice, let the fourth grade study the historical development of our ideas of justice, and let the junior in high school study the points in our society where injustice is rampant. Let the second grade study those men who have stood for freedom, let the seventh grade study the development of democracy, let the senior high school class have a seminar on civil liberties in our society."

The conclusion he reached in his talk to the church-school parents was the one his *Deputy* congregation two months later had expected to hear: "I do not believe the church is an end in itself," he declared. "Its end is the triumph of its vision of the common good. We must then be concerned with the means to these ends." He outlined what church people might do to implement social justice. "I think our religious education program should prepare our children to strive for the integrity that resides in a correspondence between words and deeds. Our aim is not the personal rectitude of the self-centered man but the purposeful action of the socially conscious person."

Drawing a lesson from *The Deputy,* Jim might have said, that each of us may be a deputy if he chooses to act on behalf of a churchman who cannot or will not act himself. Each of us may do as the priest in the play did, voluntarily go to our death, making a vicarious sacrifice for wrongs we are powerless to set right. He might have said this, but he did not. Indeed, he said the opposite. Discussing the fact that the priest voluntarily went to Auschwitz as a self-appointed deputy of the Pope, Jim said: The priest "says he went to the concentration camp so he could stand where the Pope belonged. But let us ask ourselves, did the Pope really belong there? And if he did, to what end should the priest have placed himself there? At various points in the play, Church leaders and the Pope himself suggest to Ricardo that he do what is possible—namely, work to save at least some Jews. Instead, he goes to the concentration camp. He sacrifices himself in order to show the Church really was identified with the Jews in their suffering. For me, however, there is more true religious devotion demonstrated in the saving of one Jew than in the public sacrifice of one life in sympathy for the Jews being slaughtered."

Not content to stop there, Jim continued: "In this regard I think we need to re-examine the figure of Jesus. Does his purported action in seeking or courting crucifixion provide a worthy example of religious devotion for our own time? Should we ask ourselves, thinking in purely human terms, why did Jesus permit himself to be seized? If he was not just the victim of circumstance, what purpose did he think would be served by his death?"

It was a bold question. But he answered it with his next sentence.

"Both Gandhi and the priests in South Vietnam have shown us that one person, and especially a world-recognized figure, can exert influence on the course of events by slowly or dramatically sacrificing his life."

After all, then, he believed in the Deputy's indictment of the church, even though in charity he was not willing to lay the indictment upon a single individual, the Pope, when so many others were also responsible. But it was clear too that he believed a man might profitably go to his death for a cause. In one of his first sermons at All Souls, he told the congregation: "There are some things more important than life itself." His views had not changed in the interim. Now they were more explicit. "American Society is today indicted for what it is doing to the Negro," he said. "In that struggle we should be prepared to make any sacrifice." When these two statements are put together his meaning becomes all too clear. In the struggle to give the American Negro his full rights as a citizen a man should, if necessary be ready to sacrifice his own life.

12 ❦

The Light Within

DURING the six weeks in June and July, 1961, when Marie was in Casper with the children and Jim was alone in Washington, he decided to give up his post at All Souls Church. Although he remained with us three years more, the idea was never afterward absent from his thinking.

His fellow ministers were often needling him about getting a church of his own, he told me. "Why don't you be a man," they would say to him in ministers meetings when I was not present. "Why don't you get a church for yourself instead of working for somebody else?" Denominational officials would say the same thing to him. "A man ought not to hold an assistantship very long," they would tell him. "He has to get out on his own." In June, 1961, Dr. Dale DeWitt, Regional Director in New York, sent a hearty recommendation to the Department of the Ministry of the Unitarian Universalist Association in Boston regarding Jim. "He should not stay in the Washington church more than two or three years more," he added, "although at present he can still gain much there." The next year, DeWitt gave him an excellent rating and again added, "He should not stay more than two years at most in his present post." This did not represent an appraisal of the impact of the Washington post on Jim's development; it was rather a statement of the fixed policy of the Association with regard to ministers in the assistantship role.

Persuaded that this was the wisest course to follow, Jim came to me in January, 1962, to tell me that he intended to leave during the next summer and would be assuming a new post in September. We talked a long time about the ministry, the various types of churches, the nature of an assistantship, and the problems that were built into that kind of a post. We talked about All Souls Church and about his role with us. I told him again how well he was doing, how much the people thought of him, and how well I myself thought of him. I told him of my very great expectations for his future.

We discussed the matter further on several different occasions. When we had worked the problem through it became clear that except for preaching, all Jim really wanted was already in his hands at All Souls Church. In fact, in no other church in the denomination could he find a combination of opportunities and assignments so much to his liking. He liked the constant immediate personal contact with so many of the people his post as administrator involved him in. He liked the increasing role in the community affairs his post gave him. He acknowledged that our method of operation gave him a real sense of responsibility and freedom except from time to time when we clashed with each other or with the Board on matters of basic policy.

It was not the ordinary assistantship, he readily agreed. (This was before he had formally been made Associate Minister.) He was in no sense my lackey or errand boy as assistant ministers sometimes are. He felt that he was a minister of the Church in his own right.

As to the preaching, I wholly understood his problem, for preaching had from the beginning been central in my ministry. We laid plans to give him much more experience in this area. Meanwhile, I urged him to talk the whole matter over with Howard Wahrenbrock, Chairman of the Board during Jim's first two years at the Church, and with Benjamin Ostergren, then Chairman of the Board. Both told Jim how highly he was regarded by the people of the Church and urged him to reconsider his decision to leave.

In the end he did reconsider. On April 17, 1962, he wrote to the Department of the Ministry and told them of his decision to remain at All Souls Church. "Preaching is the only aspect of the ministry in which I have not had a substantial experience as a part of my work at All Souls," he stated. "This coming year I will devote much more of my time to this than I have done in the past."

Jim's agreement to undertake more preaching at All Souls Church, however, was a complex matter. It involved, in the first place, the well-established traditions of that particular church regarding its pulpit. These were by no means inflexible, but Jim's theory of preaching and its relevance to the physical and psychological demands of a large metropolitan church created a problem. While he had outgrown the theological concepts of his youth, while he no longer believed in the Holy Spirit in any exact sense, yet his belief in the working of the subconscious, and of giving expression to one's deepest yearnings, was close to it.

In 1961 he had told the congregation:

"For as long as I can remember, and it is as true today as it ever was, what I have always thought of as the light within has been of more importance to me than anything else in life. As I have tried to think recently about how to describe that which I find important, I can only come back to this one thing—the light within. I feel a deep harmony in this with some of the things that you will all remember that Dr. Howlett has been saying in recent weeks. For it seems to me, as he has said, that it makes no difference what one calls this inward light, if you call it God, or if you don't. It is not increased by the names that we give it nor is it diminished if we do not give it any name at all."

During his five years at All Souls Church Jim returned to this theme again and again. But he personally always shied away from using the term "God." "It is difficult if not impossible for many to believe in God," he said in June, 1963. We can't believe because we aren't able to imagine what we ought to try to become. Therefore we can't name God. It is our task," he concluded, "to take the light within and deliberately and consciously set it before men. This is to live. It is a most difficult instruction. It is impossible, but it is absolutely necessary." He called it "keeping faith with the best that is in us."

What does the inner light tell us? Jim was perfectly clear on that too. It tells us, he said on many an occasion, that respect for the supreme worth of every human personality must come first. That is a broad generalization, but Jim reduced it to specifics whenever he spoke. In fact, it may be said that most of his preaching consisted in spelling out for his congregation what the doctrine of the dignity of man means, and what it requires of us in various situations. This was his theology, and once he got it worked through it never troubled him again.

For this reason Jim thought that a sermon welled up from deep within a man's inner self. A sermon, for him, was never a statement of belief. It was an occasion for personal witness, a time when he told people what had happened to him, the experiences that claimed him.

As Jim saw it, the sermon was a kind of confession. Thus, for him the writing of a sermon was a means to an end, not an end in itself. The writing was the preparation for preaching: it was not the thing to be preached.

His feelings on this matter were very deep. They went all the way back to his Princeton days. Jim had come to the seminary with no little experience in public speaking, much of it preaching, and with the knowledge grounded in experience of his ability to hold an audience. When he got his poorest grades at the seminary in his speech courses, he was greatly disappointed. But he understood why. In the period when Jim was at Princeton the department laid great stress on perfection in diction and enunciation, on cultivating a deep resonant voice and projecting a properly magnified image of the minister. The men were taught to preach not more than twenty, or at the most twenty-five minutes, to spend each morning in rigorous sermon preparation, to outline their sermons far in advance, and to have the manuscript finished and typed by Friday. One professor in answer to the standard student's question "What shall I preach about?" liked to answer "About God and about twenty-minutes." On top of all the emphasis on technique, the student was constantly impressed with the awesome urgency of bringing the very word of God to sinful men.

All this was foreign to Jim's mystical feelings about preaching which he had tested in experience. He was most effective when he felt most deeply what he was saying. He was least so when, manuscript in hand, he tried to follow the techniques of the homiletics classroom. He liked Prof. Beeners because he seemed to understand the problem. Although Jim had never gone back to the seminary since leaving the Presbyterian Church, he went around to look up Beeners in January, 1963, while attending some ministers' meetings at Nassau Tavern. It was the year Ronald Engel was at All Souls Church. They roomed together at the conference. Perhaps he imagined it, but Ron thought he detected a nostalgic mood in Jim at finding himself in these familiar surroundings once more. They went to the bookstore together. This was somehow important to Jim. He bought J. B. Phillips' translation of the New Testament. Ron felt that this was nostalgic in a deeper sense, for the New Testament had been the center of Jim's theology in Princeton days. Then they went to see Beeners.

"Jim," said Beeners, "I never understood your change to Unitarianism. You were about the most fundamentalist of all my students. I felt you were unused to the university approach to religion, and that it had thrown you."

Jim's reply was oblique. He had no inclination to discuss theological differences now. Whether or not he quite realized it, he was seeking to re-establish a broken connection with an earlier part of his life he had completely cut off. His break with Princeton had been primarily intellectual. As he thought of it in the intervening years, he realized how much he had gained there, how greatly he had enjoyed the community life with the students. Heretofore, Jim had merely pushed aside the Princeton experience as if it had never been. Now he sought to face it, to remember what he was, how he had felt, and make it all a part of the living present.

That night before they went to sleep, Jim and Ron began talking about Jim's Princeton days, his change to Unitarianism, and the reasons for it.

"To me it was hypocrisy," Jim said simply, "to say you believed one thing when you really believed something else. So I got out."

"But doesn't it go a lot deeper in you?" Ron asked. "Your problem is not merely creedal. It goes all the way through to the basic issue of words versus action, doesn't it? What you say as against what you do. There is a part of you that will always be impatient with words of any kind, Presbyterian, Unitarian, Christian, or atheist, unless they match what a person does."

"A part," Jim replied, recognizing the truth in what Ron said, "maybe the biggest part. But I believe too in the importance of words and how you use them. Beeners made a great difference to me here at Princeton because of his method of using words. He was willing to let a student take any position he wanted to as long as he expounded it clearly, forcefully, and consistently. He thought how you spoke was a matter of your whole personality. He took more interest in me as a person than anyone on the faculty, and he did more to help me speak than anyone since my high schools days. I long to be able to speak effectively, to give my thoughts the most powerful expression possible."

From time to time this side of James Reeb made itself felt when he occupied the pulpit of All Souls Church. That was why it was so easy for me to believe him when he said that regular pulpit experience was what he sought in leaving All Souls Church. A very important factor in his final decision had to do with his success in preaching. Here he believed in and doubted himself both at the same time. I felt, and often told him, that he could become one of our ablest preachers. But he never thought that in saying this I was being anything more than encouraging and kind.

"I hate preaching," he once said to Robert Post, who was Chairman of the Board during Jim's fourth year at the Church. "I shake when I get into that pulpit." He said the same thing to a number of other people. Yet he loved it too. He knew that most ministers feel shaky when facing their congregations, and he knew too, for many people had told him, that the picture he gave as he stood in the pulpit was not one of terror, but one of calm, confident self-possession, animated by a deep moral and spiritual commitment.

Jim preached his first sermon at All Souls Church in accordance with his own theory of preaching: no manuscript, just notes, although the points he wished to make were carefully thought out in advance. While it had not been a disaster, it was far from a resounding success. Thereafter he suffered the tortures of the damned whenever he went into the pulpit. He was torn between the demand of the congregation for a finished discourse and his own deep belief in the importance of the freshness, immediacy, and sense of urgency of which he felt a manuscript robbed him. His problem was further complicated by the fact that as he went around to neighboring fellowships and newly formed churches, his sermons done in the old manner were usually well received.

Yet Jim was aware of the importance of careful statement in any kind of discourse, as his sometimes meticulous dealing with a committee statement shows. He was aware of this in preaching as well, and it constituted a further obstacle for him. As he would force a committee to weigh every word in a statement they proposed to issue, so he would weigh the words he dashed off in a moment of inspiration, discard them and start again. Often he was prodigal with the use of his time in the preliminary stages of sermon preparation, as he would write, rewrite, cross out, interline, discard, write again, and discard again what he had written.

The recurring agony James Reeb went through in preaching to the congregation at All Souls Church was due to these clashing standards. As a result, almost invariably when he was to preach, he faced the moment of truth, 11:00 A.M. Sunday morning, with the knowledge that he was not as well prepared as he wanted to be. As a further result he frequently went well over the standard thirty minutes allotted to the sermon because he had more material than there was time for. When his thought was carefully prepared and tightly knit, as in *The Deputy* sermon, the congregation made no complaint. But when he seemed to be unable to disentangle himself from what he wanted to say, although no one criticized him, they were not all inclined to be charitable, and Jim was desolate.

There was still another problem he faced in connection with sermons where two sets of values were in conflict with each other. Jim believed deeply in self-discipline, and he knew how to practice it. He would have found it no trouble to set aside and hold to the necessary time for adequate sermon preparation. But his equally profound belief that a minister should always be available to whoever needed him made that very difficult for him to do. Then too, he felt there was a certain self-importance, alien to his nature, implicit in locking yourself up with a sermon. Jim was at All Souls Church morning, noon, and night, in particular during his first three years there. His office door was always open except when he was counseling. But that kind of accessibility renders continued constructive thought impossible. It was a conflict Jim never resolved.

During his second year at the church, Jim read the autobiography of John Haynes Holmes, the great liberal preacher in New York in the last generation. He was accustomed to underline the books he read, often heavily, but the only underlining in the volume is in the chapter on preaching. There he underlined and double checked in the margin these words of Holmes: "Years ago I discovered that if my preaching was not to collapse utterly, I must deliberately even ruthlessly hedge myself about with impassable barriers. It is now three decades or more since I received any callers at my study except by special appointment." Holmes then detailed other measures he took to assure privacy and concluded: "All this may sound silly, self-conscious, self-important. Why should a preacher take himself so seriously. To which question the answer is obvious—he must take himself seriously if anybody else is ever to do so."*

Jim once chronicled for Marie his agonies in the course of sermon preparation. Strewn through his letters to her in June, 1961, when she was in Casper awaiting the birth of their fourth child, are several references to a sermon he was scheduled to preach June 25. On June 8 he wrote:

"I have been busy at the church and so far have had no chance to read or do any preparation on my sermon. Do you have any suggestions about a topic? I need a subject that will appeal to my heart and the congregation's head. This is not an easy combination. I must decide soon. I had wanted to talk about the Freedom Riders but Duncan talked about this in last week's sermon and besides it is outdated now.

"I may take a crack at the Eichman trial. The place of anger in the religious life and/or something on honesty or free will and determinism in daily actions. But no one topic seems to strike fire and no one has occupied my mind so that I have some thoughts already going about it."

Subsequent references follow in order:

"I am still looking for a sermon subject. I don't feel particularly anxious about it—I just feel entirely empty. I can't imagine coming up with a theme in which I am interested, I think the people would be interested in, and about which I have thought enough to have anything to say about the subject."

"The latest *Atlantic Monthly* has a whole series of articles on the impact of psychiatry on American life. I have been reading them today as I thought they might be of assistance to me as I try to plan my sermon."

"The Charmian group is going to go to the Charlie Byrd [guitarist] concert Sunday night. This should prove quite enjoyable for me. By then my current work on this sermon will be completed and I can relax and enjoy the music."

On Monday, the day after the sermon was preached, he wrote:

"Yesterday was a busy day as you can imagine. I was able to get a substantial portion of my talk written but then this does limit the effectiveness of the communication. (At least it does for me.) I spent

---

* John Haynes Holmes, *I Speak For Myself* (New York: Harper & Brothers, 1959), p. 237.

quite some time working up the Invocation, Prayer, really a meditation, and the benediction. Many people seemed to find these helpful. There were mixed reactions to the sermon and as always I had a mixed reaction myself. Some parts of the sermon had wit and punch but it was as usual not as carefully constructed as it should be and not nearly as completely thought through as it should be."

The series of references conclude, appropriately enough, with a kind of post-mortem. A member of the congregation had written to Marie to tell her how well he had done. When she relayed the news to Jim, he replied:

"It was very thoughtful of X to write. I hope you can find time to drop her a line. The sermon wasn't really that good—believe me. It did have my own twists. I had good ideas but the organization needed to be far stronger. I am my own worst enemy. I get so emotionally involved I can't produce as effective a piece of thinking as I am really capable of."

At about the time he first thought of leaving All Souls, a preacher noted for his impromptu style came to the Church to deliver a sermon. Jim could not wait to hear him. He wanted to pitch his own preaching at the highest level and was eager through this man to learn how his own theory of preaching could be applied as well to a large congregation as to a small one. But Jim's disillusionment with the visiting preacher was complete. The man must have had an off Sunday, for Jim did not find him effective in any sense, nor did the congregation.

Now he was convinced, he told me, and gave his next sermon detailed preparation. Nor did he hesitate to use his manuscript in the pulpit. The sermon, entitled "Everybody's Doing It," was an attack on the astronauts who had just announced plans for building a motel, using their own names and their fame, as Jim saw it, for personal profit. The sermon was a great success, not only because of the power of his moral lesson, but also because of the tight, forceful way in which he presented it. The point was simple. Neither the astronauts nor anyone else is justified in turning anything to personal gain just because people generally are doing it.

But whether because he was too busy, or because he had not the inclination, or because his old deep-seated beliefs about preaching reasserted themselves, his next sermon, two months later, was one of the most informal and one of the least effective he ever delivered at All Souls Church. Again we talked about it. My argument to him was simple. As one who had formerly believed in and practiced Jim's theory of preaching, I had had to learn the hard way that in an auditorium so large that half the people aren't close enough to really see you, where some are behind posts and others are in an overflow hall listening to the service on a loud-speaker, whether you read word for word or speak entirely without notes, is lost on your congregation. Only the effectiveness of what you say counts. In a small gathering, of course, it is a rich, personal experience to follow a speaker as he puts into words before your eyes his deepest convictions. Under those circumstances the sense of intercommunication and participation, both for the speaker and for his hearers, is very real.

In March, 1962, Jim agreed to stay with us and also to assume a heavier preaching load. There followed a marked change in the number of sermons he preached: five in the next six months as against two during the previous year. He delivered two of them in June, one in September, and one in October. But the next did not come until the following March and the next not until June. It was not for lack of trying on my part. Jim's reluctance to preach was all too clear. I was not surprised, then, when early in 1963 he again said he planned to leave at the end of the church year. Again we talked at length several times. He talked also to the Chairman of the Board, in this instance Robert Post, and to one or two others. Again he agreed to stay on.

But now there was a difference. Jim still felt that preaching was important, but he no longer felt that for him to preach more frequently at All Souls would bring him into closer contact with the congregation.

"It doesn't matter how *often* I preach," he said to me one day. "And it doesn't matter how well I know the people. When I stand up before them, it's your congregation I speak to, not mine." I understood what he was saying, but urged a countersuggestion.

"This congregation can become yours as well as mine if you are willing to let it," I argued. "The affection these people have for you is enormous, and in most instances it is far more personal than anything I enjoy. When they call the Church, they get you, not me, unless they particularly ask for me. And the fact of the matter is, most of them now want you when they call. When they come to the Church, it is the same. You can call twice as many people by name as I can. Many more of them than I can boast are your personal friends."

All this he admitted, but it wasn't the same, he insisted. It was still my congregation, not his. One of the factors in Jim's decision to stay in 1963 was a very carefully prepared and very thoughtful sermon on prayer, preached at about that time and well received by the congregation. But far more important was his deepening involvement in the University Neighborhoods Council.

Nevertheless, the following January Jim came to me for the third time to say he was leaving. It was clear that his mind was made up. It was also clear that no further attempt to dissuade him should be made. A decision to leave, considered three years in succession, should be carried out.

Jim then notified Unitarian Universalist headquarters. In a "Personal Statement" to be submitted to churches seeking a minister, he wrote: "My experience at All Souls has been most rewarding to me and a happy one for myself and family. However, having been at All Souls for five years, it seems to me that the time has come to make a change. My primary reason is that I want to develop my preaching skills by regular pulpit work." A statement of his reasons for wanting to change made to the Unitarian Universalist Department of the Ministry enlarges on this theme. "My five years at All Souls Church," he wrote, "have given me invaluable experience and deep satisfaction. However, I would now like to have the opportunity of serving a small urban church where I could carry the whole role of the ministry including preaching."

During the spring Jim met with several committees from inner-city churches with vacant pulpits. There was an opening in Chicago he very much wanted, but he alienated that committee by his aggressiveness on the racial problem. He looked into an interracial church in San Francisco, but that fell through, largely because he did not want it. Then he went to interview the committee of a Unitarian Church in a city in the Midwest, preaching while there in a nearby church where the committee could hear him.

A day or two later we sat down to talk about it. Things had not gone as well as he had hoped.

"I am troubled," Jim said, and obviously he was. "I have been thinking about my contacts with these various church committees and the sermons I have chosen to preach. I have not been putting my best foot forward and I can't understand why. I seem not really to want to do what I am earnestly trying to do." Here was the psychologist attempting to analyze himself. He was aware that he was working at cross-purposes with himself, but he didn't know why. Nor did I, then.

Not long afterward, he came to see me again. "I am thinking of trying the Urban League and the Friends," he said. "They have inner-city projects where I might be useful if the Unitarians can't find a place for me." In the talk that followed, a lot came out that he had never quite said before. He was ready to give his full time to the amelioration of conditions in the inner city, he thought. He did not really want to be bothered any longer with the institutional problems of a church, even a church that so untiringly gave its time and money to social ills as All Souls.

I tried to tell him that he would be as entangled in administration in a post with the Friends or the Urban League as he had been with us; that all institutions are basically the same because the human animal they work with is the same. He agreed. Still he thought he would like to be involved in institutional machinery that was geared exclusively to effecting social change.

"You will also miss working in the context of a church," I said, "in particular, this one. It is virtually unique. Not only are the members almost uniformly high-minded and devoted to human welfare, which is an ideal environment in which to work as a minister. More than that, any group of church people grow fond of their minister if he comes anywhere near up to what they expected of him, and you have far surpassed the expectations of these people. They are proud of you and personally devoted to you. You are going to miss that next year. Once you have enjoyed that kind of support, things will seem a little empty without it."

"Yes, I know," he said, and it was clear that he did know—clear that for all his protestations, he knew the people of All Souls Church were his people as well as mine, neither the one more than the other, and with neither intruding upon the other, and that they would miss him as he would miss them.

He went to talk with Sterling Tucker, Director of the Urban League in Washington, but there was no opening in Washington at the time and Jim showed no inclination to seek a post with the League elsewhere. The chief problem for Jim, however, was the fact that the League's was not a direct-action program as he understood the term. It was advisory and educational. It was an action program that Jim wanted.

He next went to see Burns Chalmers at the Friends' Davis House. Chalmers told him about a new community development program they were planning to launch in Roxbury, Massachusetts, the next fall. It was to be in a slum area, a virtual Negro ghetto where the social needs were very great. The project sounded like just what Jim was looking for. An interview with Charlotte Meacham, National Representative of the Housing Program of the American Friends Service Committee, in Philadelphia, virtually settled the question. She realized Jim was the sort of man the Friends had been looking for. Thereafter, it was only a matter of formalizing the arrangement.

Jim told me of his interview with the Friends on a Friday afternoon. I had some pretty sharp questions for him. At that very moment he was waiting to hear from two or three Unitarian churches that were interested in him.

"What about them?" I asked.

"I don't expect to hear from any of them," he said. But this did not satisfy me.

"Then this is a decision to leave the ministry," I said, "at least for the time being?"

"No," he replied. "It's just that the Friends are interested. The others are not."

"But if you get your offer from the Friends Monday you don't have to accept it at once," I persisted. "You can wait and see if one of the church jobs comes through."

"Yes," he replied. "I know. But if the job with the Friends comes through I will take it."

"Then that means you have chosen to leave the church at least for a while to take on a full-time inner-city project?"

"Yes, I guess that's it," he replied after a pause. "It is really a full-time job on inner-city problems that I want." It was not until then that either of us understood what he had been trying to find out about himself a month before when he was puzzled at his seemingly deliberate attempt to make a bad impression on every church committee

he met with. It was in the most literal sense a moment of truth for us
both; a moment in which we faced together the fact that he really did
not want what he had supposed for three years that he wanted—a
chance to face his own congregation each Sunday and to serve them
as their responsible head throughout the week.

There was, of course, a side of Jim that wanted this very much. A
thoughtful man does not easily give up or change the ambitions of a
lifetime. Knowing this, and still not sure in my own mind about him,
still not sure that he was sure about himself, that afternoon I wrote the
Midwestern church where he had previously been interviewed. After
the letter had been sent I told Jim about it. He was not pleased. It
was the first unilateral action I had ever taken on anything in which
he was involved.

"You would never have given me permission to write it," I said.
He acknowledged as much. "It was important to get the facts before
the committee," I continued. "They were wondering about your
potential and were acting—or, rather failing to act—out of ignorance. In fairness to you, that situation had to be rectified. I am
willing for you to go out of the ministry if that is what you really
want to do. But I am not willing for you to be forced out by your
idealism if you want to stay in. Now at least the church has the
information on which to base an intelligent decision."

Jim was unpersuaded. Before he heard about the Boston project of
the Quakers, he might have welcomed the call to the Midwestern
church. Now it would only be an embarrassment. Now he knew what
he wanted, clearly, and without any doubts and misgivings. What he
wanted above all else—even if it took him out of the church for a
while—was to give his full time to a University-Neighborhoods-
Council-like enterprise in the midst of urban decay. The Quakers had
offered him the opportunity. All the other hopes and dreams and
ambitions: preaching, having his own church, summers in Wyoming,
the chance to see more of his parents—these he wanted too—but even
taken together, he did not want them as much as to go to the decaying
heart of a city and work among the people who were its victims.

On Monday, the Friends officially offered him the post in Boston.
He accepted at once. All Souls Church was notified by letter of his
resignation and of his new position with the Friends.

Once again Jim Reeb was making a major change in his life's

work. Once again he reached the decision to change his occupation because he believed that he could thereby serve his fellow man in his need more completely than he had ever been able to do before. Once again he gave up a post where he was beloved for his devotion and competence. Once again with the blessing of his former associates who sorrowed at his departure, he moved on. In Gandhi's *Autobiography* he once underlined these words:

"All other pleasures and possessions pale into nothingness before service which is rendered in a spirit of joy."

13 ❧

Man Needs Help

IT WAS to the central themes of his life that Jim turned for his farewell sermon to the people of All Souls Church in July, 1964. On this occasion he found the time for preparation in accordance with his own standards of what constitutes effective preaching, in any auditorium of any size. He did not use a manuscript. The following quotations are taken from a tape recording. His title was "Tempted to Violence." It was an emotionally charged service. He knew it was the last he would conduct for a group of people whom he had come to care for very deeply and of whose high regard and affection for him he was well aware.

For his pastoral prayer he used a prayer written two thousand years ago by the Roman stoic, Eusebius. He had found it, he told his congregation, in an article by Jerome Nathanson in *Look* Magazine written several years before. The prayer as edited by Nathanson read:

"May I be no man's enemy, and may I be the friend of that which is eternal and abides. . . . May I never devise evil against any man; if any devise evil against me, may I escape. . . . without the need of hurting him. May I love, seek and attain only that which is good. May I wish for all men's happiness and envy none. . . . When I have done or said what is wrong, may I never wait for the rebuke of others, but always rebuke myself until I make amends. . . . May I win no victory that harms either me or my opponent. . . . May I reconcile friends who are wroth with one another. May I, to the extent of my power, give all needful help . . . to all who are in want. May I never fail a friend in danger. . . . May I respect myself. . . . May I always keep tame that which rages within me. . . . May I never discuss who is wicked and what wicked things he has done, but know good men and follow in their footsteps."*

His Scripture reading that morning was a shocker. It was not biblical. He read Bertolt Brecht's poem "Concerning the Infanticide, Marie Farrar":

> Marie Farrar, born in April,
> No marks, a minor, rachitic, both parents dead,
> Allegedly, up to now without police record,
> Committed infanticide, it is said,
> As follows: in her second month, she says,
> With the aid of a barmaid she did her best
> To get rid of her child with two douches,
> Allegedly painful but without success.
> *But you, I beg you, check your wrath and scorn*
> *For man needs help from every creature born.*
>
> She then paid out, she says, what was agreed
> And continued to lace herself up tight.
> She also drank liquor with pepper mixed in it
> Which purged her but did not cure her plight.
> Her body distressed her as she washed the dishes,
> It was swollen now quite visibly.
> She herself says, for she was still a child,
> She prayed to Mary most earnestly.
> *But you, I beg you, check your wrath and scorn*
> *For man needs help from every creature born.*
>
> Her prayers, it seemed, helped her not at all.
> She longed for help. Her trouble made her falter
> And faint at early mass. Often drops of sweat
> Broke out in anguish as she knelt at the altar.
> Yet until her time had come upon her
> She still kept secret her condition.
> For no one believed such a thing had happened,
> That she, so unenticing, had yielded to temptation.
> *But you, I beg you, check your wrath and scorn*
> *For man needs help from every creature born.*

* *Look* Magazine, March 22, 1955.

And on that day, she says, when it was dawn,
As she washed the stairs it seemed a nail
Was driven into her belly. She was wrung with pain.
But still she secretly endured her travail.
All day long while hanging out the laundry
She racked her brains till she got it through her head
She had to bear the child and her heart was heavy.
It was very late when she went up to bed.
But you, I beg you, check your wrath and scorn
For man needs help from every creature born.

She was sent for again as soon as she lay down:
Snow had fallen and she had to go downstairs.
It went on till eleven. It was a long day.
Only at night did she have time to bear.
And so, she says, she gave birth to a son.
The son she bore was just like all the others.
She was unlike the others but for this
There is no reason to despise this mother.
You, too, I beg you check your wrath and scorn
For man needs help from every creature born.

Accordingly, I will go on with the story
Of what happened to the son that came to be.
(She says she will hide nothing that befell)
So let it be a judgment upon both you and me.
She says she had scarcely gone to bed when she
Was overcome with sickness and she was alone,
Not knowing what would happen, yet she still
Contrived to stifle all her moans.
And you, I beg you, check your wrath and scorn
For man needs help from every creature born.

With her last strength, she says, because
Her room had now grown icy cold, she then
Dragged herself to the latrine and there
Gave birth as best she could (not knowing when)
But toward morning. She says she was already
Quite distracted and could barely hold
The child for snow came into the latrine
And her fingers were half numb with the cold.

You too, I beg you, check your wrath and scorn
For man needs help from every creature born.

Between the latrine and her room, she says,
Not earlier, the child began to cry until
It drove her mad so that she says
She did not cease to beat it with her fists
Blindly for some time until it was still.
And then she took the body to her bed
And kept it with her there all through the night:
When morning came she hid it in the shed.
But you, I beg you, check your wrath and scorn
For man needs help from every creature born.

Marie Farrar, born in April,
An unmarried mother, convicted, died in
The Meissen penitentiary,
She brings home to you all men's sin.
You who bear pleasantly between clean sheets
And give the name "blessed" to your womb's weight
Must not damn the weakness, the outcast,
For her sin was black, but her pain was great.
Therefore, I beg you, check your wrath and scorn
*For man needs help from every creature born.**

Each time he came to the refrain, he read it with increasing emphasis. Now the congregation knew this was to be his valedictory. They knew from their knowledge of him that the refrain of Brecht's poem was to be the theme of his sermon as it was the standard of his life. Those in the congregation who did not know him knew it too. Everyone present in the congregation that morning could tell by the way he read the lines that they were in that moment, not Brecht's, but Jim's own.

But you, I beg you, check your wrath and scorn,
For man needs help from every creature born.

* From *Selected Poems of Bertolt Brecht*, translated by H. R. Hays, copyright, 1947, by Bertolt Brecht and H. R. Hays. Reprinted by permission of Harcourt, Brace & World, Inc.

Without realizing it, perhaps, he had reverted to one of the themes that had come to full focus in his thinking ten years before at the Philadelphia General Hospital: What is to be our attitude to those who do wrong? It was the same question he had asked in Miss Shidler's Latin class ten years before that when they were discussing why families got on the relief rolls in Casper and what one's attitude toward them should be. Formerly he had thought in theological terms, of God's forgiveness and man's sin. Now in his full maturity, his concern for the wrongdoer remained as strong as ever, but his concern with the attitude of the righteous had shifted. Now his interest centered upon the understanding of men. When you see wrongdoing, he pleaded through the words of Brecht, withhold your wrath and scorn, for those who do wrong need your help, not your condemnation.

The Jim Reeb who asked the people of All Souls Church to look to their attitudes toward the unfortunate knew far more about the ways of men than the young man who had preached about God's forgiveness. He knew too how much we are what we are by virtue of the kind of parents we had and all the other forces that impinged upon us in our infancy and early youth. He knew how human drives are repressed only to assert themselves in wry and unsuspected ways. In his copy of Erich Fromm's *Beyond the Chains of Illusion* he had underlined these words:

"Our awareness of primitive impulses is hidden from us. . . . Repression means distortion in the consciousness, not that you are rid of it. . . . It means that the unconscious forces have gone underground, and determine man's actions behind his back."*

Throughout his ministry at All Souls Church he had insisted that each of us needs to understand that he has his darker repressed side, whether he believes it or not. We need to understand that the darker side makes us do things that are not rational, things that we in our better moments do not want to do. Despite the harm we do, we become reconciled to one another when we see that this is true, he insisted in sermons and in conferences and in discussions. In a sermon entitled "The Reformation of the Conscience" preached early in his second year with us, Jim reminded the congregation that everyone

* Erich Fromm, *Beyond the Chains of Illusion* (New York: Pocket Books, Inc., 1963), p. 99.

is responsible for the problems that now beset the Negro in the United States. The recognition that this is so, that we are *all* responsible, binds us together, he said. This recognition is deeply religious in quality because it is the function of religion to bind men together in their common humanity.

When he had finished reading the Brecht poem, the congregation wondered what more he had left to say. The sermon had, in effect, already been preached. They already knew his message. Anything further would be an anticlimax.

But they were wrong. When Jim rose to deliver the sermon itself, his emotional state became clear to all. For an eternity, it seemed, he stood facing them, uttering no word. He cleared his throat, he shuffled papers, cleared his throat again, then at last he spoke.

"As many of you know, certainly the people of the congregation, this is the end of a very happy five years for me with you. In leaving, it is especially important to me that you understand my going was in no way any change in that sense of affection that I hope that I have conveyed to you and I have certainly sensed from all of you to me and to my family. And that is why it was very difficult and required a little determination."

Then he told them of his temptation, because this was so, to do a valedictory on the theme "If I had One Sermon to Preach." He thought he had resisted the temptation, but wasn't sure, because he wanted to sum up his thoughts that morning. He asked that no one present report what he said because he was not speaking to the public, only to them.

After the preliminaries, he moved immediately to the race question. He talked about the race riots that had already taken place that summer in Harlem, Brooklyn, and Rochester, New York. "I cannot agree," he said, "with those who say that we don't need to expect such riots in the District of Columbia. I must say to you on the contrary that there is in the street in the Negro community every much as bitter a feeling toward the police in general as I can only imagine that there is in Harlem and Rochester."

He did not speak of police brutality, but of indignities committed by the police when arresting Negroes, needless, infuriating, demeaning indignities. He predicted that such treatment would produce an inevitable reaction. "Many people," he continued, "seem to feel a great sense of dismay about this, who seemed to feel that once we had had the march on Washington and once we had the civil rights bill, things were just inevitably going to be easier, that somehow we had done it. And I can say to you only that I think that this is the most dangerous kind of self-delusion; that we've not in any way done it, and that just to the extent that we think we have, we're going to be dismayed when we find out that we have not."

He did not defend the New York rioters: he sought rather to explain what they did. There are two reasons for these riots, he said. One is despair. "But the other is a new sense of self-respect. There was a period in this country, it seems to me, when the majority of the people had their foot on the neck of the Negro, and he still acted like a gentleman, and that was in part because the Negro did not know himself whether or not it was right that someone had his foot on his neck. But that day is gone forever. What the Negro now knows is that *no* man has a right to have his foot on his neck."

The Negro, he said, has "a new sense of self-dignity out of which will be born a greater sense of taking responsibility for their own future, but out of which must also be born our sense of understanding of what it is that is involved. We must not misinterpret the situation. We must not let the backlash, as it were, increase because we continue to see that Negroes do what people call push. There is going to be ever greater pressure for more progress, for now the Negro knows that there is only injustice that stands between him and a better way of life. That's going to make relationships often difficult, and in many ways testy, but it is up to us to contribute understanding, to try to interpret to the community as a whole what is happening, why things are as they are."

Pleading for white understanding of the temptation to violence in the Negro because of his long oppression and his newborn hope, Jim put it in a wider setting. Temptation to violence exists throughout our country, he asserted, among people of every walk in life. He spoke of the impact of the war in Vietnam on people's thinking. "It is an ugly war," he said, "and it contributes to the belief that violence is the way to solve international problems." He spoke of the campaign for the Presidency just then getting under way, and, though a supporter of the Democratic party, denounced those who were then comparing Republican extremism to the Nazis. "This kind of thinking," he said, "will set the people of this country at each other's throats."

At this point, as the congregation could see him coming to the conclusion that the temptation to violence objected to in the Negro lurks in all of us, depending upon what our frustrations are, he became quite discursive. The thirty minutes' time that tradition allotted to the sermon at All Souls Church had run out, but Jim kept on, the people following intently. They were used to that with him, and in any case today they didn't care. There was no restlessness in the auditorium as he dealt with the criticism of the Supreme Court, the need to arrive at some understanding with the Catholic Church on aid to education, the need for continued cooperation of religious leaders on social issues, in the manner that they had worked together for civil rights. He then defended the police, pointing out the difficulty of the job they are given to do. "They need our support," he said. From that he moved to housing and its importance to the Negro, and thence to the importance of the congregation as a congregation taking a stand on social issues. We must support the government in its attempts at social reform, he said.

Returning to the race issue once more, he commended the sense of fellowship he found in the people of All Souls Church, Negro and white together. "But," he warned, "the Negro people who come here are going to have to be willing and, indeed, choose to call upon themselves the epithet of Uncle Toms. There is no other way but that both white and Negro people as they stand together reject racism, whether it is of the white race or whether it is of the black race. On the one hand you're going to be Uncle Toms, and on the other you're going to be radicals or Reds. And there must be a willingness to understand, it seems to me, that in the atmosphere in which we may exist, there may not be a great deal of glory on either hand for those who want to go down the road of integration, of progress, with all speed, without violence, without hatred; and that we will have to continue to say to each other, this is not an issue between white men and black men; this is an issue between people that have different values, and there are some people in the Negro community that hold values that have to do with respect for individual dignity, and there are some people in the white community that hold these values, and these people are standing on a common battle line and it has nothing to do with whether their skin is white or black. Neither group must permit itself to be inhibited by the bigots or the racists lest we all go down the drain in a sea of hatred."

It was 12:15, but the congregation was still listening with rapt attention. This was a man's personal testimony: this was his philosophy of life. He had so much to say and so little time to get it all in. Then he came to what was obviously the peroration. The congregation sensed it by his manner. "There is in each one of us this temptation to be violent," he repeated. "And I would say only one thing further. Never have I been a part of a congregation where there was so much common affection for the people for each other, and yet even here, as issues have come along that have been important to us, I have had difficulty restraining within myself those feelings that arise when one not only has a different opinion from a different person, but then also jumps to making that person somehow unworthy of consideration. If this kind of thing can so easily arise in our own beings here where the issues are not of life-and-death matters, how much more easily must it arise in people who are suffering beyond anything that we can well imagine for ourselves. If we are going to be able to meet their need, we are going to have to really take upon ourselves a continuing and disciplined effort with no real hope that in our lifetime we are going to be able to take a vacation from the struggle for justice."

He paused and bowed his head. The congregation bowed their heads too. It was the concluding "prayer."

"Let all who live in freedom, won by sacrifice of others, be untiring in the task begun, till every man on earth is free."

It was indeed a summing up. But one question remained. How far does our "continuing and disciplined effort" go? Jim did not say. There wasn't time. But those who had followed his preaching through his five years at the Church knew the answer he would give. All the way. In one of his first sermons at the church he had asked: "Is there nothing worth risking the end of one's life for? Are there no dreams or goals so important that we can risk our own destruction to gain them?" His answer had been "Yes." And had Wilbur Beeners been present that morning he might have recalled that Jim had reached the same conclusion in a student sermon preached more than a decade before. "A Christian," he had said then, "willingly chooses to sacrifice himself that other men might be saved. Wherever right is struggling with wrong he takes his place in the battle line. Wherever men are in misery and sickness he gives of himself to relieve their suffering."

When the service was at last concluded there was a long line to greet him at the door, to say good-by and to wish him well in his new work. It was deeply moving as one by one they came up to press his hand and to tell him how much he had meant to each in some particular way. Jim found it hard to maintain his composure, so warm were the expressions of affection from so many of the people.

"Leaving All Souls Church was the most difficult single thing I ever had to do," he wrote Mildred Reynolds the next fall. "I was sure it was right but it was very painful. This was especially true because I thought it really required breaking off the relationships so I wouldn't have any future involvement with the people in any way. I have had and will probably always continue to have the deepest respect for the peace and harmony of the church."

To Rev. David Osborn, a former colleague in the Washington area, he said several months later: "It is a hard thing to do to leave a church. I didn't know how much it would mean." Osborn noted Jim's use of the present tense, which indicated that Jim still felt the wrench even then. For this reason Jim steadfastly refused to return for the send-off the church wanted to give him in the fall. The decision to go with the American Friends Service Committee had been made too late to give the party in the spring.

"I can't, and you mustn't ask me," he said to me in September when I went to Boston to urge him to come. We always supposed that later he would change his mind. But James Reeb, who believed that some things are more important than life itself, never came back for the send-off party All Souls Church wanted to give him. Whether he might later have changed his mind, we shall never know.

14

The Work That Had Hardly Begun

JIM'S TERM with All Souls Church was officially concluded September 1 when his work with the Friends in Boston began. But he had the month of August for vacation, which meant that his work at the church was concluded July 31, a few days after his farewell sermon.

During July he went up to Philadelphia for a few days' orientation at the Friends Center. Then in August he went to Boston to find a house into which to move his family by September 1. He hunted for some time, but could find nothing satisfactory. The problem was, the Friends wanted him to live in the slums of Roxbury or Dorchester where their new program was to be developed. This was something Jim was very eager to do. He was at one with the Friends' conviction that the Community Relations Director of their Boston Metropolitan Housing Program (Jim's title) should live among the people with whom he was to work. Since the project was to be centered in Roxbury, it was there that Jim concentrated his search.

About August 20 he telephoned Marie to come up and look at some five houses he had lined up. None was satisfactory, he said, but they were the best he could find. There was one Jim was willing to settle for, but Marie put her foot down. It simply would not do. He and she together looked for three days but found nothing. Marie then had to return to Washington to be with the children. She went back discouraged, and Jim, even more discouraged, began house hunting again.

Then suddenly he found a place. It was on Half Moon Street in Dorchester, a fine, well-built roomy house on a street where homes were individually owned and people took pride in them. He wrote to

Ronald Engel early in the fall: "3 Half Moon Street is about 6-8 blocks from the Blue Hill Protestant Center. It is in the midst of one of the most deteriorated areas in Boston. Even though within Boston our mailing address is Dorchester as it would be Roxbury if we were there.

"It took me many days of looking to find this house. It is three floors—11 rooms and full basement, plus vacant lot across the street with a rather steep slope topped by trees and bushes. It was difficult to find this house. In the first place almost no one wants to encourage you to move into the slum. I remember one lady who when I asked her if she wanted to sell her house asked me if I was crazy when I told her I really wanted to move into the neighborhood. The frustrations of many persons caught by the forces of change in what they believe to be bad neighborhoods are severe and very destructive of neighborhood morale.

"The Negroes are no help in this regard. They think any white person who would move into an area they would give anything to escape from is just stupid (naïve) or is slumming. Of course what I have just said is an overstatement and I wish we could talk so I could tell you about the exceptions. The people were really nice and tried very hard to be helpful.

"After you find a house it is a major job to get it financed. Banks are reluctant to give loans. Insurance companies don't want to give adequate coverage and the FHA has a hand in making many of the difficulties worse. They to some degree still operate on the principle a changing neighborhood, or a unified neighborhood, is a bad neighborhood and the property values therefore are correspondingly lowered. They are lowered by the general level of appraisals. Few families that would buy houses in the inner cities have the money to use conventional financing, most need FHA."

During the course of his house hunting, Jim stayed in Watertown with Mr. and Mrs. Thomas O'Sullivan. Mrs. O'Sullivan was a member of the Boston AFSC advisory committee on the Boston housing program. They found Jim a constant delight, full of laughter and fun. There was an impishness in him they readily responded to. They were struck in particular by his excitement over a collection of fossils he brought along in his car in order to save on the eventual moving expenses which would be calculated by the weight of the load.

Spreading the various specimens out on the living room floor, he explained their origin, gave their age, and told of their meaning for the evolution of life on earth.

The impression Jim made on the O'Sullivans was typical of the impression he made on everyone. The Boston committee had at first been quite skeptical of Jim's potential. They hadn't thought of looking among churchmen for a candidate for Director of their project, and they were somewhat dubious about the mild-mannered man who came for an interview. But their doubts were dispelled as they began to see that James Reeb was committed to the principle of human dignity. It was his desire, they perceived, to bridge the chasm between people. He made no distinctions as to who people were. He took them all as individuals, even those in the power structure.

"How do you feel about leaving the ministry?" the committee members asked him.

"I am not leaving it in taking up this kind of work," he replied without hesitation. That he never ceased to think of himself as a Unitarian minister working for the Friends was made clear in many different ways. In his work in Roxbury, for example, he always introduced himself as Reverend Reeb.

Ronald Engel, describing Jim's attitude toward himself, the ministry, and the church while in Boston, said later:

"The University Neighborhoods Council tells us much about his understanding of his work as a Unitarian minister. Human reconciliation was the self-conscious goal of his ministry. Social justice was the structure that he believed social relations had to take before reconciliation could be achieved. Community organization was the new institutional vehicle that he saw as able to contain the goal of reconcilation, and still give tangible expression to the imperative for justice. Thus Jim always worked in two directions at once and this he saw as a single direction: toward a greater inclusiveness of membership in the community organization and toward greater justice in the community by programs of social reform. This was a terrible tension to maintain, but it was present in whatever he did. His co-workers found it difficult to understand that, for Jim, there was no 'enemy.' If there was something to be fought, it was the urge toward exclusiveness which he found within all men. We can see why Jim came to devote a major part of his ministry at All Souls Church to the

University Neighborhoods Council. The community organization became for him a second church, and he brought to it the same understanding and dedication that he had brought to All Souls."

One of the most important aspects of the move to Boston was a by-product of it. There Jim found himself suddenly on a forty-hour week for the first time since his YMCA days in Philadelphia. He had most of his evenings free and most of his weekends as well. Marie had preferred not to go to Boston because of the problems she would have to face there in connection with the children. But it proved to be one of the happiest times in her life. In his letter to Mildred Reynolds, who knew the work load he had carried at All Souls Church, he wrote:

"This job has changed my personal schedule. There are no specific weekend responsibilities. Can you imagine me with Saturday and Sunday to myself? Marie and the children can't quite believe it is true. While a substantial part of my time has gone into working on our house, there have been a number of occasions when we have gone to the beach, or on other type trips. I like this schedule, and I feel no desire to have a seven-day job again."

During the winter he wrote to tell his parents about buying a pingpong table with money they had given him for Christmas. His letters tell also of family visits to museums and to some of the many historic shrines in the Boston area. In a letter to Ronald Engel in February, he wrote:

"We are resuming our Friday night birthday festival. We celebrate the birthday of someone born during the particular month. We have a cake, candles—someone tells about the person and we sing happy birthday."

The new job seemed just right, in character no less than in the hours of work demanded of him, and James Reeb seemed just right for the job. His immediate superior was John A. Sullivan, a former newspaper man and radio-TV news executive, who in his near-fifties had given up his career in business for a position with the American Friends Service Committee. As he explained it to his friends who were puzzled at the switch: "I am now doing what I want to do." To Jim, he was a warm and understanding friend, always ready with fatherly counsel and always ready to talk Jim's problems through with him, however long it might take. The two made a perfect combination. John was inclined to be moderate; Jim was dynamic and impulsive. John was able to fit more readily into the organizational structure than was Jim, and was more patient with its operation. Both, however, were at one in their ideals and in their desire to put them into practice in the real world.

John Sullivan's title was Executive Secretary of the New England Regional Office of the AFSC. The office was on Brattle Street in Cambridge. For the first few months, Jim's office was there too. When he came on the job, Daniel Richardson and Robert Gustafson, the two field workers who were to assist him, had already been employed. He liked them both and they liked him. They liked in particular his ready, disarming smile, for they very soon learned that it was completely genuine. They admired, too, his obvious feeling that if anybody was to be hurt as a result of a decision or clash it was to be he. Gustafson found Jim a little bumptious and overeager at first, and Richardson thought him a little insecure in the hail-fellow-well-met manner which belied the seriousness underneath. Richardson often felt Jim overdid his effort at friendship.

"I want you to relate to me not as a Negro, but as a man," he would say. This would hurt Jim, who would drop his head and say that that was what he wanted to do. Then Dan would be sorry, for he understood that the fault was only Jim's overeagerness to surmount the racial barrier.

His old penchant for detail, both in gathering information and in preparing statements, exasperated his fellow workers now and then. They understood his concern to get things right and know what they were about. But they found it frustrating all the same. The advisory committee had the same feeling at their meetings. Jim presented each case with far more detail and supporting evidence than anyone wanted. John Sullivan explained this to him, and Jim was grateful, although he did not altogether change as a result.

Often the advisory committee was eager to know what Jim would like to do, but he would not say. The committee often thought him too cautious in pursuing his project. The members felt he did not need so much data before going ahead. Often when they asked for recommendations, Jim would hold back. They wanted him to make proposals for discussion and exploration, but Jim would wait for directions, which were never forthcoming.

Jim found the situation no less frustrating than they. He, too, wanted to get on with the program, but he felt keenly his reponsibility to the Cambridge office of the AFSC and its advisory committee, who, in turn, were responsible to the national organization. Whatever Jim or his two field workers did would reflect credit or discredit on the entire organization. One day Jim remarked to Dan Richardson that he had been much freer at All Souls Church than he now was. Both he and the committee felt hampered by the newness of the program and their realization that seemingly trivial decisions might later prove to be direction-setting.

This was not, however, because the Church was able to achieve any greater degree of freedom in its operation than was the American Friends Service Committee in its projects. Freedom of the individual within the institution was the goal for both, but always and of necessity a man's freedom is limited by the needs of others, and in an institution it is limited also by the judgment of others. Whenever a co-worker disagrees on a plan of action you either have to overrule him—which in your respect for his freedom you do not want to do—or submit to him—which robs you of your own freedom. The ideal is, of course, to find a middle way, but a middle way that all can agree upon is not always to be found.

All this Jim well knew. In the University Neighborhoods Council, where as Chairman he had presided at the meetings, he was noted for his concern that each individual member be treated with respect as a person. The views of each were given a hearing and carefully considered even though the speaker might be a minority of one. "He never confused the person and the problem," William Stuart Nelson said of him. "He might become very intense in the course of an argument, but once it was concluded, the person returned to his normal relationship to Jim." He was able to let people be themselves at a meeting because he accorded them full respect. It was because of these personal characteristics over and beyond his experience in neighborhood development that the Friends had chosen him for their Roxbury project.

What got Jim down from time to time in his Boston job was the new role he found himself playing. In Washington, he had been first the challenger, then the dynamic leader: challenger of the ways of the church; dynamic leader of an assembly of community organizations

he himself had drawn together, the members of which looked to him.
Now he was part of a much larger organization and answerable to its
leadership.

A trivial incident which became a major bone of contention illus-
trates his problem. A representative of the Boston Action Group
stopped in at the AFSC office on Blue Hill Avenue one day. He
had a picture, clipped from a newspaper, showing a white police
officer beating a Negro with a club.

"Here's something to hang up on your wall," he said, "that'll show
the folks what police brutality is."

"I don't think that's the kind of picture we want to hang up," Jim
said.

"Why not?" the man demanded in some indignation. "Don't you
think the people need to know what is going on?"

"They know," Jim said very quietly. He always spoke with a very
soft voice when he was disturbed.

"Then hang it up," said the man from the Action Group perempto-
rily. In the end, and after a somewhat heated argument, Jim flatly
refused to put up the picture. The visitor from the Action Group was
confirmed in the impression that he had gained from others that
James Reeb was not really an action man, and said so to his face. Jim
was too thoughtful, he said, too cautious, too deliberate, too concerned with the interests of his organization. Had the visitor seen to
the heart of the man he was talking to, he would also have seen that
he was rather a man of peace who would not hang in his office a
picture that might be considered to be inciting in character. He would
have seen, too, what we are not often given to see in each other, that
he had plunged Jim into deep despair by what he said.

The Action Group man was soon on his way, pursuing some other
matter. But the incident remained with Jim from then on. Now *he*
was the institutionalist dragging his feet when he ought to be up and
doing. Now *he,* who heretofore had carried the banner for action in a
group of high-minded people who he thought should be more active
than they were, was being chided by activists for inaction. He knew
his two staff assistants felt this way about him, as did many others as
well. He reflected ruefully that John Sullivan and even Mrs. Ruth
Batson, head of the Education Committee of the Boston branch of
the NAACP and a member of his advisory committee, had told him

on more than one occasion that he might well be less cautious in his program, less detailed in his preparation, and instead get on with the work in hand.

All this Jim had foreseen with that extraordinary understanding of human nature that he possessed. One day after the decision to go to Boston had been made, we were talking about the problems of administration generally. Soon we got around to the aspect of it that concerned us both the most: how do you keep an institution that is dedicated to high ideals true to its own ideal: specifically, where is the cut-off point between sound administrative policy, where the ideal is always present but common sense is never absent, and expediency, where the ideal is sacrificed through excessive caution: the old issue of *The Deputy*. Jim smiled partly at me but more to himself. Looking thoughtfully at his feet stretched out at the end of his long legs, he said:

"You know, I have often wondered what it will be like next year in Boston. We are going to build an organization there of which I will be in charge. Then I'll be sitting where you are: the responsible head of the enterprise. I have often wondered what I will do when some self-appointed hunk of glory working under me comes pounding into my office and wants to do something good in itself, but which I know will wreck my organization. What will I say to him?"

Jim knew what he would say, as I did, for no man ever had a greater sense of responsibility than he. And now, in Boston, this was his problem just as he had foreseen. His sense of responsibility to the American Friends Service Committee was so great that it hampered him in his work even though the advisory committee and John Sullivan told him that he let these things concern him too much.

Jim's problem was that he never got used to the Quaker method of operation. His enthusiasm for it at the outset was great. "My relationships to my superiors have been of the best," he wrote Mildred Reynolds. "Their point of view and methods are so right from my point of view. Here I sense a genuine respect for the individual in dissent. He isn't looked upon as a troublemaker. He is seen as someone who should be listened to carefully. After all, he is speaking out of a 'concern.'" Yet a few months later he was finding this all very frustrating when he wanted to get on with his work.

"Nothing is ever settled," he said to Rev. David Osborn, when he visited him in January. "We can reach a consensus but someone can bring the question up again at the next meeting and we have to go through it all over again."

On one occasion, however, Daniel Richardson thought he saw the man Washington had known, the dynamic community leader, not the cautious project head, trying conscientiously to keep within organization policy. One evening they went out to Billerica, one of the suburbs of Boston, to talk about their work to a group interested in fair housing. After Jim's talk there was an open-forum discussion. No members of the advisory committee were present. Jim, the crusader, eager to enlighten suburban ignorance as to inner city blight, waded in with full vigor. Here, as Jim urged them to break the suburban color line, Dan saw he was ready to go all the way. He made his points without caution in the full vigor of his own conviction. It was a stirring evening for everyone present, particularly for Dan, who that night felt he really understood his boss for the first time.

As Marie and Jim had foreseen, there were problems with the children at school. Although they could easily have arranged to send them to the schools in another district, they chose to send them to the neighborhood schools where the rest of the children in the area went, although they were the poorest in the entire city. Karen and Anne experienced little difficulty, Steven was still too young to go at all, but John, now twelve years of age, found himself among boys whose everyday pattern of life was more rugged than anything he had known heretofore. In December, Jim finally had to intervene in his behalf. He went first to see the principal, then, having made no progress, turned to Mrs. Ruth Batson.

"What school is the boy in?" Mrs. Batson asked.

"The Patrick Campbell School," Jim said.

"How could you put your boy there?" she asked. "It must be ninety-five per cent Negro. Anyone coming to that school looking strange is in trouble. Take him out."

There was a long pause.

"I can't do that," he said.

"Why?" she demanded. "I wouldn't send my children over there. He won't learn anything. Nobody cares about that school."

"But I live here," he said. "Everybody else who lives here has to send their children to that school. They couldn't send their children outside the district even if they wanted to. They can't afford it."

"Well, you make me, a Negro, feel ashamed," she said. "What do you want me to do?"

"I thought you might speak to the principal about it," he said. "You could do it more effectively than I could."

"How does John feel about this?" she asked.

"He's a little frightened," Jim admitted, "but we have talked about it and I think he'll be all right."

"Has he ever had Negro friends?" Mrs. Batson asked.

"Yes, many," Jim replied. "That isn't the problem. It's the toughs who take his lunch money away from him."

Mrs. Batson saw the principal. When he learned the names of the two boys who were chiefly responsible, he said he thought he could handle it, and did. A few days later Jim called Mrs. Batson again.

"I want to thank you," he said. "Things are going much better now. But you are right about the school. The children aren't learning a thing."

"All right," she said, "let's do something about it."

Out of this conversation came a plan whereby Jim would keep careful and detailed notes as to what his son was getting. They would then have a white parent in a white school keep notes on what his child was getting. At the end of the year a comparison of the two would prove the case against the Patrick Campbell School and the handicap the de facto racial segregation placed on the pupils who attended it. But it took Mrs. Batson until February to find a white parent who would participate in the program, and the plan was never carried out.

Although much of Jim's time during his first two or three months in Boston was consumed with the necessary business of setting up an office and getting the operation running, by December he was ready to develop projects of his own, the kind of thing which he had always done with great skill and enthusiasm. A glimpse into his many activities while finding his way around, may be seen in a report covering a period of only ten days late in November and early in December, 1963.

During this time, besides his effort to find a suitable office location, he attended meetings of, or talked with representatives of, an impressive list of community organizations concerned with his general area of interest. They included the National Association of Intergroup Relations Organizations, the Boston Conference on Religion and Race, the Mayor's Committee on Civic Unity, the Tenant and Community Relations Program of the Boston Housing Authority, Fair Housing, Inc., Association for Boston Community Development, Massachusetts Committee on Discrimination in Housing, Mayor's Advisory Committee on Urban Renewal, Massachusetts Freedom Movement, Call for Action, and many more. Jim always knew exactly what he was about and whom he was with. His report is strewn with the names of people, places, dates, and groups and are a model of clarity and readability.

By the beginning of the new year, he was in high gear, doing the work he loved, helping the poor and the dispossessed, the downtrodden and the hapless, to find a better way of life, specifically the Negro who because of his color suffered the most. Living in Dorchester, with his office not far away just over the Roxbury line, he was able to achieve a sense of identification with the Negro. By living within his ghetto in a great American city, he was able to demonstrate his concern more effectively than he could have done in any other way. Some of those among whom he lived and worked thought he was foolhardy and a few in the beginning suspected his motives. But as each came to know Jim as a person, their doubts vanished—soon they began to admire him for what he was doing, and to love him for what he was. They found in him a warm-hearted friend who cared for their suffering without seeming to notice whether they were black or white. They quickly saw, as the people in Washington had seen, that his greatest concern was for the Negro, because he, more than anyone else, needed help.

Jim's first real chance to get his teeth into a project came with the new year. On December 31, 1964, there was a fire in a brick tenement house at 24 Hammond Street, Roxbury. Two adults and two children lost their lives. The building was gutted, which left some thirty families homeless. The Red Cross helped relocate the families. To follow up, the American Friends Service Committee decided to contact each family afterward to see how they were getting along and whether further assistance was needed. As Jim and his staff worked on the case, things began to come out that were disturbing, among them the fact that there were not enough exits for so large and hazardous a building. They decided to inspect it. In this, as in everything, Jim was thorough to a fault. He took a great many pictures, checked the building and fire codes, talked with architects, insurance men, and city officials.

All through January and February, he worked on the report the American Friends Service Committee planned to present on the Hammond Street fire with recommendations regarding code enforcement and a citizens committee to study the codes. Early in March he went to see one of the city officials to tell him about the report and to recommend the formation of a citizens committee to study the codes. He found the man belligerent, seeking to trip him on his facts and constantly challenging his statement on the ground that he was not an expert and knew nothing about fires. Jim reported the incident in his official log kept for the AFSC office as follows:

"The most frequent reference [in the interview] was to my ignorance of fires. He made statements such as 'You are no expert,' 'You can't say anything about this fire that would have any meaning.'' He said I was simply stirring up trouble. He said the whole thing was a red herring.

"I then tried to get on to the exits. I said I believed they were inadequate. He responded that I had no basis for any such statement. I did not know enough about fires to be able to make any such statement. I was just looking to create a sensation in the press and 'if you are wrong I will murder you.' He repeated this several times and quite angrily."

Toward the end of the interview, Jim reported, the man "became even more agitated. He said we were just out to try and get some publicity for our organization which we otherwise would not have. He could not remember the name of our organization when I arrived. He said it was his duty to defend the Fire Department. They had nothing to be ashamed of. He said he would stand up and be counted. He allowed as perhaps there wasn't much more for us to talk about. I said I agreed, but I wanted to ask one last question—'How do you murder people?'

"This set off the volcano. He stood up, got quite flushed, stood over me and shook his finger in my face and shouted that this whole thing was because 'those people died in the fire' and we were determined to make some big issue out of it. I am sorry I can't report word for word, but the point was that Negroes had died and we were out to make a big fuss just because they were Negroes. He took my question to mean the Fire Department murdered people. He said when his son was killed nobody looked into that to see who murdered him. Why was that? [His son, a city employee, had been killed in the line of duty.] I did my best to explain that I had been asking what he meant when he said 'I will murder you.' He said I had meant something else. I explained I could not possibly have meant what he suggested because I thought the Fire Department was responsible for saving many people's lives in the fire. He calmed down and we parted company."

Jim then described further steps he took following the meeting to make sure the AFSC case was absolutely tight. "I felt these precautions were necessary," he wrote. "So long as I may be 'murdered' to say nothing of the AFSC, I thought we should supplement our evidence in every way." No one complained about Jim's thoroughness and attention to detail in this case. His report was dated March 3, 1965.

There is no measure for James Reeb's work in Boston. He had really not begun it when it was cut off. If analogies from other phases of his life are any indication, he would soon have adapted himself successfully to the Quaker way, made the most of its advantages, and circumvented whatever difficulties he found in it. He soon would have developed a wide following devoted to him personally because of his intense and continuing desire to draw very close to the people with whom he worked, and because of his ability to relate to them. We would expect him to have expanded his own organization, to work through those already in the field, as in fact he was beginning to do, and to start new ones not yet in existence.

But all these things lay in a future that never came. A week after Jim finished his report on the Hammond Street fire, the terrible threat made against him metaphorically by a city official in Boston, Massachusetts, was carried out literally by a self-appointed vigilante in Selma, Alabama.

15 ❧

Selma

ORDINARILY Jim and Marie didn't look at television in the evening. It was often late when he got home. There was always a lot to say, and anyway they liked the newspaper next morning better. But Sunday night, March 7, they turned on the eleven o'clock news. Martin Luther King had scheduled a march that afternoon to begin at the city of Selma and go to the state capitol at Montgomery. George Wallace, governor of the state, had said that the march would not take place.

"I cannot promise you that it won't get you beaten," King had said to the Selma Negroes when calling for the march. "I can't promise you that it won't get your house bombed. I can't promise you won't get scarred up a bit. But we must stand up for what is right." In the light of King's resolve to march and Wallace's order forbidding it, Jim and Marie, like millions of other Americans that Sunday night, were eager to know how things had gone.

The march that afternoon was pivotal because it set in motion the Alabama voter registration drive of the previous fall and winter which had gotten nowhere. To push it further, Martin Luther King early in 1965 had decided to pinpoint the drive in Selma, a city of 30,000 people, where the Negro lived in almost total subservience to his white master. The usual methods of nonviolent protest having brought no result whatever, the march from the city along U.S. 80 to the state capitol fifty miles away was designed to dramatize the situation further.

With the battle lines drawn and the eyes of the nation fixed upon Selma, some 650 Negroes and a few whites began the march Sunday afternoon, March 7. But the little column got only as far as the outskirts of the city. There they were confronted by a phalanx of

Alabama state troopers who stood in a solid line across Route 80, shoulder to shoulder, three deep. They were equipped with billy clubs, side arms, and gas masks. At the side of the road stood a sheriff's posse, both mounted and on foot. They stopped the march, first with an order, then by charging, with billy clubs swinging, and lastly with tear gas. All this was laid before the eyes of the nation on television that night and broadcast to the world by word and picture. Jim and Marie, like millions of others, watched the pictures of this savagery aghast.

Monday morning Jim went to the office as usual. There was the report on the Hammond Street fire to be gotten out, there were appointments to be met, and there were a dozen other things to do, all important, and all of consuming importance to him when he closed the office door Friday night. But this morning his mind was not on his work. While he met his appointments, talked on the phone, went here and there, before his mind's eye he could see policemen equipped with gas masks clubbing down helpless Negroes already blinded and choking with gas: pitiful defenseless men and women who asked only that they be permitted to register to vote, a right guaranteed them by the Constitution of their country. This was not the lawless beating of helpless citizens by the criminal element in our society so much reported and deplored in the press: this was the beating of the helpless by the agents of law enforcement equipped with the arms and instruments given them to protect an unarmed citizenry.

About noon Jim's telephone rang. It was the regional office of the Unitarian Universalist Association. Martin Luther King had issued a call to the clergy of the nation, they said, to join him in a second march from Selma scheduled for the next day, Tuesday. A telegram from King had been received at Unitarian Universalist headquarters shortly before. They had notified the regional men, who in turn were notifying individual ministers. Would Jim care to go? He couldn't say right off, he told them. He would have to see. But he was in full sympathy with the call and hoped the response would be strong.

Jim hung up with a heavy sigh, and for a long time he didn't speak. He just sat where he was, half slumped in his chair, staring straight ahead, seeing nothing, thinking. He wanted to go. He wanted to go very much. This he knew with total clarity. He felt an almost irresist-

ible impulse to call Marie, put on his coat, and head for the airport at
once. He knew there were risks. He had seen with his own eyes how
the Alabama authorities proposed to deal with freedom marchers.
The next time, the injuries might be much more serious. But these
reflections did not lessen the impulse which had seized Jim like an
external force. They increased it. All the blows should not fall upon
the heads and backs of the Negroes, he thought. They had already
suffered enough. It was time now for privileged white people who
believed in integration to stand with them and take some of the
blows too. If that was to be Jim's lot, he was ready.

But then came the second thoughts that always follow the first
impulses born in high excitement. What about Marie and the children? It did not occur to him that he might never return from
Alabama. After all, they were not killing the freedom marchers except very occasionally in lonely spots after dark. But there was a
real chance that he might be hurt badly, perhaps incapacitated. What
would he do then? What would Marie do? And John, the girls, and
the baby?

Jim reached for the phone again and dialed Rev. Virgil Wood,
leader of the Blue Hill Protestant Center and the area representative
of the Southern Christian Leadership Conference. They had known
each other in Washington and had become fast friends in Boston.
Wood had also received the call through his headquarters, and was
planning to go.

"I want to go too," said Jim, "if I can be helpful and if I am really
needed."

"You are very much needed," Wood said without equivocation.
"Everyone who can go is needed. In the first place, it is important for
you to be there as a human being. Secondly, it will be an eye-opener
to you to see for yourself what can happen to protesters in the South
—not just to see it on television but to be there and take a whack or
two of your own. But most of all," he went on, "and I am speaking as
a Negro, I think it is important for a white man to stand with the
Negro in whatever hell-hole he finds himself. It is important for white
people to share in the sufferings Negroes have had to endure."

"Yes," said Jim, "I've been thinking about that. To me it's the
most important part of it. I think I will call and see if I can get a

plane reservation. Then I will have a place if I find I can go." He made the reservation, then called John Sullivan. They talked at length. Sullivan said yes he might go provided he thought he had his work well enough in hand to leave it.

"We are asked to go only for tomorrow," Jim said. "I have a lot of things in process, as you know, but I should be back at my desk sometime Wednesday."

"It's your decision," Sullivan said again. "But speaking personally, I'm glad you're going. You will be representing all of us. I'd like to be there too. I can feel I am in some way, through you."

Later that afternoon Jim called Unitarian Universalist headquarters again. The response was excellent from all across the nation, they told him, and very good in the Boston area. They had about a hundred men going, they thought.

"I will be with you if I can make it," Jim said. He still had not made up his mind. And he had not yet talked with Marie, although he had called to tell her of Martin Luther King's appeal.

It was a busy afternoon, what with the things he already had scheduled that day and those that had to be attended to for the morrow. The other two staff members were out most of the day on appointments in connection with the Hammond Street fire report. When they got back to the office about 4:30 P.M., Jim spoke of the call to Selma and said he was thinking of going. There was no discussion of the matter. They did not try to persuade him one way or the other. It would only be a brief period—forty-eight hours at most. The other two could manage during his absence, they said.

A revealing picture of his wide-ranging interests and concerns is seen in the items he left on his desk that night: the report on the Hammond Street fire, still to be checked; notes from people who asked his assistance in securing garbage disposal; and pamphlets on non-violence issued by the Friends. One lay open at a quotation from George Orwell which read: "If you want a picture of the future, imagine a boot stamping on a human face—forever."

That evening Jim arrived home a little earlier than usual. Marie was in the kitchen and he went straight out to see her. The moment she looked at him she felt a kind of thump inside.

"Come upstairs," Jim said. "I've got to talk to you." Marie led the way up to their bedroom at the front of the house, cold fear slowly creeping over her as they went up the back stairs and along the hall. Jim, following close behind, closed the door to the bedroom as they went inside.

"I want to go to Selma," he said. "There has been a tremendous response to Martin Luther King's call from all over the nation. Many of the Boston Unitarians are going. I want to be there too. I can't just sit at home."

It was the old Jim of high school days, who, with utter distaste for fighting, had permitted himself to be drafted when he could so easily have been deferred; the old Jim who felt that where others were called upon to risk their lives for something he believed in, he was called upon to do so too.

At the time of the Korean conflict when he was in Theological School, he had come very close to volunteering. Again in the summer of 1962, when Northern ministers were first beginning to go south to help in the civil rights struggle, he had come close to going. Here was a cause he completely believed in, both its purposes and its methods. Only his deep commitment to his family had prevented his going then. In the end he took them to Wyoming. The following summer he had found the identity with the civil rights movement he sought by remaining in Washington through July to work with the University Neighborhoods Council. Only his loyalty to his family caused him to go back to Casper in August.

Marie stared at Jim wide-eyed and unbelieving. She was accustomed to maintain her composure under all circumstances. But now her lower lip began to tremble. She thought of what they had seen on the TV screen not twenty-four hours before. She thought of their four children, their need of him, and how much this year in particular had meant because of the time he was able to spend with them. She thought of the man himself to whom she had given so much, and who had become the heart and soul of her life. He was looking intently at her. At last she spoke.

"I don't want you to go," she said very quietly. "There are others to go. You belong here."

"No," he replied. "I belong there. It's the kind of fight I believe in. I want to be part of it. Every man who can go is needed."

"All right," she said in a voice he could hardly hear. "I know how deeply you feel. If you must, you must."

They faced together the danger. He might be hurt. He might be thrown into jail. Their resources were very meager. He had taken a very substantial cut in salary to go to Boston. On top of that they had had to buy a house, and had had to turn to Jim's father and one or two friends for help on that. To make ends meet, he had given up his health and life insurance policies in the Unitarian Universalist Ministers Association.

"We'll manage—somehow," Marie said, her voice breaking for the first time. Now tears stood in her eyes. "And I know you'll be all right. It is important that you go."

That night there was no time for ping-pong, for there was much to do before the plane left. He took time to read to the girls. The children caught the air of excitement, but it was nothing new to them, as their father always seemed to be rushing off to attend to one thing or another. When the stories were over and the girls and Steven tucked into bed, Jim said good night to John, and he and Marie set off on a succession of errands there was barely time to attend to. First, there was the matter of money. They hadn't enough on hand to manage such a trip; the banks closed but there were grocery stores where they might get a check cashed. The first two they tried would only give them twenty-five dollars. That did not seem to them to be enough, so they rushed off to another which they reached just before closing. There they got another twenty-five dollars.

Then there was the matter of a traffic ticket to attend to. On Saturday night Jim and Marie had gone out to dinner and on the way had been stopped for speeding. It was one of those traps the police set after an accident where everyone who exceeds the technical limit is picked up. Jim, who was less than five miles an hour over it, would have gotten by with a warning but for the fact that he had forgotten to take his license and registration. The officer seemed to be impressed with Jim's embarrassment but told him he had to see his papers to complete his record. Could Jim bring them over to the station house Monday? Jim, thinking it no trouble at all and glad to get off so easy, readily agreed. But now it was a problem. There was hardly time enough to do it, but somehow they got it in.

In all the frantic preparations Marie was guilty of no conscious sabotage, but it seemed to her that night that the fates were with her as obstacle after obstacle got in their way. Returning from the police station, they were stopped again, this time for slowing down rather than stopping at a stop sign. Again it had been a technical rather than a real offense. Jim had obviously been ready to stop if a car had been coming the other way, as the officer could clearly see. Again he got off with a warning, but that, too, took time. At last they made the airport with even a few minutes to spare. Marie did not go in. There was a great deal of activity at the entrance and no place to leave the car. Then, too, she wanted to get back to the children. She left Jim at the curb.

"Good-by," he said, kissing her. "I'll be back soon."

Her words echoed his. "Take care," she added. "We will be waiting for you."

In deep anxiety she pulled away from the crowded entrance and made her way alone back through the city to Dorchester.

Jim was feeling rather downcast as he walked into the waiting room where the passengers on the chartered plane were to gather. But once inside his mood soon changed abruptly. The room was crowded but in the throng he seemed to see friends everywhere. In all, more than a hundred Unitarian ministers and laymen were going from the Boston area. He found himself greeting old friends as he would at a gathering of the Boston Ministers Association. On the plane he was given a registration form to fill out. Beside his name Jim wrote "Unitarian Minister."

The trip to Atlanta was short, at least it seemed so, there were so many people to see and so much to talk about. Jim fell in with Robert Hohler, Henry Hampton, and Rev. Orloff Miller, all members of the Unitarian Universalist headquarters staff. All three were, like Jim, ardent civil rights men. He had known Orloff Miller since his first year at All Souls. Miller was Director of the College Centers program of the denomination and had often visited him in Washington in connection with Jim's program at American University, and at Howard also. Robert Hohler, was the Laymen's League Executive, and Henry Hampton had charge of denominational promotion and publicity. He was the first Negro to be given a high staff position with the Unitarian Universalist Association.

Their plane, which had departed at 11:00 P.M., arrived at Atlanta in the early morning hours. Planes for Montgomery, the next leg of the journey, would not be available until 7:00 or 8:00 A.M., they were told. Jim's group wondered where they could nap a little in the meantime, and, upon noticing that there was no one in the Hertz office, went inside. Jim and Bob Hohler took a divan each, Henry Hampton took a chair, and Orloff Miller curled up on the floor. Later Jim took the floor, Orloff the chair, and Henry the divan. Somehow they passed the rest of the night.

With daylight, planes to Montgomery became available. Apparently they were shuttling back and forth. Around 8:00 A.M. the group arrived in Montgomery where Southern Christian Leadership Conference cars, traveling in pairs, took them to Brown Chapel in Selma. They had had no breakfast, but they didn't really notice it. Both excitement and anxiety were too high for eating. Everyone expected real trouble on the march for which they were assembling. Then there was the excitement of seeing still more old friends. At the Atlanta airport they saw so many Unitarians, they had the eerie sense, as Bob Hohler put it, that they were attending a surrealistic meeting of the General Assembly of Unitarian Universalist Churches.

There were, of course, many more whom they did not know, for the response to Martin Luther King's call for assistance had far exceeded anyone's expectations. Clergy and laymen from all over the nation were converging on Selma. The gathering marchers were interracial, inter-class and inter-religious in every respect. There were college professors in their tweed coats and baggy trousers, and construction workers in overalls. There were Protestant ministers in business suits, like Jim, and others in the various kinds of clericals they wear. There were Roman Catholic priests and Roman Catholic nuns. Jim's heart must have swelled as he saw them all. There could be no doubt now. This was where he belonged. This kind of response to Martin Luther King's call represented everything he believed in.

Like the others, Jim left his suitcase at the Brown A.M.E. Chapel parsonage, the headquarters for all the activities. No sleeping assignments had as yet been made. Outside he joined the ever-growing throng gathering for the march later in the day. It was already obvious that SCLC was not prepared for the enormous response that their appeal for help had evoked. Robert Hohler described the scene in his Laymen's League publication as follows:

"Sylvan Street in Selma, Alabama, is anything but sylvan. It is a tired cracked city street that goes through the heart of the George Washington Carver Housing Project, a Negro development. On it, also, is the Roy Brown A.M.E. Chapel. The project, the church and the street serve as the staging area and rallying place of the Selma civil rights drive. There are hundreds of men, women and children in the street. We go into the church which is jammed and we sit on the floor beside the pulpit. A young SNCC worker is speaking. 'I hope we're gonna make up our minds that if anyone gets whupped out there today, it ain't gonna be our women.' Then he and another boy, not more than 17, demonstrate the ways in which we can throw our bodies over a woman who has been struck down by a trooper and how we can offer our backs and shoulders to their clubs."*

For Jim, Selma was another time of reunion. Not only was he constantly meeting his Unitarian friends from around the country, he also met some of his former Washington friends. At one point he spotted Father William Wendt and Father Geno Baroni, of the University Neighborhoods Council, standing together. He strode up to greet them.

"I knew you'd be here," he said with his customary enthusiasm and wide smile. They shook hands warmly and began exchanging news on the UNC and Jim's work in Boston.

Meanwhile, there had been a great amount of activity at the highest levels of the national government, and among local officials, with Martin Luther King and his men. When King issued his call for Northern clergy to join with him in his march on Tuesday, everyone from President Johnson down sensed danger. On Monday, while the ministers were packing their bags, getting plane reservations, and converging on Selma by road, rail, and air, highly placed officials or their representatives started for Selma, too. John Doar, Assistant United States Attorney General in charge of civil rights, arrived. FBI agents began coming in. President Johnson, deeply apprehensive and eager to avoid another scene like that of Sunday, sent as his personal mediator LeRoy Collins, former Governor of Florida, now Chairman of the Community Relations Service established by the Civil Rights Act. Col. Al Lingo had also come to Selma in command of one

* *The Lamplighter,* Special Issue, April 1965.

hundred to five hundred Alabama state troopers—the estimates vary. Many of them were known to be Klansmen. They had come determined, fully armed, and battle-ready, not to protect the rights of the citizens of Alabama, but to enforce the laws of a police state.

At four-thirty on Monday afternoon, four of Martin Luther King's attorneys went to the office of U.S. District Judge Frank M. Johnson, Jr., no defender of segregation. They sought an injunction against the Dallas County police, preventing them from interfering with Tuesday's march. Johnson said he could not grant an injunction without a hearing and forthwith scheduled it for Thursday.

"Call off your march," he advised, "until we can get the legal aspects of the case settled." King was reluctant to agree to this because there was now no way to stop the influx of clergy at that very moment gathering from all over the North. It would be a great frustration and a victory for the segregationists if they all arrived only to find that there was nothing for them to do. To wait until Thursday was not possible, even if desirable. There was no way in which the Negro community could house and feed so many visitors, and most of them probably could not remain so long in any case because of their other commitments. But if he was to stage another march, Martin Luther King felt he needed the protection of the law. He did not want to see Sunday's scenes repeated.

A conference was called for King's top leaders. While they were in session, the Attorney General of the United States, Nicholas Katzenbach, telephoned. He pleaded with King to go along with Judge Johnson's request and postpone the march to Thursday. He promised that if he would, government attorneys would come to Selma to help plead his case. But by this time it was clear to King and his men that the march had to be held on the morrow, with or without the protection of the law. The plan finally agreed upon was a compromise which, like many a compromise, was neither this nor that. King would march on Tuesday as planned, but he would stop in time to be sure that no trouble developed.

Tuesday morning, he was ready to begin his march as his Northern white clerical "troops" poured in from all over the nation. To clear with Judge Johnson, King's lawyers returned to his office to inform him of their decision. This time, without a hearing, Johnson issued an injunction, enjoining the march until after the hearing on Thursday.

King was now confronted with one of the most difficult decisions of his career—to march and break the law, which he had never done before, or not to march and frustrate the throng of supporters, most of whom had traveled all night and at great personal expense to demonstrate their belief in the right of Alabama Negroes to vote. His years of leadership told him that this could not be. He knew that any announcement on his part of postponement in the face of the injunction would be, in fact, an abdication of leadership which someone else who was ready to march would seize. The question before him was clear. It was not whether to march, but how he was to do it in the face of an injunction issued by a United States court.

LeRoy Collins, speaking on behalf of the President, finally proposed a plan to which all agreed. Mayor Smitherman of Selma, Col. Lingo, and Sheriff Clark would let King's men march in the direction of Montgomery to the place on the far side of the Edmund Pettus Bridge on U.S. Route 80 where Sunday's march had been halted. At that point the troopers would again stop the march. King would then lead the marchers back without further demonstration. Lingo even outlined the route King could follow, drawing a rough map for him.

As the number of clergy and others waiting in front of Brown Chapel continued to grow through Tuesday morning, word of the injunction against the march slowly got around. Many of those who were gathered there were deeply concerned. They, like King, believed in law and order. They believed in demonstrating but within the law. James Reeb belonged to this group. But the temper of the crowd as a whole, particularly the Alabama Negroes themselves, was exactly as King had predicted. They were determined to march, injunction or no. They were by no means alone in their views. At an impromptu meeting in Brown Chapel held during the morning, many national leaders spoke in favor of marching in spite of the injunction. They gave many reasons, but few of them dealt with the root issue Jim was turning over in his mind as he often had before in discussions of civil disobedience. Jim believed in a law that was higher than the law of the state. But what he sought there, as he often had before, was a

principle by which to decide when a man might set the law of the
state aside in the name of a higher law and when he was merely
taking the law into his own hands because of a conviction that might
be important to him but might not be to others. Jim's penchant for
logical consistency plunged him deep into thought while most of those
about him waited impatiently for the march to begin. At this point
Virgil Wood saw him standing more or less alone by the Brown Chapel
steps. He went over to shake his hand. Jim seemed so absorbed that
Wood at first felt he was intruding.

"Are you going to march?" Jim asked.

"I certainly am," Wood replied.

"I have been wondering about the injunction," Jim said. "It is a
heavy responsibility deliberately to break the law."

"Yes," said Wood, slipping away unnoticed by Jim, who seemed to
want to be alone to think.

Throughout the morning and into the early afternoon there had
been no word from Martin Luther King. At last, around 2:00 P.M.,
when the marchers had been waiting in the hot sun for many hours,
he appeared.

"I have made a painful and difficult decision," said King with
obvious emotion, "I have made my choice. I have got to march. I do
not know what lies ahead of us. There may be beatings, jailings, tear
gas. But I would rather die on the highways of Alabama than make a
butchery of my conscience! There is nothing more tragic in all this
world than to know right and not do it. I cannot stand in the midst of
all these glaring evils and not take a stand. There is no alternative in
conscience or in the name of morality."

To the waiting marchers, what he said was not reassuring. It was in
fact intimidating, and King has been much criticized both for what he
said and what he did and did not do. In his defense it should be
pointed out, however, that from the beginning he has conducted his
protest movement within the law. He did not depart from the principle that day. It is also true that neither he nor anyone else could be
sure that the more or less symbolic acts planned for that day would
not result in violence before the day was over. After all, his marches,
participated in by unarmed men and ending not in battle but in
prayer, were never more than symbolic in any case. Should he have

revealed the agreement with LeRoy Collins to his marchers? Only his critics think that he should have. The marchers, as always, were content to take their directions from him, realizing that someone who knew what was going on must make the decisions and give the orders while the rest followed after.

On that Tuesday afternoon in Selma, the marchers, knowing nothing of the agreement, feared a repetition of Sunday's attack by the police. Now it has all come true, Jim must have thought. All those things I have been saying all my life about being willing to sacrifice yourself for others and about what is important in life, goals worth dying for, that sort of thing: now I shall know whether I really meant them or not.

He was not afraid, yet his heart was beating hard and his throat was dry as the march itself began at 3:00 P.M., with Martin Luther King leading the way. They walked down Sylvan Street to Water Avenue, followed along the Alabama River, past the Selma City Hall to the Edmund Pettus Bridge. There they met a U.S. Marshall sent by Judge Johnson to stop the march. King listened to the reading of the injunction and responded that he must continue. The Marshall said he had no intention of stopping them, and stepped aside as the column moved onto the bridge.

The Edmund Pettus Bridge arches sharply across the Alabama River. Going up the Selma side, the marchers could not see what lay ahead of them. But as they reached its crest, they could look down onto U.S. 80 leading southeast out of the city toward Montgomery. There, stretched across the highway not far off, stood the same phalanx of state troopers that had blocked their way on Sunday afternoon. King, leading the march, walked up to the troopers and stopped as an order came through a police bullhorn commanding him to halt. Might they kneel and pray? he asked. Permission was granted and the long line knelt for prayer on the hard pavement. It was about 4:00 P.M. When the prayers were concluded, the police, in a surprise maneuver, stepped aside. Now before the marchers stretched the road to Montgomery unobstructed. But King was not to be trapped. Turning around, he led the column back along the route they had come, passing the astonished marchers who still stood where they had halted when King drew up before the state police.

Slowly a sense of relief came over them as they realized there was to be no violence. But as they turned around and started back, not in a line of march, but informally by twos and threes and fours, a feeling of frustration began to grow among them. What had they accomplished, they wondered, after coming so far at such cost in time, money, and personal inconvenience, not to speak of the anxieties of those they left behind? Had they accomplished anything? They didn't know, but they would soon find out. They were to reassemble at Brown Chapel where King would speak to them again.

At one point on the return journey Jim found himself walking beside Rev. Clifton Hoffman, Executive Secretary of the Mid-South District of the Unitarian Universalist Association. Hoffman's office was in Atlanta. He had driven over for the march and was going back that night. Wouldn't Jim like a ride? Jim was very grateful. He had a lot to do back in Boston, he said. He had to get back as soon as he could and had been wondering how he was going to do it. When they reached Sylvan Street, he put his suitcase in Clif Hoffman's trunk and, with the others, went to Brown Chapel.

As Martin Luther King rose to address the disappointed marchers, he faced a very real dilemma. They were still unaware that they had participated in what had been essentially a drama, the scenario for which had been written out in advance. Yet not quite. For there was always the chance that the forces of segregation might introduce a new maneuver that would break everything wide open. King still did not know what would have happened had he accepted what looked like an open invitation to keep going when the police stepped aside. Believing it to be the part of wisdom to say nothing about his agreement with Governor Collins and the others, he called the day's march a "confrontation." "At least," he said, "we had to get to the point where the brutality took place. And we made it clear when we got there that we were going to have some form of protest and worship. I can assure you that something happened in Alabama that's never happened before. When Negroes and whites can stand on Highway 80 and have a mass meeting, things aren't that bad." He concluded his remarks by urging all who could to remain for the march on Thursday after official permission had been gained. "Perhaps you may do something for the nation that will save it," he said.

The Unitarians and Universalists now gathered in a group at the foot of the steps to Brown Chapel to meet one another and to make further plans. Jim went over to Hoffman.

"I think I'll stay," he said.

With that he took his suitcase out of the car and waved good-by as the others drove off, leaving Jim in Selma.

16 ❦

A Man Becomes a Martyr

ONCE the march was over, the anxiety past, and the decision
to remain had been made, Jim, like the others, suddenly realized that
he was almost faint with hunger. He had had nothing to eat since his
supper with Marie and the children the night before. But where to eat
in this hostile town? They had been warned not to venture alone into
the white section and, even in groups, they were to be very careful.
Neither Jim nor the others had any desire to provoke anybody. That
was not what they had come to Alabama for. They wanted only to
remain quietly with the Negroes and the civil rights workers until the
time came for another demonstration that could be made to count.
Where, then, to eat?

Someone suggested their inquiring at SCLC headquarters which
was only a few blocks away: it was in an insurance office, they were
told, Boynton's. Jim fell in step with Rev. John Wells, a friend and
fellow colleague in the Washington area, and Rev. Orloff Miller,
with whom he had been off and on ever since they met on the plane
coming down from Boston. The young woman behind the desk at the
Boynton Agency, Mrs. Diana Bevel, wife of Rev. James Bevel, one of
the Selma civil rights leaders, was very friendly.

"Do you prefer to eat with your own kind?" she asked politely.
They said they would prefer a Negro restaurant or one that was
integrated, if there was such a thing in Selma. At this she smiled
broadly.

"There surely is," she said. "Eddie's place. It's only around the
corner from here. You'll see the sign—Walker's Cafe. It's right in the
middle of the block."

The group moved off toward the restaurant. Jim now found himself walking with Miller and Rev. Clark Olsen, minister of the Berkeley Fellowship of Unitarians in California. Olsen, after frustrating de-

lays crossing the continent, had reached Selma too late for the march but had been able to join the Unitarian group at the foot of the church steps following King's speech. Olsen had been greatly disappointed at arriving late because two of his parishioners had given him the money to come on their behalf and on behalf of the Berkeley Fellowship. But he was consoled by the fact that the real march had not yet occurred and that he was really in time after all.

"Eddie's place" proved to be in one of those border areas you find in Southern towns where Negro establishments and those belonging to the poorer whites are intermixed. It was so crowded they could hardly get inside. Seeing this, another group of Unitarian ministers coming up behind them decided not to wait but to go on to the next corner where they saw a sign for another restaurant called the Silver Moon Cafe. It was a "white" restaurant, the men found to their surprise, but they were so hungry they thought they would go in anyway, consoling themselves with the thought that by doing so they were helping to take the pressure off Walker's.

"But we felt," one of them wrote later, "an atmosphere of hatred, anger, hostility (almost as an evil pressure) and were aware of unsmiling, unfriendly white faces pointed in our direction. We dimly heard taunts and jeers. I looked inside at the grim faces there, and suddenly I was afraid. I turned to the others and asked if they felt what I was feeling. They did, and we turned and walked back down the street, into the safe and friendly Negro restaurant."*

Meanwhile Jim, Orloff Miller, and Clark Olsen waited their turn at Walker's. At last they were seated. They all had a big chicken dinner —it was the only thing the restaurant had left to offer, but no food ever tasted any better to them. The chicken was fried southern style and there were lots of mashed potatoes and gravy. Before they finished, it was 7:30 P.M., and it was dark outside. They were next to go to Brown Chapel where there was to be another meeting. Jim asked if they would wait while he telephoned Marie about his change in plans. She was expecting him to return that night.

Her emotions were very mixed as she talked to him on the long-distance telephone. She already had the news that there had been no violence on the march that afternoon, and she was much relieved. She and the children had been all excited to think that he might be com-

---

* Richard Norsworthy, in *The Liberal Context* (Spring, 1965), p. 5.

ing home that night, but when he told her that he was staying overnight and would be back the next day, she made no objection. Now
that the march was over she felt he was safe. Jim then spoke with
John and Karen, and after assuring Marie again that he would be
back soon, hung up.

Olsen and Miller were waiting by the door for him when he came
out. For a moment they discussed whether to go to the left or to the
right. They had come from the left, but the right was the shorter route
to Brown Chapel, so they went that way, falling in step together,
Olsen on the inside, Miller in the middle, and Jim nearest the curb.
They had gone but a step or two when they became aware that four
white men on the other side of the street were coming toward them
from between some parked cars. Instinctively they quickened their
pace, but they did not break step and they did not run.

"Hey, niggers," one of the four called. "Hey, you niggers," he
called again, coming up on the three ministers from behind. Their
attitude as they came on was even more menacing than their voices,
and the men felt they were in for trouble. The other two increased
their step a little more. Jim did not, nor did he look around. Olsen,
however, glanced back, just in time to see the leader of the group take
a vicious swing at Jim's head with a heavy stick. He hit him square on
the left temple and Jim fell to the pavement on his back.

Orloff Miller immediately dropped to the sidewalk according to the
technique taught to civil rights workers, face to the ground, hands at
the sides of his head. One or perhaps two men began kicking and
pummeling him. "Now you know what it is like to be a real nigger,"
he heard one of them say. Clark Olsen, who by now was several steps
ahead of the other two, was attacked by one of the four, who began
pounding him with his fists, knocking his glasses off and breaking
them.

It was a hit-and-run attack. In half a minute it was all over. With a
kick at the kneeling Miller, and another at the prostrate Jim, they
fled. Clark bent to help Orloff whose face was cut but who was
otherwise unhurt. Then they both turned to Jim. He lay flat on his
back, conscious but dazed, and could say nothing. There was no sign
of injury. Helping him to his feet, one took his right arm and the
other the left. By now he was trying to speak but he was incoherent

and they could make nothing out of what he said. He did, however, appear to be able to stand, even to walk with some assistance. At the moment they had no idea how badly he was hurt but they knew they must get him to a doctor as soon as possible.

Looking around in the expectation that someone might come to their aid, they saw no one on the sidewalk at all. Where should they go? Who would help them? Might they be set upon again? They did not know. SCLC headquarters, they thought: they could get help there. Somehow they continued on around the corner by the Silver Moon Cafe to the SCLC, Jim half walking, half staggering between them, and leaning heavily upon them.

At last they reached Boynton's Insurance Office. Mrs. Bevel immediately got an ambulance from a Negro funeral home next door and called the Burwell Infirmary, a Negro hospital, to alert them to the fact that the three men were on the way.

Dr. W. B. Dinkins, the head of the infirmary, was waiting for them when they arrived. He patched up the scratches on Miller's face but saw at once that Jim had been seriously hurt. He noted that Jim's eyes were already beginning to glaze over.

"You will have to take him to Birmingham where they have a neurosurgeon," Dr. Dinkins said. "I'll call the University Hospital so they will be ready when you get there.

Then followed a series of delays and frustrations that will remain as a nightmare to Clark Olsen and Orloff Miller the rest of their lives. First the local police came. They were sympathetic. Whether or not they were segregationists, they did not condone this sort of thing. Miller and Olsen helped them make out their report. Meanwhile, Dr. Dinkins arranged for a hospital deposit check. "The hospital in Birmingham tells me you will need it on arrival," he said. Orloff Miller then called Dr. Homer Jack, Director of the Department of Social Responsibility, Unitarian Universalist Association, at Brown Chapel. They agreed that Miller and Olsen would accompany Jim to Birmingham and see to whatever arrangements were necessary there.

Dr. Dinkins then rushed Orloff Miller back to SCLC headquarters where they picked up the deposit check. Meanwhile, the ambulance with Jim in it drew up at the door and at last they started for Birmingham. In the ambulance were the driver, an attendant, Dr.

Dinkins, Clark Olsen, Orloff Miller, and Jim—three Negroes, and three white men. With the siren wailing and a police car following, they ran through red lights as they pushed through Selma toward the edge of town. But there the police car fell away. This in itself was alarming. Negroes and whites do not drive around together in the Deep South in the daytime, let alone at night, and especially after a Freedom March. In no case do they go together on a lonely highway. But they had no choice. Off they went in the darkness along U.S. 22 to Birmingham.

They had not gone far when they had a flat tire. But they dared not change it. So they turned around, and riding on the rim and flapping tire, they limped back toward town looking for a place where they might safely telephone for help. Soon a car with some men in it came up behind them and began to follow them. Who were they? They didn't know but it alarmed them further. All they wanted was to make a telephone call. But in Alabama that is not an easy thing for a Negro to do. Most Negroes don't have telephones and no Negro goes into a white establishment for any purpose except as a menial. None of them thought it was safe for either Orloff Miller or Clark Olsen to try. At last they came to a radio station where the driver used to work.

"I think they will let me telephone from here," he said, and turned in. While he was inside telephoning, several cars pulled in at the station, all with white men in them. They looked them over and drove on.

After what seemed like an hour, but was really only ten or fifteen minutes, the second ambulance arrived, followed once more by the Selma police. Jim was tranferred to the new ambulance as more cars filled with white men drove in, looked them over, and went on. Before they could get started, a Dallas County sheriff's car drove up. The sheriff's men got out with flashlights, shining them in the windows, in the occupants' faces. Then one of them opened the rear door. The men inside were terrified, knowing the mental set of the sheriff's deputies. He asked Olsen and Miller their names and had them retell the story of the attack. They complied with his wishes while the clock ticked on.

"Could you provide us with a police escort on the highway?" Olsen asked.

"It won't be necessary," they said. "We'll radio on ahead." Dr. Dinkins, meanwhile realizing the need for a second car, had telephoned back for his own automobile. Civil rights workers always travel in pairs in the South. While they waited for his car, they worked on the ambulance siren which was broken, but to no avail. When Dr. Dinkins' car arrived at last, he got into it and fell behind the ambulance as they set out once more for Birmingham, still ninety miles away. By this time it was after nine o'clock. More than an hour and a half had elapsed since the attack.

The ambulance was in poor shape. The brackets intended to hold the stretcher in place were broken, so Olsen and Miller sat and held it steady throughout the trip. It was a harrowing ride, but whether by good fortune or extra care or both, they made it safely to Birmingham by 11:00 P.M.

It was to one of the finest medical institutions in the South that Jim was taken. The University of Alabama Medical Center is a large complex of red brick buildings located near the center of the city of Birmingham. It is modern in every respect. Fully equipped with all the complex machinery and laboratories of modern medicine, it boasts an outstanding medical staff. When Jim arrived, the hospital was in complete readiness.

He was rushed at once to the emergency room. By 11:30, four hours after he had been struck, they were operating. A respirator was inserted in his throat to enable him to breathe. Examination of his head showed his skull had been completely crushed on the left side by the viciousness of the blow. A huge blood clot had developed as a result. The brain damage was so severe the doctors entertained virtually no hope for him from the start. The part of the brain that mediates the vital functions of the body, such as breathing and the beating of the heart, had been destroyed.

Word reached Marie only a little before the news went on the air to the nation in the nightly news broadcast at 11:00 P.M. Eastern Standard Time. Dr. Homer Jack in Selma had telephoned Dr. Jack Mendelsohn, minister of the Arlington Street Church in Boston, which Jim Reeb attended, and asked him to call her. Mendelsohn, also deeply interested in civil rights, had been of considerable help to Jim as he began his work in Boston, and they had become good friends. In order not to alarm Marie needlessly, Mendelsohn was purposely vague in what he said and tried to be as reassuring as possible. This was about 10:45 P.M. The children were by now all fast asleep.

The people of All Souls Church, like Jim's friends and associates in Boston, those he had known in Philadelphia and elsewhere, heard the news for the first time on the eleven o'clock broadcast. That was 10:00 P.M. Birmingham time, while Jim was still en route to the hospital. The newsmen did not mince words. Jim was seriously hurt, they said. But Marie did not hear the broadcast. It was some time later that night when she learned the truth.

Spontaneously, Jim and Marie's friends began coming to her aid. When Tom O'Sullivan heard the news, he simply got in his car and drove over to 3 Half Moon Street. He didn't know what he could do but thought there might be something. He never left the house for the next four days, as he answered the door, the telephone, dealt with the press and the friendly callers. The next day he was joined by Harold Olsen from Washington, brother of Art, also a close friend. He too came uninvited just to help. On Friday Jack Lamb arrived. A number of other Boston friends came too.

Marie was up most of Tuesday night. Fortunately the children were not wakened by the commotion. She talked with the hospital, with her parents and Jim's by long-distance telephone, and began making plans. She would go to Jim as soon as she could. That was all she knew, and at the moment that was all that mattered. Jim's father would meet her at the hospital. Mrs. Reeb and Mrs. Deason, Marie's mother, would come to Half Moon Street to run the house and look after the children.

All night the telephones rang as people madly called one another, the hospital, Selma, and the Reeb home in Boston to get more information and see what could be done. A team of neurologists from the Massachusetts General Hospital offered to go to Birmingham if needed; a neurologist from Howard University declared his readiness. Close friends tried to call Marie and couldn't get through. They did not know her financial situation but wanted her to know she must not think about expenses. Everything possible must be done. Money would be raised; expense must not be a factor and she must not worry. They themselves would pitch in. Many of them, unable to do anything more, wrote her a note enclosing a check and assuring her that more help would be forthcoming if needed.

The wire services, radio, and TV news systems were equally busy. The next morning, Wednesday, March 10, 1965, the name of James Reeb, until then known only to his friends and co-workers, was on the tongue of every newscaster and on the front page of every newspaper in the land. As the afternoon and evening papers came out, Jim's picture was there too, with more or less accurate and detailed stories of his life, together with the statement that his prognosis was poor. Everything that medical science could do had been done at the Birmingham hospital the night before.

At 7:40 P.M. Wednesday, the hospital issued the following official bulletin:

The operation [on James Reeb] was performed by three physicians with three nurses, one nurse anesthetist and operating personnel in attendance.

Following heart stoppage there was closed chest massage and the injections of a stimulant into the heart. Three physicians were in attendance along with nursing personnel during and following the cardiac arrest. Artificial respiration was supplied through an automatic respirator.

The patient is in the Recovery Room receiving intensive care with constant attendance by physicians and nurses. Oxygen is being administered through an automatic breathing device. The heart and other body functions are being continuously monitored by devices developed for use here in cardiac surgery patients. Apparatus to lower the body temperature and to regulate heart function is standing by. A highly qualified team of neurosurgeons and other specialists are in constant attendance.

Meanwhile, between phone calls, I too made plans to leave for Birmingham as soon as possible, and by mid-morning Wednesday was on my way to Atlanta. Changing planes there, I met Marie on the Birmingham flight. John Sullivan was accompanying her. With newspapers on our laps containing Jim's picture and life story, we talked hopefully yet fearfully. Approaching Birmingham, we arranged through the pilot who radioed on ahead to have a cab waiting for us by the plane to save our having to run the gauntlet of photographers they had met in New York. We went straight to the University Hospital, going in through the emergency entrance, again to avoid the press.

James Crank, Associate Director of the hospital, was there to meet us as we came in, and before the press had learned of our arrival, he ushered us upstairs to the doctors' suite, and from there we were taken at once up to the recovery room where Jim was. There we saw him, lying on one of those rolling stretcherlike beds they use in hospitals, a sheet over his body and an enormous bandage wound round his head which was turned somewhat to the right. A tube had been inserted in his throat just below the Adam's apple, and all about were machines busily at work sustaining his life. Doctors and nurses no doubt get used to these glistening mechanical laboratories dedicated to preserving human life, but they are a chilling sight to the rest of us.

Marie walked up and stood very close to Jim's side. For a long time she remained there gazing at him, weeping silently, the epitome of human anguish. A doctor looking at the scene would have known that this man was already what the medical profession calls "clinically dead." That is to say, his body was no longer capable of maintaining life functions for itself. The machines were not helping him to recover. That was no longer possible. They were only delaying a death that was now inevitable.

But we did not know. We could recite the strange-sounding medical words we had heard the night before: multiple skull fractures; large blood clot on the left side of the brain; decompression operation; tracheotomy." But we understood better the ominous words we had heard from Mr. Crank but a few moments before: "Still in critical condition. Has not yet left the recovery room: prognosis poor."

We went back downstairs, shattered. Mr. Crank led us to the doctors' suite again, where we were granted the seclusion so necessary for those whose grief is great. He and the hospital staff could not have been more considerate of our feelings or our needs.

Then almost at once began the going and coming of which there was never an end until Jim died. Orloff Miller and Clark Olsen were among the first to appear. They wanted to express their sympathy to Marie, and they knew she would want to hear the story of how it happened. We asked them if they could come back a little later, which they were glad to do. Dr. Homer Jack came; Rev. Gerald Krick, who had been with Jim part of the time; Rev. Lawrence McGinty, minister of the Birmingham Unitarian Church; Dr. Joseph F. Volker and Dr. R. S. McMillan, both of whom were on the hospital staff and also members of the Unitarian Church, stopped by. Others included William Evans, Senator Edward Kennedy's Administrative

Assistant; A. M. Secrest of the Community Relations Service, representing Governor LeRoy Collins; the Attorney General's personal representative, and many others.

Toward dark Mr. Crank came to see me.

"I have the entire press downstairs in my office," he said, "TV, radio, newspapers, the works. So far I have been able to hold them off on the promise that they can interview Mrs. Reeb."

I protested that this was impossible. She had already been through more than anybody ought to be asked to endure. The answer would have to be No. But Mr. Crank was not to be put off. Quietly, considerately, he pointed out what we, isolated as we were, did not realize—that James Reeb, our Jim, was now a figure of international significance: that whatever our own feelings might be, we could no longer consider them alone. The world now stood at our doorstep, for James Reeb was now a citizen of the world. Slowly we came to see that Jim Crank was right.

But there was Marie. What of her? I personally had no doubt of her ability to hold such an interview, provided it was not too long. The dignity and self-possession she exercised on all occasions in Washington and the extraordinary stamina she had shown on this dreadful day left no doubt about her ability to answer questions from the press, if she could bring herself to try. Only when she was alone, or as nearly so as she was able to be, did the tears fall. Even then she wept silently. Her courage was an inspiration to everyone who dealt with her.

When we proposed the interview, her first reaction was that she couldn't go through with one. We talked about it for some time. She understood its importance. She understood the obligation she was under despite her own overwhelming sorrow. We tried to assure her that strength would come to her in the ordeal. But there was a further anxiety. Even supposing she were able to maintain her composure, what would she say? Her mind was numb. She couldn't think. The press was glad to give her a set of questions so she could go over them in advance. She reviewed them one by one, thus removing the numbness from her mind so that words would come when she summoned them during the interview. The questions submitted to her were as follows:

1. Was your husband's decision to come to Selma a mutual decision between you and your husband?
2. What were some of the reasons he gave for wanting to come to Selma?
3. Did you have any communication with your husband after the march and before he was injured?
4. Do you feel Rev. Reeb was aware of the full potential of violence? Were you?
5. Do you think the cause for which your husband came to Selma merits these consequences?
6. How did you first learn about the attack?
7. What have the children been told?

About seven o'clock Marie said she was as ready as she would ever be. We called Crank and went downstairs to his office. There, ringed around the room, was a battery of TV cameras; in front of them there was a second ring of news photographers standing two or three deep. Kneeling or squatting in front of them was a group of reporters, pencils and pads at the ready. As if unseeing, Marie walked behind Crank's desk and sat down beside Edgar Needham of ABC, who was to ask the questions. He did not use the neatly typed sheet he had prepared but spoke to her directly, and very gently. Every question he put was confined to the topics referred to there.

In a voice that was very low, but wholly distinct and clear, Marie made her response. She told how Jim had come home the night before and how they had gone up to the bedroom where he had told her of his desire to go to Selma. "I told him that I would prefer that he didn't go," she said. Was her husband aware of the potential for violence in the explosive Selma situation? "Yes," she replied. "I'm sure he was aware of it." Was she aware of the danger too? She nodded, but her affirmative reply could not be heard. There was a pause. Marie was near the breaking point with the whole world watching as she relived those moments, now seemingly years away, but only twenty-four hours past.

Had she heard from her husband since he left for the march? "Yes," she said. "Jim called about eight Monday evening. He said the march had not gone as planned, but that everything was fine and he would be home Wednesday morning." In answer to other questions Marie explained that she had first learned of the attack at 10:45 P.M.

Tuesday. "I told the children this morning as soon as they woke up that their father had been hurt," she said. "The younger ones did not fully understand but the thirteen-year-old was quite upset."

Why had Jim gone to Selma? What were his reasons? Marie's voice was a little stronger now as she said, "One of the reasons was the march that occurred Sunday. After he saw that, he felt he had to go. He couldn't stay home and do nothing when he was so much needed there."

"Was the cause worth the risk of death?" Needham asked. Again Marie paused, and when she spoke her voice was again very low. "I don't believe I could answer for myself," she said; "only for Jim. For him, any consequence that might occur would merit his coming."

The interview lasted but a few minutes. When it was over the men and women of the press waited in silent respect while Marie made her way through the packed room to the door. I felt that hardened group of news men and women would have applauded if there had been any appropriate way to do so, their sympathy and admiration for the courage and tenderness of this stricken woman had been so great. The moment she stepped outside they made for their telephones and typewriters as her story and pictures were broadcast to the world.

When we returned to the doctors' suite, a bouquet of yellow roses stood on the table in the middle of the room. It was from President and Mrs. Johnson.

About eight o'clock, Jim's father arrived. He and Marie immediately went upstairs to see Jim. It was a broken man who came back half an hour later. He had not noticed the machinery. He had only seen his boy.

"When I looked at him, I knew he was done for," he said to me later.

We then called in Clark Olsen and Orloff Miller. Quietly, with great restraint, but with deep feeling, they related every incident of the evening before in all the detail they could recall, from the informal assembly of the Unitarians at the foot of the Brown Chapel steps to their arrival at the hospital much later. The recital took an hour. It was new to us all and left us quite literally speechless. When they were through, no one said anything for some time. Marie sat staring at them tearless, unbelieving. Jim's father, periodically striking his left palm with his closed right hand, shook his head as if to deny all he had heard. The rest of us sat stupefied, numb, and cold.

Meanwhile back in Selma, the situation grew increasingly tense. The news that three ministers had been attacked near Walker's restaurant, and that one of them had been badly hurt, was first announced at Brown Chapel at the meeting to which Jim and the others had been going at the time he was struck down. Soon after, Martin Luther King returned to the church to speak warm words of praise for the three men. Then he added that things had gone too beautifully in Selma that day. "The beasts had to strike back," he said. "Now our [white] brethren know something of what it's like to be a Negro in Alabama." He then led the group in silent prayer for the three men. No one yet knew how serious Jim Reeb's injury was. Rev. Ralph Abernathy, King's assistant, followed with instructions about the next day's activities and the meeting was dismissed.

The following morning at Selma they met in the church again, while Jim lay unconscious in Birmingham. Now everyone knew he was on the critical list. An undercurrent of anger was growing in the group and the leaders were concerned. The urge to express their outrage and sorrow in some overt manner was almost uncontrollable. Andy Young of the Southern Christian Leadership Conference rose to remind them that nonviolence was the discipline of the civil rights movement. He urged them to follow the leadership. We know what is going on, he told them. You who are the participants cannot always know. Rev. James Bevel reiterated the point. No one was to devise and execute any impromptu marches. They were only to march when the leadership told them to; they were only to go where the leadership said; in everything they were to keep to the standard of total nonviolence. "You can't push the philosophy of Jesus by using the methods of Caesar," he said. No provocation could justify their turning to violence.

It was decided to march on the Court House that morning, since the court house in the South is the symbol of oppression to the Negro, and since it now specifically symbolized the struggle for voting rights toward which the entire Selma protest was directed. But the march was blocked at the end of Sylvan Street by Sheriff Clark and Wilson Baker, Commissioner of Public Safety. They said flatly there was to be no march on the Court House that day. Official guardians of the law stood three deep across the road, although a single line would have served their purpose amply. They who but three days before had clubbed to earth a group of unarmed Negroes after reducing them to impotence with gas, could not believe the marchers would now remain nonviolent. Despite the fact that Tuesday's peaceful demonstration had been conducted while many of the marchers' relatives and friends lay wounded in a nearby hospital, and that now in the attempted march to the Court House walked many with bandages still wound round their heads, the Alabama law enforcement authorities were unimpressed. Accustomed to using violence themselves they expected to be met with it and they were ready. Behind their massed forces were their parked cars, lined up in a solid row like a kind of wall to fall back to if necessary as a second line of defense.

But it wasn't necessary. On reaching the police line, the column halted. There was no bodily contact and no pushing. It was what the leadership again called "confrontation." The column remained where it halted, not dispersing until 5:30 P.M. when there was another meeting in Brown Chapel. This was the one thing the Alabama authorities were not prepared for: a moral indictment of Alabama law enforcement, carried out by Negroes and whites who would not fight but who would not yield.

At the meeting, prayers were said for Jim and tributes were paid to him as a symbol of all that they stood for. Then they began making plans as to what they should do next. A second march on the Court House was decided upon. That march, stopped by Baker, was transformed from a confrontation into a vigil, and from a vigil into an eloquent, visible, silent day-long, night-long demand that they be permitted to walk to the Court House steps but a few blocks away. Everyone who stood or sat or knelt in that line knew it might well have been he or she who had been struck rather than Jim Reeb. But it *had* been Jim, so they kept their vigil for voting rights and for him, and prayed for him all through the night.

The Medical Center arranged for Marie and Jim's father to sleep in private rooms at the hospital that night, Wednesday. John Sullivan and I were taken to the home of Rev. Lawrence McGinty. But we slept only briefly and were back at the hospital early Thursday morning. After breakfast we had a chance to talk to the doctors involved in the case. They told us plainly what the situation was—that only mechanical means were keeping Jim alive, and only further heroic measures could sustain him any longer—specifically a pacemaker, a machine to keep his heart beating. It had already stopped twice and had been started again by stimulants. I have always opposed these measures, but heretofore only in theory. Now with a life I cared about at stake, what was I to say? There seemed only one thing to say, and I said it.

"If what you say is true," I said, "then we are living a lie. Jim is really already dead." They agreed, but said that as doctors they felt obliged to do what they had done. There was, however, no chance of recovery whatever, they explained. But it must be Marie and not they who should decide not to take any further steps to sustain Jim's life.

"Then," I said, "tell her about it in such a way that she will not feel she is called upon to let Jim die. She cannot make a free decision unless she understands that to introduce a pacemaker now or to take any further steps would only prolong the illusion that has been maintained long enough." They agreed. This was to have been their approach, they said; to tell Marie that the end was at hand and that even a pacemaker could postpone it only in a technical sense.

Meanwhile, I went out to talk to Mr. Reeb. He was standing alone on a bridge between two of the buildings, which had become a favorite spot of his. But I could find no words for what I wanted to say. Eventually he found them for me. After we had stood together silently for some time, he said, and the words lay deep in his throat:

"I believe that Jim's going to die."

I nodded. "The doctors have just told me so," I said. "They are in telling Marie now."

"Then there is something we've got to settle," he said. "I think Jim believes in cremation. I don't and his mother is very much against it. What do you think?"

"I do," I said, "and I know Jim did." We talked some more, agreeing that he would talk with Marie about it when the doctors had finished.

But Marie's mind was perfectly clear on the matter, he found. She recalled that in the last letter Jim had written to her in July, 1961, before flying to Wyoming to join her, he had said that if anything happened to him his body was to be cremated at once and his ashes strewn on the prairie in Shirley Basin at the petrified forest. After but little discussion, it was agreed that the hospital should arrange for cremation immediately upon Jim's death, and that the ashes were to be shipped to Mr. and Mrs. Reeb's home in Wyoming.

Now we could no longer even hope. We could only wait for the end that was now inevitable. We knew what we were to do when the time came. And the time had come, yet it was not really here because the machines were at work, giving us false hope, creating the illusion of life when life was no longer possible. In the late afternoon Marie and Jim's father with Bob Foulkes went upstairs to see Jim once more. Bob had come down from Philadelphia. He knew it was too late, he said, but he just wanted to be there. For a long time after they came back no one entered the room where we were. It was the longest afternoon I have ever known.

At 7:00 P.M. word came downstairs that Jim's heart had stopped again. This time no measures were taken to start it up again. It was the end of the road. James Reeb was a martyr to the cause of civil rights. A little later the telephone rang. On the other end was the President of the United States. He spoke first to Marie, then to Mr. Reeb. He talked for some time, telling them of his own deep personal feelings at Jim's passing. Then he said:

"I will have a private plane waiting for you at the airport tomorrow morning to fly you direct to Boston. And when you are ready to go to Wyoming, I will provide for that flight too."

While Bob Foulkes arranged accommodations for them at a nearby motel, I secured a night flight to Washington. Our vigil was ended. Now it was for each of us to return to our accustomed place, there to strive for the ideals for which this man whom all of us so much loved had given his life.

Back in Selma where just forty-eight hours before Jim had been struck down, a soft cold rain was falling. But the line that stretched along Sylvan Street from the police barricade to Brown Chapel did not move. They were keeping their vigil for Jim. The news of his death reached them about 9:00 P.M. A low moan rose from the bedraggled column. There was no singing now. Rev. Richard Leonard of The Community Church, New York, gave a short eulogy. There was a prayer, and that was all.

17

The March to Victory

WITH THE announcement of Jim Reeb's death, a cry of rage rose from all over the nation and echoed around the world. The United States Congress rocked the next day with speeches denouncing such brutality and calling for government intervention. The headlines of the world press blazed with the story. President Johnson was overwhelmed by phone calls, telegrams, and visiting delegations. Continuous picketing was maintained at the White House. Several thousand clergy converged on Washington for a protest meeting. They sent a delegation to see the President, who talked with them for two hours. When the delegation reported back to the larger body of clergy, gathered in a nearby church, that the President was doing all he could, there were cries of protest from the group. They wanted nothing less than the U. S. Army in Selma to protect the demonstrators.

The President was, in fact, doing all he could. Deeply moved by Jim's death, "that good man," as he called him, he was already preparing a draft of a voting rights bill and the speech by which he intended to lay it before Congress. It was for this reason that he agreed to see the delegation of clergy that gathered in Washington on Friday, March 12, the day after Jim died. The impact of Jim's death on him was noted by the civil rights leaders of the District of Columbia whom he also received that day. I was among the group, and in the course of the discussion had an opportunity to thank him on behalf of the Reeb family for all he had done for them. He was visibly moved at the mention of Jim's name. Lee White, who came to the memorial service at All Souls Church as the President's personal representative, told me that Jim's sacrifice had played no small part in causing the President to lay the voting rights bill before a special session of Congress the following Monday evening.

Governor George Wallace of Alabama bore the brunt of the anger that rose from people everywhere. His club-wielding state troopers had set the pattern for the club-wielding civilian who felled James Reeb. His refusal to change or modify his position after the attack, and his futile attempt to justify himself to the President, only served to aggravate an increasingly dangerous situation. What people wanted, but Wallace would not grant, was an end to the police state in Alabama, an end to the regime of state-enforced tyranny designed to keep the Negro in second-class citizenship.

Meanwhile, an Air Force Jet Star touched down at the Birmingham airport to take Jim's father and Marie back to Boston, back to her now fatherless children. John Sullivan accompanied them. They had to run the gauntlet of photographers and newsmen at the airport both in Birmingham and in Boston. They did so again at Half Moon Street. Then, home again at last, after a tearful reunion with her mother, Jim's mother, and John, Marie took the three younger children upstairs with her to tell them their father was dead. They still thought he had only been hurt. John knew better. Dr. Mendelsohn had told John the night before. How had he taken it, everyone wanted to know: with the same steely self-composure that marked his mother and his grandfather and grandmother, each of whom had, like John, lost the one man in the world they cared about most.

That afternoon, in memory of Jim, the Boston Symphony Orchestra, at its regular Friday concert, played the "Dance of the Blessed Spirits" from Gluck's *Orpheus*. It was the same selection they had played a year and a half before on the announcement of the assassination of President Kennedy.

Then began the memorial services and marches, in Selma, in Washington, and in Boston; at St. Olaf, Princeton, the Philadelphia General Hospital, the West Branch YMCA; in great cities and small towns all over the United States and in many foreign countries as well. No one now knows nor will ever know how many tributes were paid to James Reeb in church services and special meetings held everywhere, in editorials, songs, and poems. Republican and Democrat, Protestant, Catholic, and Jew, rich and poor, Negro and white, all poured forth their lamentations and praise. The river became a torrent and the torrent became a flood. Over and over they echoed the resolve, "He must not have died in vain." The cause of the Negro in the United States must succeed. Perhaps the most remarkable tribute was paid him by the official Roman Catholic newspaper of the Diocese of Worcester, Massachusetts. They proposed sainthood for James Reeb. How he would have laughed at that yet how honored he would have been.

"Is it heresy to think that a Unitarian Universalist minister is a saint of the Church," the newspaper asked, "and to wish—and pray —deep in our hearts that the American hierarchy in a true ecumenical spirit would recognize him as such and petition the Holy See for his canonization? We think not.

"America has needed a model, a symbol of Christian love such as we have not had before . . . now we have him in James Reeb . . . he was what we would hope to be: A true witness to Christ in the marketplace . . . he lost his life; but he won that for which we have all come to earth."

What happened at Princeton, Jim's theological seminary, was typical. As the students made their way to the regular chapel service the morning after Jim died, they found one of their number, a Negro, walking back and forth before the chapel steps, carrying a sign which read: "Why pray if you are not involved?" Some stopped to talk to him, but none joined him and they all went inside where Dean Homrighausen led the student body in prayers that their hearts might be cleansed of contempt for those not of their race, class, or creed.

After lunch, faculty and students met together in the Campus Center for a discussion of the meaning of Jim's death and the meaning of the civil rights cause to them personally. They set up a committee to plan strategy whereby the students and faculty could become involved. They agreed to continue the discussion and to embark on the voluntary raising of funds to enable those who wished to and had not the means to go to Alabama. The discussions continued afterward. Said Dean Homrighausen later: "We will never be the same again."

In Jim's home town, Casper, Wyoming, a march was planned from the center of town to the Natrona County High School which Jim had attended as a boy, where a memorial service was to be held. The march was led by three of Jim's classmates, Dr. Joseph Murphy, Attorney Frank Bowran, and Mayor Patrick Meenan, and Rev. Peter

Koopman of the Presbyterian Church. It was they who paid him tribute at the high school, together with Roy Wilkins of the NAACP, who flew to Casper for the service. In Sioux Falls, South Dakota, Jim's old friend Art Olsen, now teaching at Augustana Lutheran College, organized and led a march and memorial service there. He, like Jim's high school classmates in Casper and thousands of people in cities and towns across the country who had not known his name a week before, marched and sang and prayed in his memory, and for the rights of the Negro in the land of the free.

Funds to provide for Jim's widow and children sprang up spontaneously everywhere; other funds were established in his name to provide further resources for the civil rights struggle. A hundred thousand dollars was raised in his name in a single evening in a show entitled *Broadway Answers Selma,* the proceeds to go to the civil rights cause. Many of the most famous actors and entertainers in the nation took part.

Full scholarships for the Reeb children were set up at Temple University in Philadelphia and Howard University in Washington. How much money was raised for Marie and the children and for the civil rights movement generally in Jim's name, or because of his martyrdom, no one will ever be able to say, for there is no way to measure it. To say that hundreds of thousands of dollars were given by tens of thousands of people would not be to exaggerate.

Besides the special services and marches held everywhere, uncounted churches across the land memorialized Jim during their regular morning service the Sunday following his death. We did not plan to do so at All Souls, because our formal memorial service at which the family would be present was scheduled for the following Tuesday. But it didn't make any difference. The people came to the church that Sunday morning to pay their tribute to Jim, and because he was so much in the minds and hearts of all of us, the service and sermon were in effect a memorial to him. For the congregation gathered at All Souls Church that morning was not like any of the thousands of others gathered elsewhere to honor him. Those who met at All Souls were his friends; almost every one of them had known him personally, worked with him, laughed with him, fought with him. They had been inspired by him, lifted up, consoled, advised, helped, comforted, and on occasion thwarted when he felt they were wrong. But most of all, they had been loved by him, and they had loved him in return.

The church was filled to overflowing long before 11:00 A.M. when the service was due to begin. The parish hall, equipped with a loud-speaker and used for overflow on Sundays, was soon filled also. And still the people came. Extra chairs were brought in for every available space. At my invitation, people then sat on the edge of the lower platform that stretches across the front of the church, on the pulpit stairs, and even on the pulpit chairs themselves. And still they came, standing three, four, and five deep at the back of the church, as many as could crowd inside.

An hour after the service was concluded, we reassembled in the church for a march down the sidewalks of Sixteenth Street to Lafayette Park, where a citywide, inter-church memorial service and civil rights rally was to be held. Other marchers joined the procession as it moved slowly toward the park opposite the White House. Fifteen thousand people gathered there to pay tribute to the fallen minister. The symbolism of the occasion was perfect. This was not the first civil rights march to have left All Souls Church and move southward to the public area at the heart of the nation's capital. On August 28, 1963, when the great "March on Washington" was held, Unitarians and Universalists had assembled at All Souls Church for a service preceding the march. Then, one thousand strong, they had gone to the Lincoln Memorial with the other two hundred and fifty thousand who gathered there that memorable day. A month later, following the bombing of a Negro church in Birmingham where four children had been killed, the people of Washington who cared, of all faiths and political parties, assembled at All Souls Church to walk down Sixteenth Street to Lafayette Square for a memorial service. Jim had been one of the initiators of that demonstration. Then on Sunday afternoon, March 14, we did it again, but now for him, and for the cause for which he gave his life.

A memorial service in Selma was held the next day at Brown Chapel, with a great gathering of national dignitaries present. Martin Luther King gave the principal address. From the church they marched to the Court House to lay a wreath on the steps in memory of Jim. Among those in the march, unnoticed by the newsmen who were all about, was Rev. Truman D. Nabors, Jr., minister of the Mt.

Hebron Presbyterian Church of Ellicott City, Maryland, who had grown up in Selma and whose parents still lived there. He had visited with them, but spent most of his time in Selma in the Negro section, sleeping there as well. "It was a liberating experience," he said later, "just as Jim's influence on me back at the Philadelphia General Hospital was liberating. I went to the spot where he fell and just stood there to pay my own silent tribute to a man who had given my life a new dimension."

Tuesday, March 16, All Souls Church held its memorial service, conducted by Dr. William Stuart Nelson, Jim's old friend of the University Neighborhoods Council, by Dr. Dana McLean Greeley, President of the Unitarian Universalist Association and by me. Besides President Johnson's personal representative, Lee White, Vice President and Mrs. Hubert Humphrey, Senator and Mrs. Edward Kennedy, and a host of other high officials of church and state were present. Marie and John, Jim's father and mother, Marie's parents, and other members of the family came to Washington for the service. This was the family service in the church which Jim and Marie still thought of as their own.

Thursday, at the Arlington Street Church in Boston, an ecumenical service was held which Marie and her father and mother also attended. It was sponsored by the Boston Conference on Religion and Race. Speakers included Dr. Mendelsohn, minister of the church; John Sullivan; Rabbi Roland B. Gittelsohn of Temple Israel; Rt. Rev. John M. Burgess, Suffragan Bishop of the Episcopal Diocese; and Rev. Gilbert H. Caldwell of the Union Methodist Church. Richard Cardinal Cushing of the Roman Catholic Archdiocese of Boston was to have been present to deliver the prayer, but was ill. The Most Rev. Thomas J. Riley, Bishop of the Roman Catholic Archdiocese, read the Cardinal's prayer on his behalf. John Sullivan gave the eulogy.

The next day the President's private plane flew the bereaved family to Casper, which was to be their new home. As they left 3 Half Moon Street, they closed the door forever on this phase of their lives. Back in the Wyoming Jim loved, where his father and mother still lived, and where Marie's father and mother lived too, they could begin again. With Marie and the children on the plane were her father and mother, Jim's father and mother, and his Aunt Hazel. A small group of relatives and friends was at the Casper airport to meet them,

among them Bob Reed, Jim's old friend of high school days. A
memorial service for him was held at the First Presbyterian Church
on March 21. Bob Reed gave the tribute, and Rev. Griffith Williams,
now of Minneapolis, assisted in the service.

While marching and rallies continued all over the country and the
name of Jim Reeb, the martyr, became a symbol of the civil rights
movement, the attention of the people still centered on Selma. Things
remained at a complete stalemate there, with the marchers maintaining their column facing the Selma "Wall" night and day, through rain
and hot sun, until permission to march to the Court House steps
was at last obtained. It was granted for Monday, March 15, following
the memorial service for Jim at Brown Chapel. After the march and
the service, most of the white Northern participants in the demonstration left. But some held on, some went home and came back, and
some new recruits came in while the legal battle was fought to gain
permission for the march to Montgomery. At last it came, and Sunday, March 21, the great march from Selma to Montgomery began.
Ralph Bunche and many other nationally known religious and civic
leaders joined Martin Luther King for the occasion.

The line of march was guarded by 1,900 federalized Alabama
National Guardsmen, perhaps 100 FBI men, 100 federal marshalls,
and 1,000 U.S. Army troops. As many could start the march as
wished, but seventeen miles out of Selma where U.S. 80 becomes a
two-lane highway, the number was reduced to 300 who would be
permitted to continue. These were equipped with bedrolls, pup tents,
and other supplies. Food was trucked out, portable latrines followed
the marchers, together with garbage trucks and ambulances. There
would be three stops at Negro farms along the route, all arranged for
in advance, and a fourth just outside Montgomery at St. Jude's
Roman Catholic Center.

The federal government was determined to avoid any further incidents. Demolition experts searched under bridges and passes along
the line of march; soldiers probed fields along the way for mines.
Every side road was sealed off by armed troops. There were no
mishaps while the eyes of the world watched the little army of 300,
mostly Negroes, plod the fifty miles toward the state capital.

Another call had gone out to Northern clergy and others to assem-
ble at St. Jude's on the night of Wednesday, March 24, or early on

the 25th for the final stage of the great march. From all over the country they came, by bus and car, train and plane. Thirty thousand people, walking six abreast in an orderly column two miles long, marched into Montgomery the next day. The throng drew up in the great area before the Alabama State Capitol, where famous entertainers sang to them and famous civil rights leaders spoke. It was not primarily a memorial service for Jim Reeb, although people often spoke of him. It was a victory celebration for voter rights demonstrations in the South. Yet Jim Reeb was present in that gathering in a way that no one could measure but everyone felt.

That night the brutality always latent in the segregationist movement was revealed once more. The marchers departed from Montgomery without incident. But in the darkness on the now famous Route 80, a young mother, Viola Liuzzo, a white woman, was shot dead. She was driving with a Negro to Montgomery from Selma where she had just taken a group of marchers who had no other means of getting home. And so another white martyr was added to the cause of civil rights for the American Negro.

The battle of Selma was over. The victory had been won. The voting rights bill was on the way through Congress. Jim Reeb and Viola Liuzzo lay dead. But the war in which they gave their lives was not over, and would not be for a long time to come. Others were yet to give up their lives in the struggle. While 30,000 civil rights marchers stood before the Alabama State Capitol listening to speeches about civil rights, the flag of the Confederacy, defeated at arms almost exactly one hundred years before, flew from the top of the mast above the State House dome. Beneath it was the state flag of Alabama. A diminutive stars and strips fluttered from a little pole set in the lawn far below.

Was it all worth the price of a man's or a woman's life? In particular for us, was it worth the life of a man like Jim Reeb, even though his death had given the movement great impetus? Asked that question, Marie had said: "Jim would have thought the movement worth any sacrifice." How well she understood him. In a sermon to the people of All Souls Church preached two years before, he had said: "It is of the nature of prayer that we are given more than we are prepared to receive . . . insights, understandings, aspirations . . . rise from the creative levels of our minds to challenge our usual patterns of thought and conduct. [They] call us to assume new roles, summon us to renounce evil and denounce injustice, prompt us to live in peace and harmony with all men. It was such an experience that men have had in mind in speaking of the need to surrender to the will of God."

Then he said: "Yet for the joy of serving truth some men will surrender. We cannot know for sure who they are. We presume we know the great poets of our day. We are thankful for the light they give. Yet it is altogether possible that the careful eye of history will pass them by and instead recognize enduring greatness in the work of a man no one considers is of any consequence."

How could he know; how could he have dreamed that he was speaking of himself? Yet perhaps he did. An admirer had written to him some time before:

"I want to thank you for the wonderful concept you shared with us last Sunday. The more I think about it, the greater my admiration grows. This is the sort of thinking we need—the country needs. I wish you could take this message to everyone. Have you thought of publishing it? I believe a national magazine or newspaper might well be interested in something with so powerful a punch and so unique a point of view. It should be shared with the most possible people. They really need it.

"Don't be shy or modest about your ideas. One of the things I believe is that liberal religion needs a prophet. Maybe you are he."

Some who did not know him have said that Jim gladly died for the movement in which he believed. It is not so. Given the choice, he would rather have lived for it. Like the others who went to Selma, he was willing to run the risk the Sunday gassing and clubbing indicated was present in Alabama. But Jim did not think of himself as a civil rights hero. He thought of himself as a worker for the cause. But he was ready, like the others, to pay a high price if necessary—whatever price was asked of him.

A single blow by a man tempted to violence beyond his power of self-control caused the careful eye of history to single out this man for greatness. Yet the blow alone was not enough to explain the reaction of the nation and the world to his death. It was yet more because of the man, about whom relatively few had known heretofore, whom the tragedy disclosed. Here was a man fit in every way for the greatness now thrust upon him. A lesser man than he could not have borne such a burden. The world was shocked at the murder of a defenseless minister who asked only that citizens of a race other than his own be permitted to exercise their right to vote. But when men looked to see who he was, they found that James Reeb in his private life was all that a civil rights hero might be expected to be. "He was marching long before he decided to march in Selma," as a colleague at the Philadelphia Y put it.

"We shall find no security in existence," James Reeb had said in one of his first Washington sermons, "if the mere continuation of our life is our final goal. Man never has been willing and never shall be content merely to live." Then he asked rhetorically: "Is there nothing in life worth risking the end of one's life for?" All the world now knew that for James Reeb there was.

"Are there no dreams," he asked, "so important that we can risk our own destruction in order to make them come true?" He had answered that question in the affirmative. The dream of freedom for the American Negro was for him a dream so important that he could risk his own destruction to make it come true. James Reeb, the martyr, like all the martyrs in history, had found something greater than himself to which he could give himself completely— something great enough to make the early termination of his own life seem worthwhile. One man, felled on the streets of Selma, set thousands to marching for civil rights who had never marched before, and set millions to thinking, who, before he died, had not thought it made any difference.

Two days after his death, Marie received the following letter. A medal was enclosed with it. The letter read:

"Dear Mrs. Reeb:

"Twenty years ago I was awarded the enclosed medal. The citation read in part—'volunteered to accompany a platoon of light tanks in order to point out targets for their effective fire—he advanced through the street of town in advance of the armored vehicles—firing his sub-machine gun at targets of opportunity.'

"Your late husband, Reverend Reeb, volunteered to accompany his fellowmen against a force of greater threat to the principles of our country, than my opponent, the German soldier.

"Reverend Reeb was unarmed except for his convictions, his 'Armed support' was the songs and prayers of the oppressed.

"Would you please give this medal to your oldest son, John—his father was a much braver American than I.

Sincerely,

John D. McCarthy"

In the Wyoming he loved, south and west of Casper in what is known as Shirley Basin, we scattered Jim's ashes, the last physical remnant of a living human body once surging with vitality, animated by love and the highest idealism. But the ashes of flesh that was once warm, and bone that was once strong, are a poor reminder and symbol of those we have loved and lost. So are monuments of stone. That is why Jim asked to have his mortal remains become a part of the prairie, to return to the earth whence he came.

Those who go there now see what he saw when he went there first, earth and sky, sage brush and a few clouds on the far horizon. No gravestone mars the scene. But those who go there may come closer to him than any monument could bring them, if gazing at the wide prairie and the vast dome of the sky they sense the scene as well as see it, as Jim did; if they let it become a part of them, as it became a part of him. At the decaying center of any American city, where poverty and deprivation stunts and warps young children, those who seek Jim Reeb may find him too. Wherever a human being lifts up his hand to aid another in distress, they will find him. And above all, of course, in the civil rights movement: there we shall find him most easily, for his life by that magic alchemy through which men and movements merge is now the life of the movement itself. His soul is its soul. His sacrifice has been transmuted from tragedy into victory —the ultimate victory of right over wrong and good over evil. Jim would not have called for vengeance upon his attackers. Neither has his widow nor his father and mother. He would have called for the understanding and forgiveness that breaks the chain of evil through the power of love. So too, under the burden of an intolerable sorrow, have they.

Index